The Saxon and Norman Kings

Blackwell Classic Histories of England

This series comprises new editions of seminal histories of England. Written by the leading scholars of their generation, the books represent both major works of historical analysis and interpretation and clear, authoritative overviews of the major periods of English history. All the volumes have been revised for inclusion with the series and many include updated material to aid further study. *Blackwell Classic Histories of England* provides a forum in which these key works can continue to be enjoyed by scholars, students and general readers alike.

Published

Roman Britain
Third Edition
Malcolm Todd

The Saxon and Norman Kings
Third Edition
Christopher Brooke

England and Its Rulers: 1066–1272
Second Edition
M.T. Clanchy

Crown and Nobility: England 1272–1485
Second Edition
Anthony Tuck

Church and People: England 1450–1660
Second Edition
Claire Cross

Politics and Nation: England 1450–1660
Fifth Edition
David Loades

Politics without Democracy: 1815–1914
Second Edition
Michael Bentley

THE SAXON AND NORMAN KINGS
Third Edition

Christopher Brooke

BLACKWELL
Publishers

Copyright © Christopher Brooke 1963, 1978, 2001

The right of Christopher Brooke to be identified as author of this work has been asserted in accordance with the Copyright, Designs and Patents Act 1988.

First published by B.T. Batsford Ltd 1963
Second edition published 1978
Third edition published by Blackwell Publishers Ltd 2001

2 4 6 8 10 9 7 5 3 1

Blackwell Publishers Ltd
108 Cowley Road
Oxford OX4 1JF
UK

Blackwell Publishers Inc.
350 Main Street
Malden, Massachusetts 02148
USA

British Library Cataloguing in Publication Data

A CIP catalogue record for this book is available from the British Library.

Library of Congress Cataloging-in-Publication Data

Brooke, Christopher Nugent Lawrence.
    The Saxon and Norman Kings / Christopher Brooke. – 3rd ed.
        p. cm. – (Blackwell classic histories of England)
    Includes bibliographical references (p.) and index.
    ISBN 0-631-23130-7 (alk. paper) – ISBN 0-631-23131-5
    1. Great Britain – Kings and rulers – Biography. 2. Great Britain – History – Anglo-Saxon period, 449–1066. 3. Great Britain – History – Norman period, 1066–1154. 4. Monarchy – Great Britain – History–To 1500. 5. Normans – England – Kings and rulers – Biography. 6. Anglo-Saxons – Kings and rulers – Biography. I. Title. II. Series.

DA28.1 .B7 2001
942.01′092′2–dc21
[B]
                                                                            2001025985

Typeset in 10.5/12 pt Sabon
by Kolam Information Services Pvt. Ltd, Pondicherry, India
Printed in Great Britain by T.J. International, Padstow, Cornwall

This book is printed on acid-free paper

To H.E.W.

Contents

Illustrations

Preface to the Third Edition

I am very grateful to Al Bertrand and Blackwell Publishers for giving this book a new birth. It has been a fascinating exercise to study the state of knowledge and the views of the author nearly forty years ago – and to bring them into a new century. There have been revisions at many points, and two new chapters especially reflect what is new. First, I select some parts of the field which look very different in 2001 from their aspect in 1963. In two of these I have had a special involvement. When I was elected President of the Society of Antiquaries in 1981 plans for a major research campaign at Sutton Hoo had been becalmed, and it was my business – in collaboration with many others, especially Sir David Wilson, then Director of the British Museum – to refloat the project. In 1983 we were able to recruit Martin Carver to direct the campaign, and in my last year as President he and I worked together to smooth the many difficulties which remained: this he has described in his *Sutton Hoo: Burial Ground of Kings?* (1998, pp. 46–50). In 1984 my own direct involvement ceased – save for delightful visits to the site and talks with the Director – but it has been a special privilege to admire the progress of a great scholarly enterprise from the touchline. Long before that Harold Walker, the inspired schoolmaster to whom the book is dedicated, had sadly died: he left his notes on the Bayeux Tapestry to me, with the instruction that Nicholas Brooks was to have access to them – and from this sprang the article by Brooks and Walker which has laid the most secure foundations for modern study of the Tapestry. I have also expounded, in chapter 1, the difference between 'the English people' and 'the kings of the English', so often confused in earlier discussions: for it is much clearer to us now than it was even forty years ago that human societies are not naturally grouped in nation states; that there has been and should be infinite variety in the shape and influence of political units. Thus we have learned to sit at the feet of the great historic federations, of Switzerland and the United States – we have even learned to admire the Holy Roman Empire. But we have also learned, from Rees Davies and others, that intense local feeling existed, and in some senses grew, in our period – culminating in the twelfth century, when the aspirations of western Christendom were as fragmented as ever in recorded history, and also at their most cosmopolitan. Out of such paradoxes is human history fashioned.

The other new chapter is on Queens. They had a small place in the first edition, and a larger place already in my interests; and the numerous studies of queenship, and of women's history in a wider context, have made far clearer than I could hope for in 1963 the role that queens played in our period.

As I explain below (pp. 3–7), Brooks and Walker and the many other excellent articles which the Tapestry has inspired, have still not revealed all its secrets. The Bibliography, which is entirely new, lists my other principal debts – but special homage is due to Simon Keynes and Michael Lapidge for all things pre-Conquest; and to Marjorie Chibnall, whose editions (especially of Orderic) have been constantly in my hands – and to whom the whole community of Anglo-Norman scholars is indebted for taking over the mantle of Allen Brown in *Anglo-Norman Studies*, and wearing it for several years. The chapter on Queens will reveal my debts to Janet Nelson, Elisabeth Van Houts and Pauline Stafford especially, and at a deeper level, to Rosalind Brooke. I am most grateful for the expert copy-editing of Brigitte Lee. In the edition of 1978 acknowledgement was also made to Mr R.H.M. Dolley, Mr C.A.H. Franklyn, Dom David Knowles and Professor Peter Sawyer.

The book was dedicated to Harold Walker, and he responded in a letter which revealed his pleasure in the gift – while hinting here and there (in a characteristic mode) that it was a history 'task' (a schoolboy essay) which had not in all respects turned out too well. He was a teacher and scholar of extraordinary range – he could expound the French Revolution and the making of the American Constitution with the same penetration and insight he showed among the Gewissae and the rapidly moving panoramas of the Bayeux Tapestry. It is a particular pleasure to pay tribute to his memory.

Preface to the 1963 Edition
(Abbreviated)

One cannot write biographies, in the usual sense of the word, of Saxon and Norman kings, and there are no portraits to show us at all clearly what they looked like. This book was bound in its nature to be different from those on kings in modern centuries. I hope I have made clear in chapter 2 what is attempted. The text is a rendering, *tel quel*, of some of what I have learned over the years from pupils, friends and teachers. A few of my many debts must be specially noted. What I owe to to Mr H.E. Walker cannot be easily summarized: what I say about the origins of Wessex (p. 87) and the Bayeux Tapestry draws heavily on his suggestions and insight. My wife and Dr [now Professor] H. Mayr-Harting read the whole book in manuscript, and the latter has also read it in proof; both have suggested improvements and eradicated many errors and infelicities, though they are not to be reproached for those that remain. I have also had generous help and advice from Dr P. Chaplais, Mr J.V.H. Eames, Professor M. Gluckman, Dr P. Hunter Blair, Dr E. Peters, Mr A. Thompson, and from the publishers.

Henry Loyn's *Anglo-Saxon England and the Norman Conquest*, which contains a number of aperçus on English kingship, and Michael Wallace-Hadrill's *The Long-haired Kings and Other Studies in Frankish History* were both published in 1962, too late to guide me before this book was written, although I had had the benefit of hearing and discussing with Michael Wallace-Hadrill a part of the new essays in his book.

Christopher Brooke

I

Prologue

From 1963 to 2001

What has happened to the themes of this book since 1963, when it was first published? Much every way: for there have been new editions of sources, new interpretations of vital texts and a host of books and articles on almost every corner of the subject. The bibliography at the end contains only a tiny number of books and editions already published in 1963. This means that a far deeper understanding of the kingship, queenship and the political history of England has been furnished by the scholarship of the last forty years.

Deeper, yet not in all respects different. The main sources remain as they were: the *Anglo-Saxon Chronicle*, Asser's *Life of Alfred*, the biographies and chronicles of the eleventh and twelfth centuries still hold sway, most of them in new and better editions. The authenticity of Asser has been vindicated and challenged again; I assume that the general consensus is, with good reason, in its favour. *Beowulf* is still the central heroic lay of the Anglo-Saxon era. Only here, further discussion and deeper research has had the paradoxical result that we know less, not more about the poem![1] A sensitive interpretation will still see it as the work of a Christian author reflecting on a pagan past, and in the current state of knowledge, the arguments in favour of an eighth-century date seem likely to prevail; but all that is certainly agreed is that the manuscript in which it survives cannot be later than the mid-eleventh century (many would say, than about 1000), and the poem could conceivably be as late as the tenth century. In that case the poet shows the kind of imaginative insight into the

---

1 The various dates suggested for the poem and the MS in which it is preserved are summarized by George Jack and Donald Scragg in *Blackwell Encyclopaedia*, pp. 62–3. Kiernan 1984 argued for a mid-eleventh-century date for both; Lapidge 2000 has restored the poem to the early eighth century.

nature of the pagan world shown by Shakespeare in King Lear – though I do not myself believe in the attempt to find a Christian mythology in that great and terrible work. But the author of *Beowulf* in any case had access to paganism still in the Scandinavian world he so lavishly describes. On this theme I have left my text little altered; for who knows where the criticism of *Beowulf* will have led us forty years hence?[2] Where recent research has altered or undermined the views expressed in 1963, I have made such adjustments as seemed needed. Some of my interpretations have been proved simply wrong: my account of the death of William Rufus has been revised to allow for the strong arguments deployed by the late Warren Hollister that it was accident not murder.[3] I had suggested that there was possible evidence of conspiracy; but this Hollister dissolved. It depended on the assumption that Walter Tirel fired the fatal arrow, and that his relations were richly rewarded; but Tirel himself denied the charge (as I admitted in 1963); he personally did not benefit; and the rewards of his relations were not all that remarkable. Accident it probably was; but we do well to reflect the staggering comment of William of Malmesbury – in most respects a warm admirer of Henry I – on the fate of Henry's eldest brother, Robert Curthose. Robert was captured after the battle of Tinchebrai in 1106 and kept in 'open confinement' until his death in 1134. 'It was owing to the praise-worthy *pietas*[4] of his brother that he suffered nothing beyond soli-tude.'[5] Kings being what they are, to sentence one's brother to life imprisonment is 'praiseworthy'; one might reasonably expect sen-tence of death...

I wrote in 1963 from the sources, and they are still in the main as they were then – though many have taken on a new lease of life in modern editions. I particularly note two crucial sources of which we know far more in 2001 than we did in 1963, each in a very different way outstanding examples of historical detective work: Martin Car-ver's campaign at Sutton Hoo, and the numerous attempts to reinter-pret the Bayeux Tapestry.

---

2   For another case in which we know less in 2001 than we thought we knew in 1963, see p. 77 on the kingdom of Lindsey. A more doubtful example is the poem on Athelstan embedded in the text of William of Malmesbury: see p. 113.

3   Hollister 1986 (first published in 1973). He also argues (p. 66 n. 2) that because the arrangement between Robert and William by which each should succeed the other had broken down at an early date, Henry's chance of the throne was not so dependent on Robert's absence on crusade as I had argued. I am not so sure: in 1100 Robert certainly still thought he should succeed.

4   'Sense of duty' (Winterbottom) is very probably the best translation; 'family feeling' is possible – brotherly love would be a mockery.

5   William of Malmesbury, *Gesta Regum*, I, 706–7.

Mound 1 at Sutton Hoo, opened in 1939, turned upside down our understanding of England – and Europe too – in the seventh century. But it was a document without context: no modern, scientific investigation of the other mounds had taken place, and it was as if a single item from a rich archive had been extracted, published, and studied – and yet no one had looked at the rest of the archive from which it came. Much was done by Rupert Bruce-Mitford and others to reinterpret the discoveries of 1939; and the numismatists meanwhile redated the coins to suggest a burial date of c.625 rather than c.655.[6] At last, between 1983 and 1997, under the direction of Professor Martin Carver, with the support of the Society of Antiquaries, the British Museum, and other bodies, a major campaign of archaeological research was mounted on the site.[7] This involved research in many disciplines, and extensive study of the wider context throughout Suffolk, England and north-western Europe in the early Middle Ages. In accordance with the rules of research archaeology, something was left for future generations, with yet more advanced techniques, to investigate. But nearly a quarter of the site was uncovered, and the whole surveyed, and we now know most of what it has to tell us. It was clearly a cemetery dedicated to kings or great nobles; the manner of burial and some of the grave goods show a close link with Scandinavia; the coins and other elements show some relationship to the kingdoms of the Franks – and some of the objects came from Byzantium. It is most naturally explained as the cemetery of a pagan royal family – though baptismal spoons among the grave goods in Mound 1 hint at a Christian influence beginning to make its way. This has long seemed to fit Rædwald (died c.625 – more precisely, between 616 and 627), who raised Christian and pagan altars in the same temple;[8] and conversion to Christianity would naturally (in the conditions of the age) bring to a close both cremations and the accumulation of treasures for the afterlife. East Anglia seems to have had a pagan royal house for less than a hundred years, from the late sixth to the mid-seventh century. Martin Carver's conclusion is admirably cautious: 'Although the association of Sutton Hoo and the short-lived pagan royal house of East Anglia has not been proved, there are still sufficient grounds for believing it.'[9]

The interpretation of the Bayeux Tapestry was and is of exceptional importance for my account of king-making. I had had the good fortune well before 1963 of advice on this from the late Harold Walker – to

6   Bruce-Mitford 1975–83; cf. Carver 1998, pp. 34–5.
7   See p. x. There is an admirable summary in Carver 1998; we await the full report due shortly in Carver and Hummler, forthcoming.
8   See p. 47; for his dates, see S. Keynes in *Blackwell Encyclopaedia*, p. 508.
9   Carver 1998, pp. 172–3.

whom the book is dedicated – and I regard the article by Nicholas Brooks enshrining his own and Walker's views (published in 1979) as fundamental. The essence of the matter is that it was the creation of an English designer and craftsmen (probably craftswomen) working for a Norman patron, Odo, bishop of Bayeux and earl of Kent.[10] Recent work has suggested links with Canterbury, specifically with St Augustine's Abbey.[11] An attempt has since been made to argue that it was Norman work; and it is notoriously difficult wholly to distinguish English and Norman styles in this period.[12] But the attempt founders. First of all, the spelling of personal and place-names is palpably English – even the Norman Bayeux comes out as *Bagias*, a natural way for an English author to render the sound of 'ai' or 'ay': in all the Norman texts of the period which I have seen the spelling is a variant of *Baioce* or *Baiocum*. Equally striking is the ambiguity, or ambivalence, of the story it tells. In none of the recent discussions I have read is this sufficiently emphasized. The brilliantly vivid pictorial narrative has its own Latin commentary above; and at several crucial points the Latin fails to tell us what is happening. It opens with Harold consulting Edward the Confessor before setting off for Normandy – no explanation is given. The other sources are divided as to whether Harold was sent by Edward or went on his own initiative. When Harold swears his oath to William we are not told what the oath was about – even though it was central to the narrative and clearly of great importance. Most remarkable of all is the vital scene in which Edward the Confessor lies on his deathbed. It is argued below (p. 28) that the scene of his burial here precedes his death (a reversal of the order of the narrative unique in the Tapestry) precisely to ensure that a direct connection can be made between Edward's last moment and the offer of the crown to Harold. To the right a man makes the offer, and his hand meanwhile is pointing to the previous scene. The Latin here is at its most gnomic: 'Here King Edward on his [death]bed addresses his faithful men' – and below, more lucidly – 'And here he is dead'. The king addressed his faithful followers. As C. H. Dodd said of the crucial meeting of St Paul

10   The highly professional knowledge the designer reveals of the possibilities of embroidery as a craft in the service of vivid historical narrative may suggest that it was designed by a woman. We have no means of being sure, but for convenience I refer to the designer as 'she'.

11   Richard Gameson in Gameson 1997, pp. 171–3 – leaving open whether the designer was a monk or a secular artist. Elsewhere Gameson emphasizes the religious inspiration of the Tapestry – against C.R. Dodwell, who in a brilliant article reprinted ibid., ch. 7, had emphasized the secular elements, especially in the links with secular epics. For other recent studies by art historians, see the essays by G.R. Owen-Crocker and Peter Lasko in Owen-Crocker and Graham 1998.

12   Grape 1994, on which see Gameson in Gameson 1997, pp. 162–74.

Plate 1 The death of Edward the Confessor from the Bayeux Tapestry. Edward's death is the centre of a long tableau: to the left he is carried to Westminster Abbey for burial; to the right the crown is offered to Harold, and beyond is Harold's coronation. By twisting the story in this way the deathbed and the offer to Harold are brought close together: the man offering the crown to Harold whose finger is just visible points both to Edward's dying speech and to his death. See p. 4.

with St Peter in Jerusalem: 'we may presume they did not spend all the time talking about the weather'.[13] Basically, the Norman case was that Edward had designated William; Harold's case was that on his deathbed Edward designated him. The Tapestry avoids discussing William's designation by starting after it can have happened (if it did), and by making no reference in the Latin inscriptions to any message Harold may have taken to Duke William. An English observer contemplating the scene of Edward's death would naturally take it for granted that Edward was designating Harold. But the Latin does not say so – it is clearly and deliberately vague. As we have seen, strong grounds have been found for connecting the design of the Tapestry to Canterbury; and it is striking that its story is closest to that told by the Canterbury monk Eadmer, who was a boy in Canterbury at the time of the Conquest.[14] Eadmer makes Harold go to Normandy to release two relations who were hostages in William's power. There is no sign of the hostages in the Tapestry, which has Harold in the Conqueror's presence pointing towards the next, mysterious scene in which a clerk seems to be raping a nun called Ælfgyva. The natural interpretation is that Harold's visit was connected with her story, and that she was also related to him – or so it was believed in late eleventh-century Canterbury. There is no other trace of her. But the rest of the Tapestry's story, with Harold's oath to William and Edward's subsequent designation of Harold before his death, is strikingly similar to Eadmer's; and we may be reasonably confident that the designer of the Tapestry knew a Canterbury version of the events similar to Eadmer's, and was sufficiently confident of her view of the matter to preserve it in her portrayal of the Conquest – while avoiding any explicit statements which might not appeal to her patron, the Conqueror's half-brother. Historians are inclined to assume that patrons could dictate to artists how their commissions were portrayed; but artists have often had their own views. The designer of the Bayeux Tapestry was a great artist: she (or he) has sometimes been denied her full stature since so little survives with which to compare the work. It seems to me abundantly clear that the Tapestry portrays events in a manner acceptable both to an English and a Norman audience;[15] and that this was achieved by careful

13 Dodd 1944, p. 16.
14 Eadmer, *Historia Novorum*, pp. 6–9.
15 I make – as most historians do – too clear-cut a distinction between the English and Norman points of views. Thus Eadmer and the Tapestry have much in common with the fullest Norman account by William of Poitiers; so much so that William has been supposed to be their main source. This I find difficult to believe, but the ambiguities of the Tapestry are eloquent testimony to as lively a debate on the events of 1066 in the late eleventh century as in the early twenty-first.

reticence in the inscriptions. 'Great are thy powers, O silence', said Trollope's Miss Dunstable, quoting Carlyle.[16] We cannot tell what really happened. There are three versions of the designation of William – one when Edward was still an exile, the second in 1051, when Robert of Jumiéges, archbishop of Canterbury, is said to have carried the nomination to William when he was on his way to Rome, the third, also in 1051, when William is alleged to have visited Edward. In some sense or measure, all three may be true; but that does not diminish the probability that Edward designated Harold on his deathbed. However that may be, there is no doubt that the Tapestry still has secrets to reveal.

Thus the Tapestry emphasizes the links of England and the continent in art as well as politics. Some historians lay more, some less stress on the European context of the institutions of monarchy in pre- and post-Conquest England; I remain an unrepentant European. Janet Nelson's brilliant studies of coronation rites have shown how intimate the relations of English and Frankish practices were already in the ninth century – when English books could influence the Franks, and vice versa;[17] and we may suppose that these links in fact went further back still, to the days when Offa of Mercia had his son anointed king in 787, six years after the pope had anointed two Frankish princes, thirty-six after the anointing of Pippin as king of the Franks, the formal inauguration of the Carolingian dynasty. Other similar links can be observed from time to time throughout the period. Otto the Great's imperial coronation took place in 962, Edgar's in 973 (see p. 33). Cnut's pilgrimage to Rome in 1027, culminating in his meeting with pope and emperor, was an important step in the legitimation of his rule. The earliest surviving great seal, that of Edward the Confessor, is a close imitation of that of the Emperor Conrad II. In 1963 already I pointed out links with the Spanish monarchy (see p. 155). The catalogue could be extended.

It is true that George Garnett, in a fascinating article, has argued that English customs were in some respects in contrast to those in France and Germany – and that the Conqueror brought continental ideas with him in 1066.[18] I am sure that he has put his finger correctly

16 *Framley Parsonage*, ch. 48. For what follows (Edward's designation of William), the best authorities are: for the period of exile, Eadmer, *Historia Novorum*, p. 7; for 1051, via Robert of Jumièges, William of Poitiers, pp. 20–1, and William of Jumièges, II, 158–9; for the visit of William, ASC D, trans. Garmonsway, p. 176. The ASC does not mention designation, and has been often doubted; but if Robert did carry such a message earlier in 1051, a visit by William to Edward seems a very likely consequence.

17 Nelson 1986, chs. 11–17.

18 Garnett 1986.

on some local customs. But all the processes of king-making have to be seen in the political context of their day. The practice of associating the king's son with his father by anointing and coronation was innovative in 787 – but not practised again in England till 1170. The French and German precedents were not all encouraging; and the English kings might take warning as probably as being inspired by the model: it could only work if there was genuine affection or at least a convincing show of obedience on the part of the son – a show which quite often proved illusory. Again, it is notorious that Alfred succeeded though his elder brothers had left sons who might have reckoned, in Hamlet's words, that Alfred had 'popp'd in between the election and my hopes': the urgency of the Viking attacks probably determined the issue in this case, though we may allow something for Alfred's ambition. Garnett observed that late Old English coronations commonly took place some time after the new king's accession. In contrast, the Norman kings were anointed and crowned at the earliest opportunity. But in this they simply followed the example of Harold, who doubtless himself sought every means of propping up a doubtful claim that the Church's rites could give. By the same token William (however he might protest to the contrary) was a usurper; William II and Henry I both had an elder brother with a colourable claim to succeed before them; Stephen was in many folk's eyes a usurper; Henry II had to secure an inheritance based on a possibly shaky treaty with his predecessor. If we look for an innovator, it was not the Norman William, but the English Harold. Yet this is to take a superficial view of the case: throughout the history of monarchy in England, local custom has been adapted to political circumstance, English traditions to the views of a monarchy with its eyes on Europe at large: the monarchs of Europe could seek the customs of their caste in the recesses of a large room. This is particularly clear if we observe the contrast between the strength of local feeling which bound the English people, the *gens Anglorum*, and the complex of local and Europe-wide models and ambitions which inspired the kings of the English.

The English People and the English Kings

It cannot be too strongly emphasized that this book is a history of the English kings and queens down to 1154, not of the English people. The difference is fundamental. There were kings, but not kings of England or the English, in the sixth and seventh centuries already; the title 'king of the English' is of the tenth century. But already in the

590s Pope Gregory I was talking about 'the English people' – *gens Anglorum;*[19] and the phrase so appealed to the Venerable Bede that in the 730s he immortalized it in his *Ecclesiastical History of the English People.* It is not quite clear how Gregory came by the notion – he is commonly believed to have invented it; and it has often been thought to fit uncomfortably with Bede's famous description of how the Anglo-Saxon invaders comprised Angles and Saxons and Jutes.[20] Why have they all been compressed into 'the Angles' or 'the English'? It might be easier to answer the question if we knew more of the origins and nature of the invasions. But in truth, after generations of close research, we know very little of the matter. That Saxony and Jutland were important sources of the invaders of the fifth and sixth centuries need not be doubted; though Pope Gregory's own belief that the Angles came from the angle between Denmark and Germany is not quite so easily credited. What seems certain is that both Gregory's belief that they were all Angles – expressed in the early and well-recorded legend that he hoped they might (if duly converted) become angels – and Bede's that they belonged to three clearly defined tribes, are very doubtful.[21] In later times, local groups and peoples were given titles like 'West Saxon'; but the kings of the West Saxons succeeded kings of quite a different region and tribe, the 'Gewissae', who occupied a rather different area in the west country.[22] There is undoubtedly an element of later rationalization in all these schemes. However much truth may lie in some of them, far the earliest recorded is Pope Gregory's reference to the English people. But Pope Gregory lived in Rome, and may have known little about this island: when he chose York and London as the centres of his archbishoprics (which in fact became centred in York and Canterbury until the southern archbishop moved to Lambeth in the twelfth century), he showed more knowledge of the geography of the Roman provinces than of contemporary kingdoms.

What is certain is that the ruling elites of most of what we call England from the sixth century on were pagan and spoke dialects of

19 Bede i.27, 32, pp. 88–9, 110–11 (and cf. ii.2, pp. 132–5) – Gregory also refers to *Angli* and *Anglorum ecclesia.* It is true that Gregory addressed Ethelbert, king of Kent as *regi Anglorum* (Bede i.32, pp. 110–11) and Bede himself refers to Aldfrith of Northumbria as *regem Anglorum* (v.15, pp. 506–7) – but these are abnormal usages before the tenth century. Cf. Sarah Foot in *Blackwell Encyclopaedia,* pp. 170–1 and refs., who is clear that *gens Anglorum* was coined by Gregory. Maybe: I do not think we can be sure of it; but his use of the phrase was crucial to its later use.
20 Bede i. 15, pp. 50–1 – inspiring a 'vast archaeological debate' (Wormald 1983, p. 100). See also the essays in Bassett 1989.
21 For the legend of Gregory and the Angles, see Bede ii.2, pp. 132–5, and refs.
22 Walker 1956.

a Germanic language with links on the coasts of the Low Countries and Germany but surprisingly few Celtic loan words. Religion and language suggest little contact between native British and the Anglo-Saxon invader; whereas common sense, archaeology and the political history of the peoples suggest that there was constant interchange. There is thus no reliable information on the genetic mixture from which the modern English are derived – only a series of fascinating puzzles.[23] None the less, it was clearly possible for an intelligent foreigner in the sixth century and an exceptionally well-informed Englishman of the seventh and eighth to believe in the existence of 'the English people'.

At first sight it may seem surprising that this ethnic unit (as it was perceived to be) had to wait over three hundred years for political expression. But such seems to have been the case: when an English king achieved such power as to be reckoned overlord of several kingdoms he was called not king of the English but *bretwalda*. Now we do not know for sure what the phrase meant: it is likely that it implied some sort of hegemony in Britain (see p. 80); it cannot possibly have implied any special rule in Angel-land, 'England'. It was only after the Viking invasions, and the union of the non-Viking areas of England by Alfred and his dynasty, that the concept of an English *kingdom* found fortune (see chapters 9–10).

In truth, this separation of people and kingdom need not surprise us: it is only a remarkably dramatic example of a common experience. Kings and queens were dynasts, members of an international caste, set (in some senses) above the petty nationalisms of regions and peoples. Soon after the end of our period, King Richard I reigned for ten years as king of England, spending only a few months in his kingdom. He was much more at home in the large areas of France he also ruled; he married a princess from Navarre in northern Spain; he went on Crusade, settling the affairs of the kingdoms of Sicily, Jerusalem (after a fashion) and Cyprus before returning to England – only very briefly – in 1194. This was a cosmopolitan age in which those who had stomach for it travelled far. But it was also an age which saw the intensifying of many local loyalties – when Welsh and Scottish loyalties found new expression, as Rees Davies has taught us, when the descendants of the Norman conquerors called themselves Englishmen.[24] It was possible for a king to

23   On attempts to align genetic and linguistic evidence, see the penetrating comments in Sims-Williams 1998.
24   Davies 1994–7.

find and harness local loyalties; and the English people had, after all, existed in some senses for centuries longer than the king of the English.

The full ambivalence of these divergent sentiments is brought out by Shakespeare most forcefully in *Henry V*. A king pursuing a purely private and dynastic quarrel – an English king claiming to be king of France as well – precipitates a war which means some loss of life to his own people, immense destruction to the French. On the other hand, it is in some ways a heroic epic. A small English army wins a glorious victory over the French. There are moments of patriotic rhetoric, as in the siege of Harfleur:

> Once more unto the breach, dear friends, once more,
> Or close the wall up with our English dead! (3.1.1–2)

and many more during the battle of Agincourt. The chorus emphasizes the drama and, in the end, the triumph, in a manner curiously at variance with the mood of much of the play. For from the start the purely dynastic nature of Henry's claim to the French throne is strongly emphasized. The archbishop of Canterbury gives a pedantic account of the case, whose very pedantry underlines how far removed the issue is from the normal interests and concerns of the French and English peoples – and then urges Henry to war. The French dauphin sends Henry a set of tennis balls as a parody of a challenge, and this helps to make the quarrel personal and petty. The rhetoric at the siege of Harfleur is immediately followed by Bardolph's skit on it, and the comic and the sordid sides of warfare are laid bare. Some of the finest poetry in the play is reserved for the duke of Burgundy in the final act: he attempts to make peace between the kings by a brilliant evocation of a French countryside destroyed by war.

> The darnel, hemlock and rank fumitory
> Doth root upon, while that the coulter rusts
> That should deracinate such savagery. (5.2.45–7)

The images of hemlock, rust and savagery recall us to the nature of war. Most of all, the ambivalence comes out in Henry's wandering by night incognito among the English tents before the battle. Every variety of viewpoint is offered him, each more unwelcome than the one before. The common soldiers lay the responsibility for their fate securely on the king:

> Upon the king!...
> We must bear all.
> O hard condition, twin-born with greatness... (4.1.203–6)

but also, as the audience well knows, of his own making. The dilemma is most brilliantly and forcefully presented: Henry is the English king enrolled with his people under the banner of St George; but he is also a dynast with a doubtful claim to a foreign throne and a petty quarrel with the rival heir. Thus Shakespeare seems to invite us to view a king sometimes as the central, symbolic figurehead of a people – but sometimes as one of an international caste with interests quite separate – quite alien even – to those of his subjects.

The early Anglo-Saxon kings lorded it over a variety of peoples and regions. Only in the tenth and eleventh centuries did they fully and effectively climb on the bandwagon of the *gens Anglorum*, and come to bear the title of *rex Anglorum* – king of the English. Thus this book is not a history of the English people, but of the dynasties which happened to rule them.

2

The Method of this Inquiry

The further back we go from the modern world into the Middle Ages, the less material the historian has to work on. If a man wishes to study human society at work in detail, or to learn how to select the significant details from a mass of information, he will do better to study very recent history. If he wishes to understand and enjoy the detective element in history, to see how one can wring information from a few scattered clues – or if he wishes to see human nature at work in a different context from his own, to stir his imagination by studying his own remote ancestors, remote not only in time but in their thoughts and interests – then he will be well advised to study the Middle Ages, and will be richly rewarded for his efforts. This book could not hope to be a collection of biographies: the kings were too many; our information is too sparse. I have therefore, quite deliberately, made it a collection of problems: how were kings made? What did they do? How did we come to have kings at all? In the earlier chapters, by pursuing these questions, I hope to elucidate the nature of early kingship, to free it from the strange political notions which are inclined to cling to it, sometimes because of modern preconceptions, sometimes because of the lingering influence of seventeenth- or nineteenth-century historians, who saw in kingship the origins of seventeenth-century tyranny, and in royal councils the origins of parliamentary liberty.

We shall find that early kingship was surrounded by very different ideas from those to which we are accustomed; and as we pursue the story of the early English kings we shall see some of these ideas working out in practice. The early kings are rarely more than names; but as the centuries pass we find some who left their mark on English history – Ethelbert, Edwin, Offa – and from the time of Alfred (871–99) on we know something more of all the English kings than their dates and their battles. By whatever route the sources open to us I have tried to pursue these kings and reveal what manner of men they were – their tastes and interests and achievements. It is by worrying over some particular problem that we can hope best to get to know them. Why was King Athelstan so great a connoisseur of 'relics'? Was William II a religious sceptic? Was Henry I an accessory to the murder of William II? One major difficulty is that we rarely know the physical appearance of these men. No portraits, in the modern sense, survive of any of them. We have some sort of description of Edward the Confessor and the first three Norman kings; we have pictures of many kings – but they are all stylized and conventional. None the less the trappings of kingship, crowns, armour, costume, palaces, castles, and other objects more or less intimately connected with them – rings and jewels made for them, books written for them, coins struck in their name – can give us some kind of physical contact with them; and in the Bayeux Tapestry we see the story of the Norman Conquest told by an English artist for the benefit of one of the greatest of Norman lords, Odo, bishop of Bayeux, the Conqueror's half-brother. In it are shown Edward the Confessor and Harold as well as William the Conqueror. From all these sources our purpose is to find out what we can know of the Saxon and Norman kings of England.[25]

It is sometimes thought that the real pursuit of historical problems cannot be undertaken without a heavy panoply of footnotes and technical arguments. There is, of course, a great deal of truth in this, and it has been one of the chief difficulties in writing this book to make the arguments genuine without making them too technical. I have been sparing in footnotes, and avoided too elaborate a Bibliography. But I have also been aware that if we remove the element of quest, the pursuit of problems, the 'burrowing into wormholes', we remove from history a great part of its interest. The study of medieval history, especially of the early Middle Ages, is largely detective work, and there is no reason why it should not be widely enjoyed as such.

My theme is English kingship: kingship as it was known to the Germanic peoples, the Anglo-Saxons, who conquered and settled what we call 'England' in the fifth and sixth centuries; who formed a multiplicity of tiny kingdoms, out of which the kingship of England grew. The period stretches roughly from 450 to 1154. In 400 most of the island had been part of the Roman empire; in 406 the Vandals and the Burgundians broke across the the Rhine into Gaul; in 410 Alaric and the Visigoths sacked Rome itself. The Roman empire in the east

---

25   I have made no attempt to include the kings of Wales and Scotland: their story is no less interesting, but it is quite different, and cannot be treated as an Appendix to English history. But see pp. 67–70.

survived until 1453; the Roman empire in the west died in the fifth century – died in fact, that is, for its memory lingered on, a potent influence on all its former provinces. Meanwhile military disaster led the Romans to abandon Britain, and leave it a prey to barbarian attackers – from Ireland (the 'Scots'), from Scotland (the 'Picts') and from Germany. The Roman provinces were broken up into kingdoms, whose precise number and extent are quite unknown. Tradition has it that the greatest of these was ruled by a king called Vortigern in the mid-fifth century. We know that Saxons from northern Germany had visited England as pirates and mercenaries for some generations before the time of Vortigern; but Vortigern is said to have raised an especially powerful force of Saxon mercenaries under leaders called Hengest and Horsa. The Saxons presently turned on their master, and formed a kingdom of their own, traditionally supposed to be the kingdom of Kent. From then on settlers from northern Germany came in numerous shiploads, sailed up the Thames, the rivers of the Wash and Humber, settled, formed little kingdoms and confederations, and conquered the native 'Britons'. The Britons were not wholly defenceless. Early in the sixth century they found a great leader, whom tradition (probably wrongly) calls Arthur, who drove the German invaders out of a great part of the south midlands. But this success was not lasting. By the late sixth century the Germans had recovered what they had lost; they had conquered at least two-thirds of what we call England, and their supremacy was rapidly admitted in the rest.

The invaders are commonly called the Angles, Saxons and Jutes. The Saxons came from northern Germany ('Old Saxony', what we should call north-western Germany), the Angles perhaps from where Germany and Denmark meet, the Jutes (to cut a long story short) most probably from Friesland or the Rhineland. In England they met and mingled; very roughly, the Angles preponderated in the north and midlands, the Saxons in the south and west, the Jutes in Kent and Hampshire. By 600 the country was firmly settled by the 'Anglo-Saxons', and a group of leading kingdoms was beginning to emerge: the chief were Northumbria, the most powerful kingdom of the seventh century, Mercia, which, after challenging Northumbria in the seventh century, won supremacy in its turn in the eighth, and Wessex, which after a late start emerged the leader in the early ninth century. Also about 600 took place the central event of Anglo-Saxon history, the mission of St Augustine from Rome to begin the conversion of the English. In the decades following 597 missionaries both from Rome and from Christian Ireland, Wales and Scotland worked with great effort among the pagan Anglo-Saxons. In the late seventh century the English Church was firmly organized by a Syrian Greek, sent at an advanced age by the pope to be archbishop of Canterbury, Theodore of Tarsus. By that time most of the English kingdoms were Christian, at least in name; and in the eighth century, in the days of the Venerable Bede, the English Church was one of the centres of western civilization.

In the early ninth century Wessex became supreme; by the end of the ninth century it was the only English kingdom; in the tenth and eleventh centuries it was converted into the kingdom of England. This was the joint work of the Danish invaders and the dynasty of King Alfred. The Danes raided, and then settled in England in the ninth century; by 871 they had conquered most of it, Wessex excepted. The other royal dynasties became extinct. From 871 to 899 England was ruled by Alfred, an indefatigable warrior, and a man who showed exceptional imagination in the arts both of peace and of war. He just saved Wessex, and laid foundations on which his successors were able to build a united English kingdom; but this could hardly have happened if he had not been succeeded by a line of notably able rulers, his son Edward the Elder (899–924), his grandson Athelstan (924–39) and his great-grandson Edgar (959–75) in particular. The Danes were pagan, and the conversion of England had, in some measure, to start again. This was rapidly accomplished in the wake of the ecclesiastical revival of the tenth century, a movement of reform, particularly of monastic reform. The revival of English kingship, however, was rudely checked at the end of the tenth century, when Danish attacks began once again. In 1013 the Danish Swein completed the process of dispossessing the English Ethelred the Unready; but in 1014 Swein died, and it was not until 1016 that his younger son, Cnut, was firmly established as king. Cnut could command the loyalty of both his English and Danish subjects in equal measure, and so, in a special sense, was first king of the united kingdom of England.

Cnut died young; and soon after his death the kingdom reverted to the native English line in the person of Edward the Confessor (1042–66). Edward's death in 1066 was the signal for the most famous crisis in English history. He was succeeded by his brother-in-law Harold II; but nine months later Harold fell under a Norman arrow or a Norman axe at Hastings, and the Normans ruled in his stead. The period closes with the reigns of William the Conqueror (1066–87), his two sons, William II (1087–1100) and Henry I (1100–35), and his grandson, Henry's nephew, Stephen (1135–54).

Of all these kings Alfred is the one about whom we are best informed. We have a number of works written or inspired by himself – his translations and his laws; we have Asser's *Life*. This is not a masterpiece of biography, and its authenticity has been seriously questioned. The dispute continues, but must for the present be ignored. Asser's *Life* is a sandwich, made up of a version of the *Anglo-Saxon Chronicle*, with a description of various aspects of Alfred's life and activity squeezed into it; in this book I have assumed that the latter can reasonably be used as evidence of what a well-informed but not over-intelligent contemporary resident in Alfred's court thought to be true. This is now the view held by most scholars.

Alfred is the only king whose own writings survive from this period; and one of the very few we know to have been literate. Of early kings we have vignettes and other valuable information in the pages of Bede's splendid *Ecclesiastical History* (c.731), the finest historical work produced by any scholar in Europe in this period. Of later kings we have accounts in a variety of chronicles and other narrative sources; of Edward the Confessor we have a contemporary biography; of the Norman kings we have panegyrics and chronicles of various kinds. Of most Saxon kings before Alfred, and many after, we have no narrative account, beyond the brief annals in the *Anglo-Saxon Chronicle*. Of the kings of the lesser kingdoms, we usually know little but their names; of the kings of Lindsey we know nothing but their names; the kings of the Middle Angles and the Middle Saxons (if kings they had) are wholly anonymous.

The early kings, save those fortunate enough to find a place in Bede, must be pursued through one of four channels; the *Anglo-Saxon Chronicle*, genealogies, vernacular poetry, archaeology. The *Chronicle*, as we know it, was drawn up in the reign of Alfred; it was a part of that renaissance of which the king was centre, which produced works in the vernacular, rather than in the normal language of literature, Latin, because the king wished them to be understood by a wider circle. Whether Alfred himself inspired the *Chronicle* has been disputed; but it is difficult not to see in it the reflection of his interests, or to doubt that he perused a copy of it. One of the copies made in his lifetime is still preserved in the library of Corpus Christi College, Cambridge. From this and from later copies which were distributed and continued at various monasteries, we have versions of the chronicle down to the Norman Conquest and even a little beyond; one version was continued, first at Canterbury, then at Peterborough, down to 1154, and gives towards the end a famous description of the reign of King Stephen.

Sources of the Norman period are much more prolific than those of the Saxon, especially of the early Saxon. This is not mainly due to the chance of survival – though countless medieval manuscripts, of course, have disappeared. Mainly it is because far less was written in the seventh century, or in the ninth, than in the twelfth. Even comparatively literate ages, like the age of Bede or of Dunstan (died 988), produced far less than the age of the twelfth-century renaissance. Of this little, a remarkable proportion has survived. The Bodleian library at Oxford contains a copy of one of King Alfred's translations sent by himself to Worcester Cathedral; the Corpus library in Cambridge contains a ninth-century manuscript of the *Chronicle*, and a book which King Athelstan in person gave to the community of St Cuthbert, then at Chester-le-Street (later of Durham Cathedral); the Cotton collection in the British Library contains two of the five surviving copies of Bede's *History*, which were written in Bede's own century, before 800. It is no chance that we find these books in Cotton's collection or in Corpus. After the Dissolution of the monasteries, most medieval manuscripts tended to be destroyed; the invention of printing had made many of them seem valueless. But there were men in the sixteenth century like Matthew Parker, archbishop of Canterbury under Elizabeth I, who were passionately interested in the early history of the English Church – a natural interest in the wake of the Reformation. Parker and his secretaries were fanatical collectors of early manuscripts, especially of early chronicles; and Parker's collection was left to Corpus Christi College, Cambridge, of which he had once been Master. A little later there appeared a collector of equal avidity in Sir Robert Cotton, who shared Parker's interest in the Church; but was also much concerned with developing theories of parliamentary origins. It was widely thought in the early seventeenth century that our parliamentary liberties were derived from the Anglo-Saxon Witan; and this gave Cotton a special interest in Saxon charters, whose long lists of signatories or witnesses are almost our only information on who formed the Witan. It is probably true to say that the majority of pre-Conquest original charters owe their survival to Sir Robert Cotton. The practical concerns (not to say fantasies) of Parker and Cotton, coupled with a genuine devotion to the past, saved much valuable evidence in the nick of time. For this we must be grateful to them; but, for the earlier Saxon period, there was mighty little to save.

The Parker copy of the *Chronicle*, Asser's *Life* (the manuscript of which was preserved by Cotton, but burnt in the disastrous fire of 1731 and so is only known from sixteenth-and seventeenth-century copies), and other manuscripts – including one of the early ninth century in Cotton's collection – contain genealogies and lists of early English kings. From these, if treated with a certain measure of scepticism, and checked wherever possible by other evidence, we can reconstruct lists of early dynasties. It is not perhaps an inspiring thought that we ourselves might be represented to future generations by something akin to a telephone directory; but skilful probing has enabled the experts to derive much interesting information from these lists and genealogies. And the survival of early poetry, especially of the splendid epic *Beowulf* – another of Sir Robert Cotton's finds – enables us to put a little flesh on the dry bones.

Beowulf also helps us to clothe the kings and imagine the houses they lived in; and it has in these respects been marvellously supplemented in recent years by archaeology. The trowel has unearthed many relics of this period: from graves, from settlements, from Saxon and Norman churches and towns, and Norman castles. But the archaeologist can only dig up what is lasting; that is, broadly speaking, stone and pottery, metal which rust has not wholly corrupted, and bones; but not wood or cloth. It is therefore somewhat ironical that the most sensational finds of Saxon archaeology have been the wooden ship at Sutton Hoo and the timber halls of the palace at Yeavering. At Sutton Hoo the timber had rotted, but the iron bolts were still visible, and the marks of the timbers could still be traced in the soil; and in any case it was the contents of the boat which made the discovery so exciting. At Yeavering the timber had entirely disappeared. But timber halls are built round posts set in post-holes, or by driving a row of timbers into slots. When the timber rots, the holes are filled in with soil from the surface, of a different quality from that surrounding the hole. This affects the fertility of the area of the hole, so that when the soil is richer corn grown today will be higher, when less rich, lower, than over the rest of the surrounding ground. Normally this would be extremely difficult to observe. But from an aeroplane, flying low over the field in early dawn or late evening, when the sun is low, one can see the shadow cast by the higher crops on the lower; and so an aerial photograph taken under these conditions will reveal the pattern of a timber hall centuries after the timber has completely disappeared. Thus was Yeavering discovered; and the palace of the Northumbrian kings has since been excavated.

Later in the period the sources become more diverse: a regular currency provides the archaeologist with large finds of coins; growing literacy provides the historian with a mass of charters, laws and (by the eleventh and twelfth centuries) chronicles and biographies to read; more stone buildings – especially the tremendous buildings thrown up in such numbers by the early Normans – give us more substantial, visible monuments of the past; and the chance survival of a remarkable piece of embroidery gives us in the Bayeux Tapestry a chronicle and a film-strip combined: we can study events, and armour and costume, and many other things, all at once.

This is not meant to be a catalogue, and is far from complete. As we proceed, I shall try to reveal from time to time how historians use these various materials to reconstruct the past; and explain some in more detail, and introduce others not here described. In this period it is often more interesting, more exciting, more intellectually satisfying, to consider how we know rather than what we know.

3

On King-making

In Sir John Plumb's *The First Four Georges* we are introduced to four kings spanning a little more than a hundred years. The assignment of this book is seven hundred years and perhaps two hundred kings. Worse still, the large majority of them are so obscure we know only their names; a few are wholly anonymous. Yet the study of these distant figures has a special fascination: their obscurity challenges us to find every clue and follow it wherever it leads us; and if we do this we shall find that we can learn a surprising amount about the early English kings. We shall also find ourselves inspecting the roots of English kingship, of our oldest institution of government; and that too is rewarding. It will help us to understand some things about English monarchy, some of the reasons why its continuity has been so little broken; but it will only do this if we are quite clear at the outset that in most particulars the kingship of Saxon and Norman times was utterly unlike the constitutional monarchy of Elizabeth II.

Historical labels easily deceive us, and some of the most deceptive are those which surround ideas of government and kingship. Nobody imagines that a medieval king, whether of England, France or Germany, was a constitutional monarch in the modern sense. But one often hears or reads discussions on whether they were limited or absolute, elective or hereditary. No doubt we shall keep these problems in the back of our minds as we study these kings and the manner of their rule; but in the front of our minds we should be concerned with less abstract notions. If we observe how men acted and how they described their actions we shall get a much sharper focus on their assumptions; we shall see their minds more as the human mind really is, not as the mirror of coherent principles of political thought, but as the battlefield of conflicting assumptions and aspirations, without evident coherence. Human nature, the psychologists tell us, is liable to change. But the nobleman who acclaimed a Saxon king was acting on a mingling of impulses as rich, confused and intriguing as a modern voter. This is not to underestimate the interest of political theory or its influence on human affairs; as we shall see, intellectual influences utterly remote from the native tradition of the Saxon peoples played a crucial part in moulding English monarchy. But the meaning of this will only become clear as we inspect some of the peculiarities of early kingship; and the first problem is to try to discover how kings were made.

This problem has been the subject of many extraordinary notions. In 1867, in the first volume of his great *History of the Norman Conquest of England*, Edward Augustus Freeman propounded one of the most preposterous. In writing of the Witenagemot, the Anglo-Saxon royal council, he said: 'In one sense it was more democratic than anything that the most advanced Liberal would venture to dream of; in another sense it was more oligarchic than anything that the most unbending Conservative would venture to defend. Yet it may in practice have fairly represented the wishes of the nation; and, if so, no people ever enjoyed more complete political freedom than the English did in these early times. For the powers of the ancient Witenagemot surpassed beyond all measure the powers which our written Law vests in a modern Parliament. In some respects they surpassed the powers which our conventional Constitution vests in the House of Commons. The king could do absolutely nothing without the consent of his Wise Men [the Witan]. First of all, it was from them that he derived his political being, and it was on them that he depended for its continuance. The Witan chose the king and the Witan could depose him. The power of deposition is a power which, from its very nature, can be exercised but rarely; we therefore do not find many kings deposed by Act of Parliament either before or since the Norman Conquest....

'If the Witan could depose the king, still more undoubtedly did the Witan elect the king. It is strange how people's eyes are blinded on this subject.... The ancient English Kingship was elective. It was elective in the same sense in which all the old Teutonic kingdoms were elective. Among a people in whose eyes birth was highly valued, it was deemed desirable that the king should be the descendant of illustrious and royal ancestors. In the days of heathendom it was held that the king should come of the supposed stock of the Gods. These feelings everywhere pointed to some particular house as the royal house, the house whose members had a special claim on the suffrages of the electors. In every kingdom there was a royal family, out of which alone, under all ordinary circumstances, kings were chosen; but within that royal family the Witan of the land had a free choice.'[26]

Freeman had it in mind to refute the old Tory doctrine of the Divine Right of kings. He points out that there have been an infinite number of different rules of succession in different countries; that it is absurd to suppose that any one of these is more natural or eternal than another. What is strange is that he should assume that the English law was always clear and coherent, even if it changes at certain times. He lived, as do we, under a monarchy whose rules of succession were precisely defined by law: they are, perhaps, the most precise and clear-cut arrangements surrounding our modern sovereigns. When a king or queen dies, we know who is going to succeed – or rather, who has instantly succeeded; the whole royal family is arranged in order of succession, according to a coherent principle established by law; in this case by written, Statute Law.

In the early Middle Ages the law of England was unwritten. There are exceptions to this statement, as we shall see; but they do not affect our present problem. This means that succession to the throne was arranged by custom and tradition. Custom can be a very definite thing, and very tenacious; but among primitive peoples it has a way of appearing definite and clear only to the people who operate, live and assume it; of appearing to the outsider vague, indefinite, even contradictory. A special difficulty attaches to the study of early mon-archies: as time passed, practices changed, but our information is often so slender that we must try to draw a clue from here and there and form a coherent picture covering a wide space of time. A further difficulty is that at various times there was much diversity of opinion, more than has commonly been allowed; and since the succession to the throne was always a vital issue, it was frequently the subject of discussion and debate.

There were, indeed, no precise rules; but the succession to the thrones of the Anglo-Saxon kingdoms and the English kingdom was hedged round with a series of conventions, customs and assumptions; and out of the dialectic between these conventions each succession was settled – sometimes peacefully, sometimes by violence. Frequently a 'strong man armed' seized the throne; and in later centuries at least he often felt bound to justify his action, and from the way in which he justified it we can tell what rules he was pretending to have followed. If at all possible, he showed that he was related to his predecessor – that he had a hereditary claim; he argued that the people had accepted his rule in due form – that he had been 'elected', whatever that meant;

26 Freeman 1867–79, I, 113–17.

and he asserted that his predecessor had declared that he was to succeed – he had been designated by a reigning king. Our investigation of king-making must be woven out of these three threads, inheritance, election and designation; in some way or another each of these three entered into most acts of king-making in western Europe in the Middle Ages.

Freeman spoke as if a king was elected, as if monarchy was essentially elective; inheritance was respected, election was the law. This is a large and strange assumption; and we must be very wary of making assumptions.

Even the most obvious generalization about kingship, that only one person rules at a time, had numerous exceptions to it. In early days kings did not necessarily rule alone: they may indeed not normally have done so. All the male members of a family could rule together, while one king might hold a pre-eminence, so it appears, in most kingdoms. As time passed 'monarchy' in the literal sense – the rule of one man – steadily developed. In later times the Anglo-Saxon monarchies remained hereditary; not in the sense that the kingdom passed by any strict rule of primogeniture, from eldest son to eldest son, but that in the large majority of cases a king was in fact succeeded by his eldest son or nearest male relative. There are cases in which a brother succeeded although the old king had children; but usually in such cases the children were very young. There are one or two cases when it was argued that a son 'born in the purple' – when his father was king – had a superior right to one born before his father succeeded; and none of the Norman kings was the heir by primogeniture. In 1066 Edgar the Ætheling was related to Edward the Confessor more nearly than William of Normandy, far more nearly than Harold. In 1087 and 1100 the Conqueror's younger sons, William and Henry, succeeded although their eldest brother Robert was alive. In 1135 Henry I's nephew Stephen succeeded, although Henry left a legitimate daughter, and Stephen himself had an elder brother.

The succession in 1066 and the succession in 1135 are among the most extraordinary and interesting in English history. They come near the end of our period, and so are relatively well documented; and they reveal between them almost all the problems and forces at work in English king-making. They will serve us very well as examples of the various conventions and assumptions.

Edward the Confessor (1042–66) was childless. He had a nephew called Edward who lived in exile in Hungary; a cousin called William who was duke of Normandy; while the most powerful man in England after the king was Harold, earl of Wessex, who was his brother-in-law. In addition, his predecessor, Harthacnut, who was also king of

Denmark, had made an arrangement with Magnus, king of Norway, that, if either should die without an heir, the other was to succeed to his kingdom. In virtue of this Magnus had invaded Denmark and laid claim to England in 1042–3; and his claim was inherited (oddly enough) by his uncle, Harold Hardrada.

Edward's closest relation was his nephew; but Edward the exile died in 1057, and his son, Edgar the Ætheling, was too young to be a serious candidate in 1066. To William, on hereditary grounds, two objections could be raised: that he was illegitimate, and that he was related to Edward in the female line, and not himself descended from Edward's predecessors. It is abundantly clear that, if heredity had been in this instance the vital test, William would never have become king of England. It is strange enough that he ever became duke of Normandy: when his father died he was a boy of seven and the duchy was in uproar; and in the Middle Ages illegitimacy was normally regarded as a barrier to succession. He was the exception which proved all the rules; for the precedent was never followed. Henry I acknowledged at least twenty illegitimate children, including a number of sons; but none of them succeeded him.

The question whether the kingdom could pass through the female line is more complicated. The short answer seems to be that it had very rarely happened in Anglo-Saxon times, but that there was no known barrier against it. Women were as respectfully treated before the Conquest as after; but we must distinguish carefully between rules of succession and the status of women. Many societies have been matrilineal, that is, inheritance has passed normally through a female line, but this does not necessarily, nor even usually, go with a high status for the womenfolk themselves. Nor can we deduce from the attitude to women in pre-Conquest times anything about the rules of inheritance. All that we can safely say is that it was possible for property to pass in the female line under Anglo-Saxon law, but not normal. All the Germanic peoples were mainly patrilineal; but in none of them, in early days, was this a strict rule. At one time anthropologists taught us that inheritance must be either patrilineal or matrilineal; and that, if we found traces of succession in the female line in a patrilineal society, it must mean that it had once been matrilineal. This view eventually seeped through to the historians, and one sometimes hears echoes of it still. But it has long been abandoned by the anthropologists: it is quite common for systems of inheritance to contain both elements.

It is possible that succession in the female line was less rare than our records suggest. It has been the practice in many societies for men, especially great men, to recite with pride the catalogue of their

ancestors; genealogy has been a favourite form of literature (if such it
can be called) in many parts of the world at many different times. The
royal genealogies of primitive peoples are rarely historical documents,
though they often enshrine – and may preserve for centuries – some
elements of genuine tradition. Their purpose is to join the reigning
king to the ancestor from whom the kingdom derives; in some cases,
from the god who gave the kings their authority. It is in the nature of
genealogies to suggest a tidy line of succession from father to son – to
cover up more distant relationships, where necessary, and to jump
generations. Since our early records of royal Saxon families are
mainly genealogical, we may be inclined to exaggerate the patrilineal
element in royal succession. But the influence of genealogies works
both ways: from early days the love of genealogy inclined men to stick
to the male line, to insist that a king should be the direct descendant of
the ancestor who gave his name to the dynasty. In the early records of
Wessex, it is frequently emphasized that this or that king was of the
line of Cerdic; and almost all the Anglo-Saxon genealogies go back
ostensibly to Woden, the chief god of the pagan Teutonic hierarchy.

It may have helped to give colour to William's claim to the throne
that his great-aunt was Edward's mother. But it did not make William
a descendant of Cerdic, still less of Woden. William's wife was of
Cerdic's line; and his youngest son, Henry I, whose claim to be
William's heir was doubtful, married Edgar the Ætheling's niece,
Edith or Matilda, and once more brought the blood of Cerdic (and
perhaps of Woden!) into the English royal house.

In fact, of course, William was king because he had succeeded in
conquering the country: it was his strength, not his right, which
convinced the Witan that they must accept him. Conquest and usurpation were comparatively common events in the early Middle Ages;
and the ease with which a disputed succession could lead to civil war
and bloodshed helps to explain why archbishops and bishops were
prepared to accept and crown *de facto* kings, sometimes at very short
notice: they were trying to stifle dispute by presenting a *fait accompli*.
Already in the early eleventh century Swein of Denmark and his son
Cnut had been accepted and elected kings simply because they had
succeeded in conquering the country. Election gave a cloak of legitimacy to a usurper, and Cnut strengthened his position by marrying
his predecessor's widow, which gave him affinity, though not kindred,
with the house of Cerdic. William the Conqueror went further: he
asserted, and believed, that he was king by right as well as by conquest. Earl Harold had been Edward the Confessor's brother-in-law,
since Edward's queen was his sister. But this hardly made him the
king's next of kin; and since Harold was elected, and succeeded

against both Harold Hardrada and (for a few months) against William of Normandy, it might be supposed that Freeman was right, and that the monarchy was essentially elective. This, however, would be a very superficial view of the case. Edward the Confessor died on 5 January;[27] Harold was elected and crowned on 6 January. It is quite impossible that the election was anything but a formality: it must have been planned before the old king's death. It is commonly supposed that a monarchy is either hereditary or elective. This dilemma and the facts of 1066 sit ill together. None of the three candidates had a hereditary claim which would stand any serious inspection; the obvious heir, Edgar the Ætheling, was ignored until after the battle of Hastings. There was certainly a hereditary and an elective element in the English monarchy; but these were factors in a more complex situation; and to understand this, and the meaning of election, we must make contact with a third factor, the most decisive of all.

After Hastings, William might claim to be king by divine judgement as well as by conquest. Neither aspect of his title was neglected. But even in the eleventh century men hesitated to assume, without further inquiry, on whose side God really wished to be; and even in the eleventh century men could distinguish between might and right. By what right was William king?

In all probability the claim which mattered most to the two Harolds and to William was essentially the same: that at various times and in various ways each had been designated heir to the kingdom by a reigning king. Harold Hardrada's designation was remote. His nephew and predecessor, Magnus, had made, as we have seen, an arrangement with Edward's predecessor by which if either died without an heir, the other should succeed to both kingdoms. We do not know precisely what these words meant: how close a relation was implied in the word heir, whether the kingdom of Harthacnut was meant to include England as well as Denmark, whether there was any intention that the arrangement should carry on to Magnus's successor. The claim may have been exceedingly shadowy; but there is no doubt of its nature. Harold Hardrada could only claim the English throne by virtue of designation by Harthacnut. In this the Witan, or Witenagemot, can have no place at all.

Duke William's claim was more lucid. He had been designated by Edward the Confessor as his heir. The Norman sources, not unnaturally, are more explicit on this than the English, and the story has been doubted. But it seems to be assumed in the Bayeux Tapestry (see pp. 4–6). This shows us how Harold fell accidentally into William's

27 Or possibly on 4 January (see *Edward the Confessor*, p. 124 n. 329).

hands in 1064, and how William made him swear a solemn oath. It does not define the oath, but clearly implies that Harold swore to support William's claim to the English throne. It is likely that William used strong pressure; but it seems to me unlikely that Harold would have sworn unless he was compelled to admit that William had a case; and equally improbable that William would have thought of invading England in 1066 unless he had a well-based claim to the throne. There seems only one explanation, that William had been designated formally by Edward as his heir. This is most likely to have happened when Edward was most his own master, and most able to indulge his taste of giving patronage to Normans – that is to say, in the years 1051–2. In 1051 an English source records a state visit to Edward by William, to a king by a foreign duke – a very rare and singular event in this period; we can hardly doubt that it was then that Edward promised him the crown. (See pp. 137–8.)

How, then, did Harold succeed in 1066? Edward had designated William as his heir. The Witan, or the leading factions in it, may never have been happy about William's claim; they may well have been openly opposed to it in 1065–6. Harold had by then established himself as the leading man in the country, the person most likely to hold England together and defend it successfully against Norwegian attack. But we have seen that Harold's election was purely formal. The decision must have been taken in Edward's lifetime. The English sources state quite plainly that Edward granted the kingdom to Harold, and some such story is also implied by one Norman chronicler – who goes on to point out that this was either untrue or unjust, since Edward had already granted it to William. In the Bayeux Tapestry (Plate 1) King Edward's burial has been placed before his death, so as to enable the scene headed 'Here King Edward on his [death]bed addresses his faithful men' to be placed side by side with one headed 'Here they gave the king's crown to Harold'. The inscription, as so often, is elliptical; the interpretation, in the circumstances of the eleventh century, is clear. Edward had designated Harold as his successor.

This implication could be drawn even if it were not supported by other evidence. There is copious evidence, from all over western Europe, that designation by the old king was a crucial element in the making of the new. Conrad I of Germany designated Henry of Saxony, founder of the great Saxon dynasty, as his successor (919), although they were in no way related. In German history before 1077 this was the normal process, although a man could not reign until he had been acknowledged as king by representatives of his subjects. Charlemagne had designated and crowned his son Louis the Pious in his own lifetime, so that there were two kings and two emperors in Charles's last years. This plan of establishing a successor in one's own lifetime had already been tried by Offa, the king of Mercia, in the late eighth century; and was often to be followed in England, France and Spain. In the early eighth century Bede tells us that Osric, king of the Northumbrians, appointed Ceolwulf, brother of his predecessor Cenred (no relation of his own, apparently), as his successor.[28] These cases are few, but the cases in which we have any details about how kings succeeded are also few.

Freeman's account of the Witan is now seen to be profoundly misleading. Its rights are much more doubtful, and were probably more vague by far than he allowed. The Witan consisted of those leading men and counsellors (so far as we can tell) whom the king chose to summon; it advised him, but only when he asked its advice. On the other hand a king was wise to ask and take advice; and a king who was on good terms with his Witan would find it easier to enforce his will, and be much more in touch with the temper of his subjects. It may well be that designation played a larger part in king-making than election; but we must not abolish the Witan altogether. If we ask 'Why did King Edward change his mind?' we are faced with a very awkward question; so awkward that some historians have averred that he cannot have changed his mind, and that some part of the story must be untrue. This seems to me unnecessary scepticism, although I do not think we can be sure what happened in the Christmas court of 1065. The king was old and ill; he may have been more open to influence than hitherto. He may have felt that Harold was the one man strong enough to save the kingdom from chaos, and in particular to defend it against Harold Hardrada, the most noted warrior of the northern world. We may be fairly sure that he was under strong pressure from many of his subjects to prefer Harold to William. It is no doubt true that the election on 6 January was a formality; but only because the Wise Men had already made up their minds.

The election indeed seems usually to have been a purely formal process, however much lobbying may have lain behind it. It was hardly an election in our sense of the word. We assume in an election that there shall be more than one candidate; that there shall be a fixed and easily defined body of electors; and that the election shall be by some kind of majority vote. Between 450 and 1154, so far as we know, no election of this kind took place in Europe. The first known election under a majority principle took place in 1181, when Pope Lucius III was elected under the papal election decree passed at the

28 Bede v.23, pp. 556–9.

Lateran council of 1179, which laid down (for the first time) that a majority of two-thirds among the cardinals made a man pope. In the election of kings there was no majority principle, no fixed body of electors, and very often only one candidate. Why, then, do we call them elections at all?

The word elect or choose (Latin *eligere*, Old English *ceosan*) was used by contemporaries so often as to make it plain that it played an important part in their thinking. There are, however, few more obscure words in English constitutional history. Clearly there was some difference of opinion among contemporaries. The well-known writer of the turn of the tenth and eleventh centuries, Abbot Ælfric, evidently felt that there was a real element of choice when a new king came to be made: 'No man can make himself king, but the people has the choice to choose as king whom they please; but after he is consecrated as king, he then has dominion over the people, and they cannot shake his yoke from their necks.'[29] It is doubtful if either part of this statement would have been generally accepted at the time; the people did not 'choose whom they please', and every Germanic people claimed in some way or another the right to resist a tyrannical king, the right to rebel. We should not read too much into Ælfric's words: he is not stating precise constitutional doctrines, but telling his audience that kings ought not to be usurpers and people ought not to rebel – a general plea for good behaviour, not unsuitable in the reign of Ethelred the Unready.

The word elect was used in contexts where no element of choice can have been involved. Sometimes it was God who elected; and all kings felt themselves to be kings by God's grace – and so by his choice, by *His* election. But the word is also commonly used of human agents. When Henry I became king of Germany he was first designated by King Conrad on his deathbed, then, at the instance of Conrad's brother, elected by the Franks and Saxons. The Franks and Saxons were two of the four peoples who comprised his kingdom.[30] They did not choose Henry as king, they simply acknowledged him; and there is little doubt that this is the true meaning of the Latin *eligere* and the Old English *ceosan* in English sources. In many cases these words may hide discussion and arrangement; what they actually describe is a formal process of acknowledgement and acclamation.

This comes out very clearly in the description of how Edmund Ironside became king in 1016. Cnut was master of a great part of England; Ethelred was dead. To rally support to Edmund, Ethelred's

29   EHD I, 925–6, from Ælfric, *Sermones Catholici*, I, 212.
30   Widukind, pp. 38–9.

eldest son, demanded as impressive a show of king-making as could be staged. He was chosen, we are told, by the members of the Witan who were in London at the time, and the citizens (*burhwaru*) of London. From this and later occasions when the citizens of London played a part in king-making they came to make the startling claim that no king could be chosen without their consent. London was already a great city by 1016, and the leading men may have played an important part in the events of that year. But what was needed was a group to strengthen the Witan, only a proportion of whom can have been present, and a throng of citizens to acclaim the new king. The Witan and the leading citizens simply acknowledged their allegiance to Edmund; the people acclaimed him; that seems to have been all that was normally involved in an early medieval election.

The coronation rite opened with a formal demand for the people's consent. The bishops, later just the archbishop, presented, as the latter still presents, the sovereign-elect to the people for their approval; and only when this had been signified did he proceed. This is surely what Stigand is performing in the Bayeux Tapestry on 6 January 1066; and this may have been all that was involved in Harold's election. More probably some formal gathering of notables, to whom one of the leading men, perhaps one of the archbishops, presented Harold, will have preceded it. Sometimes the two processes were kept well apart. After Hastings the Wise Men (by great folly, as one of the chroniclers thought) acknowledged Edgar the Ætheling; later Archbishop 'Ealdred (of York), prince Edgar, Earl Edwin, Earl Morcar, and all the best men from London' went to Berkhamsted to submit to William and swear fealty; thus completing his election.[31] Later, on Christmas Day, he was anointed and crowned in Westminster Abbey; and the great shout of the *collaudatio* at the opening of the service so frightened the Norman knights that they set fire to the buildings round the abbey church. But the seal was put on Edward's designation, William's conquest, the Witan's submission and God's election by the sacred ceremony of anointing and coronation, according to a rite which has much in common with that employed in 1953. Thus the *collaudatio* was originally the formal act of election; but in due course became a fossilized confirmation of a formal act which had already taken place.

The final act of the king-making was the solemn confirmation by God's blessing of the process which had gone before in the rites of anointing and coronation. All that we have described so far – inheritance, designation, and election – has a long history going back into early Germanic society. Some attempt shall be made a little later to

31 *ASC*, ed. Garmonsway, p. 200 (1066).

penetrate into this obscure region. The history of the coronation
ceremony, however, is comparatively clear. In the fifth and sixth
centuries the ceremonies of election of Germanic kings were often
completed by raising the king on a shield. We do not know whether
this was ever done in England. Indeed, we have no idea what ceremonies were performed when a king was made before the days of
Offa, little enough before the days of Edgar. In 787 Ecgfrith, Offa's
son, was consecrated in his father's lifetime. This has been taken to
mean, anointed with chrism and holy oil, the central act of any
medieval coronation ceremony. It is no coincidence that this should
have happened in the late eighth century. In 751 the Frankish dynasty
was changed by a ceremony of anointing and coronation sanctioned
by the pope; in 781 two sons of Charlemagne had been anointed by
the pope in person. What is the significance of these events?

The early Frankish kings had all been drawn from the family of the
Merovings. Whatever their origin, they had reigned so long by the
eighth century that it was a considerable effort for anyone in Francia
to imagine a king not of the dynasty – even though among the other
European peoples Visigothic kings had usually been elected and
Lombard kings had only had any sort of hereditary succession for
about a century. In the early eighth century the effective ruler of
Francia was the 'mayor of the palace' Charles Martel; for a time he
dispensed with monarchy altogether, but most of the time he kept a
Merovingian puppet in being. In 751 his son Pippin grew weary of the
Merovingian farce, and applied to the pope for permission to assume
the royal title himself.

In such a situation it was natural for men in the Middle Ages, and
especially churchmen of the eighth century, to look back into the Old
Testament for precedents for what they were doing. And there they
found what they were looking for: how Samuel had anointed David to
be king because Saul had lost God's favour – even though David was
in no way related to Saul; and how David's successor Solomon was
chosen, not by primogeniture, but by 'Zadok the priest and Nathan
the prophet' (albeit acting on King David's instructions). The ceremony devised for Pippin's king-making was what we should call a
coronation; like many Teutonic kings, he had taken over crown (or
diadem), orb and sceptre from the ceremonial of the eastern Roman
empire. But the crucial event in it was the anointing. This was performed, in medieval coronations, with holy oil and with chrism; and
chrism (oil and balsam mixed) was also used in the ordination of
priests and the consecration of bishops. Small wonder that anointing
came to be regarded as having a sacramental character, as a kind of
ordination.

Some kind of anointing may have been known among the Celtic princes of Ireland and Wales before the days of Offa. But we know little of this, and little enough of the ceremonies of king-making between Offa's time and the early ninth century. From the ninth century on the English rituals have been reconstructed in the brilliant studies of Janet Nelson and others. It is abundantly clear that there was a continuous tradition of royal anointings and coronations from the early ninth century to the Conquest – often closely linked to contemporary rites on the Continent, especially in the Frankish service prepared for the anointing of the young princess Judith in 856 for her marriage to the king of the West Saxons – appropriately, based on English models. A new element entered for a time in 973, when, so it seems, King Edgar was anointed and crowned for the second time. It has been observed that Edgar's second coronation was linked to his claim to overlordship of the whole of the British Isles; it was, in short, an imperial coronation.[32] And it may be noted that Edgar's coronation in the Roman city of Bath fell just eleven years after the imperial coronation of Otto the Great in Rome in 962. We have unusually good records of the ceremony performed by St Dunstan of Canterbury and St Oswald of York at Bath on Whit Sunday 973. The same order was used from the ninth to the mid-eleventh century; and many elements in it were used in 1953.

'The holy season [of Pentecost] was approaching', writes a contemporary, 'in which it was the custom for the archbishops and all the other eminent bishops and abbots, and religious abbesses, and ealdormen and reeves and other laymen' to come to court. 'An edict went out from the emperor that they should come to him, from the east, from the west, from the north, and from the sea.' They came not to expel him or to plot against him, but rather 'that the most reverent bishops might bless, anoint, consecrate him, by Christ's leave, from whom and by whom the blessed unction of highest blessing and holy religion has proceeded' – the first of many indications of what is implicit in the words of the service itself, that the king is God's elect, God's chosen, and for this reason only (whatever the human instruments) fit to be God's anointed.

Two bishops led Edgar into the church while the choir sang an antiphon. The king prostrated himself before the altar, laid aside the crown (which he already wore), and Dunstan began the singing of the *Te Deum*, but was so moved by the occasion that he wept for joy at the king's humility and wisdom. When the *Te Deum* was finished, the bishops raised the king, and the archbishop administered to him the coronation oath. At this time, the king swore: 'that the Church of God

32 See Nelson 1986, chs. 12–16, esp. pp. 296–303.

and all his Christian people shall keep true peace under our rule at all times; that I shall forbid thefts and every iniquity to every grade of man; that I shall ordain justice and mercy in all judgements, that the kindly and merciful God may grant to me and to you his mercy' – and to this all present said 'Amen'. After three prayers, came the solemn prayer calling down God's blessing 'on your servant Edgar, whom we have chosen with suppliant devotion for royal authority over Angles and Saxons', and asking God to grant him the faithfulness of Abraham, the gentleness of Moses, the fortitude of Joshua, the humility of David, the wisdom of Solomon, and to help to nourish, instruct, fortify and build up the Church of his kingdom and all the people committed to him, ending with the anointing by Dunstan in Christ's name, and the antiphon 'Zadok the priest and Nathan the prophet' which is still in use, though now in English, not in Latin.

In the midst of further prayers, the king was given a ring and sword, symbols of royal power; then he was crowned, and sceptre and staff were placed in his hands; and a blessing pronounced over him. Then the king received the allegiance of his leading subjects, and was acclaimed: '*vivat rex, vivat rex, vivat rex in eternum*'; and his royal position defined: 'Stand and grasp your royal status, which you have held till now at your father's designation (*paterna suggestione*),[33] delegated to you by hereditary right on the authority of almighty God and by the present agency of ourselves, God's bishops and other servants; and the nearer you see the clergy standing to the holy altars, the stronger the honour you should remember to give them . . . , so that the mediator of God and men may confirm you on the throne of this kingdom as mediator of clergy and people, and make you reign with him in the eternal kingdom – Jesus Christ, to wit, Our Lord . . . .' And after further prayers, and the anointing or consecration of the queen, the ceremonies were completed by a solemn mass.[34]

By a ceremony in all essentials the same, with the *collaudatio* added, muted by the confusion without, and lacking the queen's consecration, since William's wife was still safe in Normandy, the dramatic problem of who should succeed Edward the Confessor was finally resolved on Christmas Day 1066. To understand it we have had to consider the attitude of Edward, of his subjects, of William's rivals – and finally of God himself, as understood by the English bishops. William won his kingdom by force of arms; but he

---

33 Edgar succeeded his brother, not his father, and this phrase should not be interpreted too literally.

34 Byhrtferth, *Vita S. Oswaldi*, pp. 436–8, also in Schramm 1968, pp. 241–3. For the rite itself, see Schramm 1968, pp. 233–41. Cf. Nelson 1986, ch. 16.

claimed to be king by right, and in order to do so, he had to make his claim as clear as it could be. He was related to Edward, but not very closely, and to earlier members of his line not at all. His hereditary claim was better than Harold's, but not strikingly good. He was elected, but only in a purely formal sense; the English leaders submitted to the Conqueror. The strength of his case lay in the attitude of Edward the Confessor: Edward had declared William his successor (even if he had changed his mind since), and Harold had sworn to accept William. In 1066, the principle of designation was more powerful than inheritance or election. In our second example, the accession of King Stephen, the elements are in rather different proportions; but the events of his accession illustrate very clearly the operations of the three principles of inheritance, election and designation, and so form a fitting close to our investigation of king-making.

On 1 December 1135 King Henry was 'alive and dead', in Lyons-la-Forêt in Normandy. Following the precedent set by William II, Henry's nephew Stephen of Blois, count of Boulogne, crossed the Channel, convinced the archbishop of Canterbury that he was the true heir and had Henry's dying vote, and was crowned king, probably on 22 December. In 1139 Henry's daughter Matilda, widow of the Emperor Henry V and now countess of Anjou – whose supporters were therefore called Angevins – also crossed the Channel, and adherents gathered round her. For a moment, in 1141, she was mistress of London, and victory seemed in her grasp. But she failed, and passed on her claim to her son; the young Henry invaded England in 1147, again in 1149, again in 1153, was finally accepted by Stephen as his heir in 1153, and himself crowned on 19 December 1154.

The events of the 'anarchy' raised much comment, and we have a variety of statements from supporters of both sides: chroniclers, like Stephen's supporter who wrote the *Gesta Stephani*, or Matilda's supporter, William of Malmesbury, gave the practical arguments produced in 1135 with the echo of later comments wrapped up in their own reflections. In 1139 the issue was debated before the pope, and of this we have two reports, from John of Salisbury in his *Memoirs of the Papal Court*, and from an eye witness, Gilbert Foliot, later abbot of Gloucester and ultimately bishop of London (1163–87). Gilbert, an ardent supporter of the empress, adds the teeming arguments of a fertile legal brain, which soar to the heights of law natural and divine.[35]

---

35 John of Salisbury, *Historia Pontificalis*, ed. and trans. M. Chibnall, pp. 83–5; Gilbert Foliot, *Letters and Charters*, no. 26; cf. Morey and Brooke 1965, ch. 7; Chibnall 1991, pp. 75–87.

In the early stages only two candidates were seriously considered;
but it is interesting to reflect that these emerged from a possible bag of
at least six. Matilda was Henry I's only surviving legitimate child. If a
woman could succeed, her hereditary claim was clearly very strong.
Stephen's advocate before the pope claimed, indeed, that she was
illegitimate; that her mother had taken a nun's vows at Wilton or
Romsey Abbey and was therefore not free to marry her father, and so
she must be set aside. As Matilda's supporters reasonably pointed out,
the saintly Archbishop Anselm had himself looked into this and
allowed them to marry, and the pope had confirmed his decision.
Nor had anyone dared to raise this hint in Henry's lifetime; twice,
indeed, the English baronage had sworn allegiance to Matilda as their
future queen. On the first occasion Stephen, the legitimate nephew,
and Robert of Gloucester, the illegitimate son, had competed as to
which of them should be the first lay baron after the king of Scots to
swear the oath. These oaths were reluctant, and the first, in many
folk's eyes, was rendered null by the subsequent marriage (without
baronial consent) of Matilda to the count of Anjou. There was precedent for royal widows helping to decide the succession, as in *Beowulf* and in the Danish legend well known to us from Shakespeare's
Hamlet, and, more strikingly, in the case of Queen Emma, wife
successively to Ethelred II and Cnut. This might encourage the idea
that a royal daughter, who carried royal blood in her veins, might
settle a succession. But it was assumed that Matilda's husband
would rule, not she herself. A recent precedent for a woman ruling
in her own right could be found in Queen Urraca, successor to
Alphonso VI of León-Castile; but it was an exceptional case and
had not been a success. It was generally expected that the crown
would pass through Matilda's husband to her sons. Succession in
the female line had its peculiar rules; but these raised no special
difficulty in the present case, since all the other claimants bar one
owed their claim to a lady.

The one exception was Robert of Gloucester, who seems to have
been considered. He refused, however, to be a candidate, on the
ground that he was illegitimate, and this barrier seems to have been
generally accepted, in spite of the obvious precedent of William the
Conqueror. Earl Robert is recorded to have preferred the claims of his
nephew Henry, son of Matilda and Count Geoffrey. Henry was two
years old in 1135, and, even if his claims had been seriously considered, adult direction was needed to deal with the crisis which developed. It is doubtful if the idea of inheritance, powerful though it was,
had yet progressed so far as to outweigh suitability in most people's
minds. Minors had succeeded in the tenth century; the Conqueror as

duke of Normandy had been a minor; but England was not to have a boy-king again until 1216.

If Matilda's claims were to be accepted, the obvious candidate was Geoffrey, count of Anjou, her husband; a worthy heir of the savage counts of Anjou, the man most likely to show the strength of Henry I. There were, however, certain difficulties. First of all, Anjou and Normandy had become enemies; the idea of being subject to a count of Anjou was not in the least congenial to some of the Anglo-Norman baronage. In the second place, he would rule as Matilda's husband; but the marriage was so unhappy that it was extremely doubtful whether they would be able to live together peacefully enough to rule their great dominions. By a curious chance, however, they had sufficiently patched up their differences in Henry I's last years to spend a short space together, to have children, and to quarrel with Henry. The count of Anjou was suspect in England; in 1135 he and his wife were at war against Henry.

Henry's other near relative was his sister, the countess of Blois, who was still alive: she died in 1137. No one seems to have considered the countess herself, but her two eldest sons, Theobald and Stephen, were among the strongest candidates. Theobald was count of Blois, Champagne and Chartres; one of the greatest lords of northern France. He would at least have the strength to hold the power of Anjou at bay, and the Norman barons proceeded to invite him to be their duke. While they were preparing to acknowledge their allegiance to him, however, they received a message that Theobald's younger brother, Stephen, count of Boulogne, and (owing to Henry's favour) probably the best endowed English baron, was crossing the Channel. Theobald was a trifle querulous, but refused to queer his brother's pitch. And so Stephen was able, like William II, to win the archbishop of Canterbury and have himself crowned, like Henry I, to seize the treasury at Winchester, like Edmund – and this is strongly emphasized by his biographer – to win the voice of the citizens of London, who made great capital out of an occasion on which, as in 1016, the loud voice of the London citizens was needed to hide the small numbers of the nobles who elected the king. His wife, like Henry I's, was of the old English line: a niece of Henry's queen and Edgar the Ætheling, daughter of a Scottish princess.

We have seen that Henry I, in earlier years, had publicly and strenuously designated Matilda his heiress. After his death the story was told that like Edward the Confessor he had changed his mind, and on his deathbed designated Stephen. This story has generally been disbelieved; but it was one of the two crucial issues in 1135 and the years immediately following, and the central mystery of Stephen's accession.

The other great issue was that of suitability: Matilda was difficult and quarrelsome, too inclined to remember that she had been an empress; her husband was distrusted by the Normans.[36] Stephen, on the other hand, was a leader among the barons, one of themselves, open-hearted, brave, energetic, innocent of his uncle's rapacity and perhaps of his uncle's cruelty. This alone might account in fair measure for his success; at least it may explain why he won support. But it fails to explain the most puzzling feature of the events of 1135: the rapid and decisive action which he took after Henry's death. He was crowned as quickly as Rufus had been, and against much heavier odds. Stephen was always capable of rapid action; but in later years lacked the determination and persistence to carry his actions to success. It is possible, as most historians have thought, that for once in his life Stephen saw his chance, and took it; that his rapidity of action was sufficient both to carry him to temporary success, and to push his elder brother into the background without even the trouble of an argument. It is possible; but there is another explanation.

John of Salisbury tells us that in the argument before the pope in 1139, the king's advocate, Arnulf, later bishop of Lisieux, alleged two arguments: that Matilda was illegitimate, and that Henry on his deathbed had changed his mind and designated Stephen. 'And he declared that this had been proved publicly before the English church to William, archbishop of Canterbury and legate of the holy see, by the oath of Earl Hugh [Bigod] and two knights; and that on hearing the proof the archbishop had recognised Stephen's claim to the crown with the unanimous consent and approval of the bishops and nobles. What had been done with such ceremony, could not, he concluded, be undone.' In answer the empress's advocate countered the charge of illegitimacy, and denied that Henry had changed his mind: 'As for your statement that the king changed his mind, it is proved false by those who were present at the king's death. Neither you nor Hugh could possibly know his last requests, since neither was there.'[37] Nor could the archbishop's acceptance hurt the empress, since she – to whom they had all sworn so solemnly – was condemned to the loss of her crown without being given any chance to answer the charges against her case. Gilbert Foliot is only explicit about the argument on the empress's legitimacy. This is what especially concerned him, since his case is based almost entirely on the hereditary claim of the

---

36 For a rather kinder view of Matilda, see Chibnall 1991.
37 John of Salisbury, *Historia Pontificalis*, trans. Chibnall, pp. 84–5.

empress. But he does discuss the question whether a father can disinherit a legitimate heir, to which his answer is: only for rebellion or the like, and he firmly (though erroneously) asserts that the empress was never guilty of this.[38] The argument may be academic; but it is likely that implicit in it was the charge of the royal advocate that Henry had abandoned his daughter on his deathbed. In any case we may probably take John of Salisbury's word for it that this argument was in men's minds. John was writing under Henry II, the empress's son: he had no motive for improving Stephen's case – save perhaps to discredit Stephen's advocate, a special enemy of John's. Whether the story was true is another matter. The earliest of the chroniclers, Orderic Vitalis (1136–41), William of Malmesbury (1140–1) and John of Worcester (1140–3) make no mention of the story that Henry changed his mind on his deathbed. But William and John owed allegiance to the empress when they wrote.

Stephen's biographer, Robert, bishop of Bath (1136–66), set out, it seems, in the 1140s to write a panegyric of Stephen – but only completed his work, in a different mood, after Henry II's accession. He arrives at a curious compromise. The enterprise was of Stephen's own devising; on arrival in England he was immediately elected by the citizens of London – and we are treated to a lecture on London's rights, in which the author, to put it mildly, doth protest too much. We are then told at length of a debate before the archbishop of Canterbury, whose decision, as first counsellor and as the man who would anoint the new king, was vital. The archbishop objected that he had sworn allegiance to Matilda. The answer to this is very strange indeed. Henry's design in extracting the oath and marrying his daughter to Anjou was to make peace between Anjou and Normandy. This laudable project, which makes Henry I out as a disinterested Nobel prizewinner, raised a difficulty: he knew the barons swore unwillingly. And so on his deathbed, to prevent his little scheme troubling them for ever, he released them from their oath. It is a mistake to take too seriously speeches in medieval chronicles: direct speech was regularly used as a device to give colour and drama, to enable the actors or the author to comment; no one supposed them to be stenographically accurate. But they are often, none the less, extremely interesting; and this argument has a kind of logic of its own which has never, apparently, been observed. Henry's motive is patently absurd. If peace was his aim, he needed to tie his barons by every possible oath on his

---

38 One would like to know how Gilbert Foliot described the empress's activities in 1135. Perhaps he drew a distinction between conniving at her husband's offensive activities and actual rebellion; perhaps he had conveniently forgotten the affair.

deathbed. But in fact the Angevin marriage was no guarantee of
peace, with Anjou or within his own dominions, in his lifetime. Nor
has the ideal of peace for its own sake anything in common with Henry
I as we know him; it is simply an emanation of the legendary Henry I,
the 'lover of peace' to whom men looked back, nostalgically, from the
chaos of the succeeding reign. The story is ridiculous; and yet some
story is urgently needed. The archbishop's arguments against Stephen
are cogent; how then was he induced to crown him?

The *Gesta* tells us that Henry released his barons from their oath to
Matilda on his deathbed, a story elaborated by later chroniclers. If
this is all he did – if he released them without indicating who was to
succeed, he acted either as a convinced democrat or in a fit of total
irresponsibility. The former is impossible; the latter, for Henry I of all
people, incredible. It is much more likely that the *Gesta* is repeating
the old story that Henry designated Stephen on his deathbed, in a
somewhat veiled form. But why is it veiled? When the *Gesta* was
written, or at any rate finished, Henry II was on the throne. In its later
pages, Henry is always referred to as 'the lawful heir', even though
Stephen's elder son lived to 1153, his younger to 1159. This explains a
curious element of prevarication in the book: it is in the main a
panegyric of Stephen, but written by somebody who has had to
come to terms with Stephen's failure and the Angevin triumph. He
cannot say openly that Henry I repudiated his daughter and her issue,
for Henry II claimed above all to be his grandfather's heir. Yet if he
says nothing about Henry I's deathbed, Stephen's case is gravely
weakened.[39]

Thus we have the Angevin chroniclers ranged on one side; Stephen's
advocates on the other. The Angevins had a powerful motive for
suppressing any story that Henry had designated Stephen; Stephen's
supporters an equally strong motive for pressing it. Orderic, writing
in a Normandy which had abandoned Stephen, gives no hint of it;
perhaps his silence tells slightly against it. But in the main, we have
here, as not uncommonly, a plain contradiction in the sources; and it
is only by observing the behaviour of the main actors that we can
hope to settle the issue.

Stephen acted with the utmost promptitude; the archbishop of
Canterbury argued, but agreed. The king of France supported
Stephen; the pope confirmed his coronation. The count of Blois with-

---

39 *Gesta Stephani*, pp. 8–13. The editor, the late R.H.C. Davis, argued cogently that the
early part, composed before 1147, was not much altered when the book was completed
after 1154. But this section could well have been retouched to avoid a direct implication that
Henry I had designated Stephen on his deathbed. See now Crouch 2000, ch. 2.

drew his claims; the count and countess of Anjou attacked Normandy, at first ineffectually; the earl of Gloucester, after a long pause, swore fealty to Stephen. Much of this reflects recognition of facts as they were. Disputed successions were common; acts of violent usurpation not rare. Normally the *fait accompli* had to be accepted, even by the Church, since the Church's refusal could only lead to bloodshed. What mattered to the pope was to keep England free from civil war. As for the king of France and the count of Blois, we know too little of the detailed circumstances to judge of their motives; but Theobald had little to hope for in England in any event, Louis everything to fear in France if Anjou was joined to Normandy.

The promptitude of Stephen and the acquiescence of Canterbury are the most remarkable points in this sequence of events. Stephen acted so fast that his manoeuvre must almost certainly have been premeditated; it is indeed likely that it was inspired by a stronger personality than his own. The archbishop must have been convinced by cogent arguments. Both parts of the puzzle would be explained if Stephen could indeed bring testimony that Henry on his deathbed had designated him his heir.

There are, however, two other points to be taken into the account. The archbishop was concerned to provide England with an effective king who could prevent bloodshed: civil war was imminent; he might well feel that Stephen was more suitable, more capable of winning support than the empress. Stephen was a good soldier, and already well endowed in England. Nor was he slow to make promises of good rule and obedience to the Church. Stephen may well have seemed suitable, *idoneus*, a vital factor in the Church's eyes.

If Stephen's actions surprise us, and we look for a stronger personality to inspire him, his uncle is not our only choice. Another Henry, Stephen's younger brother, abbot of Glastonbury and bishop of Winchester, played a leading part in the events of Stephen's reign. He was not always on his brother's side, but William of Malmesbury attributes to him Stephen's early success: and makes his influence responsible for the archbishop's acquiescence. William's picture, in general, is confirmed by the *Gesta*. The brilliant, turbulent, ambitious Henry may well have influenced both his elder brothers; and we may accept William of Malmesbury's word that he hoped (and no doubt convinced the archbishop) that Stephen would prove a worthy guardian of the Church, and submit to the direction of his leading bishops.[40]

40 William of Malmesbury, *Historia Novella*, pp. 28–9. On the events of December 1135, see E. King, ibid. pp. xl–xlii; Hollister 1986, pp. 162–3.

Finally, is it credible that Henry I himself should have deserted his daughter after all his elaborate schemes, and declared for his nephew? It is clear that Henry had been seriously worried about the succession to his throne for many years: he had married again, but had no children by his second wife; he had summoned Matilda back from Germany against her will; he had exacted two oaths from his barons. In all this he seems to have been guided as much by a particular notion of inheritance as by affection. One would have expected his heart to have lain with his illegitimate son Earl Robert or his legitimate nephew Stephen, both of whom he endowed with the best lands he had to give; Stephen to an almost unprecedented degree. He treated them with every mark of favour and affection, hunted with them, enjoyed their company. In contrast, he treated his daughter as a pawn in the marriage game, as so many women were treated in that age. At eight she was shipped to Germany;[41] as a young widow she was hurried back, made heir to the throne, married forcibly to a younger man whom she despised (he was a mere count), and who had no liking for her. So her father allowed her to leave her husband; then reunited them so as to ensure that his line was continued with a supply of heirs. Finally, and not surprisingly, she spited the old man: rebellion broke out in Normandy, the count openly supported it, the empress only a little less openly fomented it.

What happened on Henry's deathbed is pure conjecture. If he felt that his daughter had shown herself ungrateful – had he not laden her with honours, made her an empress, promised her a kingdom? – that would be only understandable. He was an irascible member of an irascible line; he was capable of saying anything when the fit was on him. It is intelligible that he should succumb to a temporary reaction, a feeling that he might after all follow his heart not his head; that Stephen was Henry himself *redivivus*, a younger son married to a descendant of Alfred and Cerdic, and Woden.

When Queen Elizabeth I was on her deathbed, gargantuan efforts had to be made to get her to designate James as her successor. So precise was she about her prerogative, and so little did she relish thoughts of her own death, that she put the act off to the very last moment. In the end, an incoherent sign made after she was incapable of speech was interpreted as consent, and the last barrier to James's succession was removed. Around Henry's deathbed were gathered men passionately concerned about who should succeed. The leading men at Henry's deathbed named by Orderic were somewhat slow to join or support Stephen. Hugh Bigod claimed to have Henry's word

41   Chibnall 1991, p. 9.

that Stephen should succeed, but the empress's supporters rejoined that Hugh was not present at the deathbed. It is perfectly possible, however, that Hugh was near at hand, picked up a rumour that Stephen had been designated heir, and carried it at once to Boulogne, where (so it seems) Stephen then was; and with this rumour stirred Stephen to his remarkable adventure. It is likely, I think, that Stephen thought himself to have Henry's support. Whether Henry had wished to give it we shall never know.

In Germany in the late eleventh and twelfth centuries there were signs that inheritance and designation might one day give way to election as the means of creating a new king; and in the thirteenth and fourteenth centuries this came to pass: a specific body of electors made free choice – choice so free that in the early sixteenth century the kings of England, France and Spain could all be thought of as suitable candidates. In England and France this never happened. The word election was freely used; Stephen gave out that he had been elected by cleargy and people, and the *Gesta* makes his election a key event. But he was elected by the citizens of London, not the Witan; and if Stephen could be thought of as an elected monarch, the precedent was not encouraging. In fact other ideas were more strongly present in people's minds: designation was still, perhaps, the most vital factor of all; inheritance was gaining ground, and being supplemented by sophisticated arguments from Roman and Canon Law; nor could any responsible person overlook the problem of whether the candidate was suitable for the office. Laymen and churchmen were agreed that the royal office was vital for the welfare of the people; the choice of a new king was a profoundly serious matter: too serious to be subjected to simple rules; so long as the English kings ruled as well as reigned, there was an element of uncertainty about the principles of succession. Strange as it may seem, the modern law of succession dates only from the eighteenth century.

4

The Occupations of a King

We have seen how kings were made; we have still to study how they lived: to provide them with palaces and retinues, to clothe and feed them, and fill their daily round.

The bulk of the surviving literature of Saxon and Norman times was written by churchmen, and written in Latin, the international language of the Church of western Christendom. Kings were usually illiterate. To this, as we shall see, there were notable exceptions; but it remains true that most laymen were not interested in book-learning, and that the surviving literature reflects the tastes and interests of the clergy. They have much to tell us of layfolk, but it comes to us at one remove; if we wish to make direct contact with laymen, we must look to the physical remains – houses, weapons, coins – unearthed by the trowel, and the vernacular literature composed for them, for minstrels to recite in the great halls of kings and thegns in the evenings. This was essentially not a written but a spoken literature, passed down from minstrel to minstrel, alternately refined and corrupted in the crucible of human memory. The result is that only a small proportion ever came to be committed to parchment, and of what was written down only a part survives. The student of English history is relatively fortunate. Of French vernacular literature virtually nothing survives before the late eleventh century – though from then on it is abundant; of German literature only a little survives before 1100; a fair quantity of early Scandinavian poetry was written down in Iceland about the year 1100, and is known to us from later copies; but England can boast some 30,000 lines of Anglo-Saxon verse, quite apart from the substantial remains of Old English prose.

Much of this verse is religious: paraphrases of parts of the Bible, pious legends, saints' lives, spiritual fantasies like the famous *Dream of the Rood*. The men who wrote the manuscripts in which the poetry survives were themselves churchmen, and the high proportion of religious verse in what they wrote no doubt in part reflects their tastes. But it is clear that it also reflects the tastes of many of the laymen for whom these poems were written. There is also some secular poetry; most notable of all the short epic *Beowulf*, the only complete survivor of the Germanic lays and epics of the early Middle Ages. *Beowulf* may well be uncharacteristic, in certain respects, of the literature from which it sprang – above all in being, as we shall see, a Christian poem with a Christian moral; but it reveals in vivid fashion much that we should not otherwise clearly perceive about the life of kings and the aspirations of their followers. Its date is not precisely known: it is reasonable to ascribe it to the eighth century, and it can hardly be later. (See p. 1n.)

The poem opens with the death of a Danish king. 'Scyld's hour came when he was in the prime of his strength. After a long reign the king departed into the care of God. His dearest retainers carried the beloved Danish leader to the sea's edge, as he had commanded while he could yet speak. Rime-crusted and ready to sail, a royal vessel with curved prow lay in harbour. They set down their dear king amidships, close by the mast. A mass of treasure was brought there from distant parts. No ship, they say, was ever so well equipped with swords, corselets, weapons, and armour. On the king's breast rested a heap of jewels which were to go with him far out into the keeping of the sea. The Danes furnished Scyld Scefing with offerings from their treasury that were as good as the gifts provided by those who, when he was a child, launched him alone across the ocean. High overhead they set his golden standard; then, surrendering him to the sea, they sadly allowed it to bear him off. And no one, whether a counsellor in hall or a soldier in the field, can truly say who received that cargo.'[42]

Until about sixty years ago this passage read to most readers like pure fantasy. But in 1939, shortly before the outbreak of the Second World War, the 'harbour' into which just such a ship had sailed was excavated on a windy hill above the river Deben in Suffolk. It had long been known that the East Anglian kings had had one of their principal palaces at Rendlesham, four miles away; and excavation of the burial mounds, or barrows, at Sutton Hoo itself had begun in the previous year. One of the mounds had already revealed a ship burial, but this had been previously excavated by robbers, and its main contents are lost. In 1939 work began on one of the largest of the barrows, and once again the traces of a ship were found. Then the excavators began to look in its centre, where the burial chamber should be, hardly hoping to find it still intact. As they approached it, they realized that something of interest lay underneath – sufficient

42 *Beowulf*, trans. D. Wright, pp. 27–8.

for them to halt their work, and call in a team of the most highly qualified experts to complete an extremely delicate task. Through the July days of 1939, as the war clouds gathered, gold and silver and jewellery, some of it of great beauty, the whole of unprecedented splendour and interest, were scooped from the centre of the ship. The owner of Sutton Hoo presented them to the nation; they were deposited in the British Museum, sorted and catalogued, and stowed safely away. Then the war came, and serious work was held up till it was over; for five years the experts and the not-so-expert speculated and guessed. Then the treasures were reopened and examined afresh, and proceeded to confound some of the speculation. They were examined and reconstructed in the laboratory, compared with other finds, analysed by archaeologists, numismatists and historians. In the 1980s, as we have seen above (pp. 11, 3), a major campaign was mounted under the direction of Martin Carver: and now we know, perhaps, almost as much about the site as can be known.

The burial chamber of Mound 1 contained armour, bowls, spoons and dishes, and various other objects. But it contains no body;[43] and this has deepened the mystery of whom it was meant to celebrate.

It could be the tomb of a king. Scyld's boat was laden much like the boat at Sutton Hoo. True, it was not buried, but sent out to sea. But we know that burial was normal – a barrow was made for Beowulf himself at the end of the poem; and other ship burials have been found elsewhere, most notably in Sweden. We know too that the hero of Sutton Hoo was no ordinary mortal. Numerous Anglo-Saxon graves have been excavated; few of them have even the dignity of mounds raised above them; none of them so far compares with Sutton Hoo; nothing quite so splendid has yet been excavated anywhere in the Teutonic world. Mr Boffin in *Our Mutual Friend* is described as the golden dustman, because of the great wealth he had inherited as heir to substantial piles of valuable dust. One might almost call Sutton Hoo the golden dustbin of the early medieval world, for its treasures are cosmopolitan. The lost warrior had spoons from the Byzantine empire; bowls from Byzantium and Egypt; helmet, shield and sword from Sweden; the clasps and buckles of his harness, and the lid of his purse, were masterpieces of Anglo-Saxon jewellery; the money in his purse came from Merovingian Gaul (i.e. France). We cannot be sure that this represents his personal gear: when Beowulf himself was buried, an earlier treasure was looted to provide him with suitable equipment. But the money at least is a homogeneous collection,

---

43   It is now accepted that this was due to the corrosive effects of the soil. For this and all that relates to current views, see Carver 1998.

though not English, and reveals to the expert on coins that the burial took place about 625.

It is usually assumed that the lost warrior was in fact a king. But before the days of crowns and sceptres, we do not really know how kings were distinguished from other men. The strange rack may have been a lamp-standard or royal standard; a small stag surmounted a primitive sceptre. The standard, it has even been suggested, may have been a rack for hanging scalps; scalping was a favoured pursuit among the Frankish kings in whose name the Sutton Hoo coins had been issued. It remains true that nothing so magnificent as the Sutton Hoo burial has yet been unearthed; that a fragment of what seems to have been the twin of the helmet at Sutton Hoo has been unearthed in Sweden in a grave generally thought royal – and both are distinctly more magnificent than other Swedish helmets of the time, found in graves presumed non-royal. But there is an element of presumption in this; and we must leave it to the experts to decide. In the meantime we can safely assume that, whether or not the lost warrior was a king, his accoutrements would not have disgraced a king; and if we wish to imagine an early English monarch in state dress, enthroned in his hall, we can clothe him in the trappings of Sutton Hoo.

Nor can we decide the fascinating problem of the religious meaning of the tomb. It has been suggested that the man was a Christian, and the spoons, inscribed with St Paul's two names – Saul, before baptism, and Paul, as a Christian – strongly suggest a christening present, or at least that the warrior had Christian friends. Why, then, the elaborate trappings for his voyage through the afterworld, suitable only to pagan burials? Perhaps the corpse was given Christian burial, while his pagan followers raised a traditional monument to him. Yet this hardly seems likely: it is more probable that the Church tolerated a survival of pagan practices for a space, and allowed a recently con-verted warrior to be buried in customary style. The date indicated by the coins fits perfectly the most prestigious of all the kings of the East Angles, Rædwald, who died about 625 (between 616 and 627), and of whom Bede curtly observed that he was seen to serve 'both Christ and the gods whom he had previously served' – by putting an altar for the Christian eucharist and an altar for sacrifices to 'demons' in the same building.[44]

The same mingling of pagan and Christian themes puzzles the reader of *Beowulf*. The characters in the poem seem definitely pagan, but the poem itself has a Christian moral and a Christian theme.

44 Bede ii. 15, pp. 190–1.

The palace of the Danish king is haunted by a monster called Grendel, who visits it nightly and devours such of the warriors as are foolhardy enough to sleep there. The news of this trouble comes to Beowulf, a noble of the Geats – the folk of southern Sweden, Gotland or Geatland. Beowulf sets off with a band of followers, and succeeds in killing the monster; he then kills another monster, Grendel's mother, in a fierce encounter at the bottom of a neighbouring lake, and so rids the Danish court of the whole brood. He is feasted by the Danish king and loaded with presents, mostly of gold; and then, to everyone's sorrow, returns to his own people, where he recounts the tale of his adventures to his own king, and passes on to him a share of the gifts. In return for this the Geat king makes Beowulf his closest confidant and loads him with more presents including a large landed estate. So ends the first part of the poem. Years pass: the Geat king and his son are killed, the first in a raid in Friesland in search of booty, the second in a blood-feud, and Beowulf has succeeded to the crown – chosen for his suitability by his former master's widow. After years of successful and peaceful rule, his kingdom in its turn is troubled by a monster, in this case by a dragon. The dragon lives on a mound and guards a great treasure which is hidden within the mound; some of the treasure is stolen, and in revenge the dragon lays waste the country-side. Beowulf, now an old man, sets out to save his people from this menace, and kills the dragon; but in the fight he himself receives a mortal wound. The poem concludes with the mourning for his death, and with his burial. He is burnt on a great funeral pyre, and the best horsemen among his followers ride round his pyre, as the Greeks rode round the corpse of Patroclus and the Huns round Attila's.

Beowulf portrays a society of heroic barbarians: courage, prowess in war, loyalty and generosity are the qualities most forcefully portrayed for our admiration. Personal loyalty and kinship are the principal bonds; loyalty above all, for kinship played a less conspicuous part in English society than among the Germanic peoples on the Continent. It is an aristocratic society: a society of chiefs and kings, each with his hall, in which a company of followers can gather. The following was the source of a king's power: on his capacity to inspire friends, relations and foreigners to gather round him, on his capacity to lead them successfully in war and to feed and reward them with princely gifts, depended his power and prestige. In *Beowulf* we are given a vision of a barbarian society at its finest.

Yet *Beowulf* is more than that: it is a poem with a specifically Christian moral, applicable to a recently converted barbarian people; first steps in Christian heroism. It is a remarkable fact that Beowulf only kills dragons on the stage, and hardly any human beings off it.

Germanic legends and Germanic history were full of wars and blood-feuds. True heroism does not lie there, says the author of *Beowulf*. But where does it lie? It may be that Beowulf is a Christian allegory of a primitive kind, and that the meaning is that true heroism lies in fighting spiritual enemies, devils, not human beings. On the surface lies a meaning which would be more likely to impinge on a warrior audience: 'a little less of the blood-feud' was perhaps as much as they would immediately grasp of its message; and the very existence of the society portrayed would have been threatened if all the warriors had taken to fighting dragons or tilting at windmills. The Church had taken on a tough job when it set about converting the barbarian world; *Beowulf* shows us that it took it seriously, that it was trying already to devise a notion of Christian heroism; and this ideal may well have appealed to many in its original audience.

The centre of the story of *Beowulf* is the great hall in which the Danish king and his followers gather for their evening banquets, in which the king honours his followers, in which gifts, and stories, and heroic lays are exchanged. 'Such success in arms and so great a fame attended Hrothgar that his kinsmen were eager to serve under him, and in this way the number of his young retainers increased until he had a formidable army. It came into his mind to command the erection of a building that should be the greatest banqueting hall ever known, in which he could apportion to young and old everything that God had entrusted to him, with the exception of public lands and human life. So, as I have heard, orders were dispatched all over the world for its furbishing; and in a short time the enormous building was completed. The king called it Heorot, and kept his promise at the feast, when he distributed rings and treasure. Tall and wide-gabled, the hall towered overhead; yet it was to endure terrible and leaping flames, when in the course of time a deadly feud between Hrothgar and his son-in-law should be kindled by an act of violence.'[45]

Heorot was large, but simple: an open, barn-like hall, made of wood. The remains of several such royal halls have been discovered in England in very recent years: the first, and most remarkable, at Yeavering, in Northumberland, where, as has been described, air photography revealed the traces of a series of buildings, and excavation the foundation slots and post-holes of several wooden halls. Heorot was of wood, and in the end caught fire and was burned; and this probably explains why the palace at Yeavering was several times replaced. In the 1960s what was thought to be a palace of Saxon and later kings at Cheddar in Somerset was excavated, and a group of

45 *Beowulf*, trans. D. Wright, pp. 28–9.

buildings covering a wide area discovered. But – as has happened also at Northampton – a group of halls is now thought perhaps to be part of a monastic rather than a secular complex.

The halls at Yeavering, like Heorot, were first and foremost banqueting halls; where a great king or military leader dined in the evening surrounded by his followers, the warriors of his following, who were bound to him by the tightest bonds of loyalty. Its magnificence reflected the king's glory: Heorot, we are told, was plated with gold. 'When we sat down to banquet,' Beowulf himself reports, 'the king of the Danes rewarded me generously for this encounter, with treasures and beaten gold. Songs and junketing followed, and the patriarch Hrothgar, who had a great fund of stories, told anecdotes about bygone times, and every now and then played a pleasant melody on the harp. Now and then some true and unhappy ballad was sung; occasionally the king would recount a curious legend in its correct form. . . .'[46] The proceedings were not always orderly. It was noted as a special sign of virtue in Beowulf that he did not kill his companions in his cups; and several stories are told of how feuds were begun or continued by an excited argument, warmed by the potent influence of mead in the 'mead-hall' as it was often called. In spite of such occasional disturbances, the evening was governed by a traditional order; and closed with a visit from the queen, who carried a jewelled loving cup round the hall for all to drink; then took her husband to their chamber for the night. The chamber was evidently a separate building; and in another separate building, we are told, Beowulf was lodged when a visitor at the Danish court. The palace was something like a village, a group of halls and huts, with the banqueting hall in its midst. But only the great had separate chambers. Most of the warriors slept in the hall, including Hrothgar's most trusted counsellor, who was grabbed from Heorot as he slept by Grendel's mother. Only the king and specially honoured guests could expect any privacy.

Heorot was the headquarters of the king and his followers. From it they went out by day to ride and hunt; in summer, for longer expeditions, for war, plunder and the pursuit of feuds; and also to govern their kingdom and do justice. To Heorot they returned to drink, to exchange gifts, and on more sober occasions to give counsel.

There is much talk in *Beowulf* of gold. Heorot is plated with it, the queen adorned with it; the king is an 'illustrious prince and giver of (gold) rings';[47] every important event is crowned by the exchange of

46 *Beowulf*, trans. D. Wright, pp. 76–7.
47 *Beowulf*, trans. D. Wright, p. 35.

gifts, in which gold cups and gold-plated armour are usually conspicuous. This had been a fundamental part of the life of the barbarian
warriors at the time when the Roman empire in the west fell to their
arms. Rome supplied them with the bulk of their gold; but they used it
in their own way. They accepted it as the symbol of wealth and
grandeur: a king must be able to display it in his hall, on his armour,
on his wife; he must be able to lavish gifts of gold on his followers –
but yet remain wealthier than they. This meant a constant scramble to
provide themselves with adequate supplies by loot, by levying tribute,
by themselves receiving gifts, and even occasionally, perhaps, by
trade; and it is one of the reasons why plundering expeditions play
so large a part both in the history and the legends of the fifth and sixth
centuries. It helps to explain why the greatest deposits of Roman gold
have been excavated so far from the Roman empire – in Scandinavia
and the Baltic; and how treasures from the Mediterranean world,
from Gaul and from Sweden were collected in the grave at Sutton
Hoo.

In due course the supply of gold tended to dry up. When a stable
currency was introduced in the eighth century, it was of silver – as
everywhere else in northern Europe by this date. Even in *Beowulf*
there are hints of a more stable basis of social organization. The king
of the Geats gave Beowulf a sword whose hilt was covered with gold,
but also 'a hall and 7,000 hides of land'.[48] This reminds us that land
had long been the most stable form of wealth; that as the supplies of
gold declined it tended to become the regular means of rewarding a
faithful follower. In the English kingdoms the king was the greatest
landowner, and he fed his court either by wandering from estate to
estate eating its produce, or by arranging for boat- or wagon-loads of
produce to be brought to his halls. In the late seventh century the laws
of King Ine of Wessex give us the following list: 'As a food-rent from
10 hides: 10 vats of honey, 300 loaves, 12 "ambers" of Welsh ale, 30
of clear ale, 2 full-grown cows, or 10 wethers, 10 geese, 20 hens, 10
cheeses, an "amber" full of butter, 5 salmon, 20 pounds of fodder and
100 eels.'[49] This was an indication, not a precise account; but it
reminds us vividly of the complexity of household management
before there was a stable currency or a proper system of markets or
tolerable conditions of transport. Long before the Norman Conquest,
however, currency and markets had improved beyond King Ine's
imagining; and, even though transport was dismal by modern standards, it was quite elaborately organized, and the 'farm of one night',

48 *Beowulf*, trans. D. Wright, p. 79.
49 *EHD* I, 406.

as the basic unit of royal food-rent was quaintly called, could be translated into cash, into wagon-loads, that is, of silver pennies. The silver penny was the only effective currency this country had between its institution by Offa and the reappearance of a gold coinage in the fourteenth century.

Beowulf gives us a picture of a society of warriors dedicated to loyal service to their lord, and the faithful pursuit of his and their own blood-feuds. It is quite clear, however, that this was not their sole occupation; still less the only concern of the poem's original audience. Bede describes more than one Northumbrian king as a man of learning, and to King Ceolwulf he dedicated his *Ecclesiastical History*. But the swiftest correction to any notion that Saxon kings were mere barbarians is a short glance at Asser's *Life* of King Alfred. No doubt we are in a more humane world than that of Hengest or Sutton Hoo; we must allow for much growth in the organization of the country and the arts of peace. But in Alfred's time the English kingdoms were threatened with extinction by the invading armies of the Danes. The *Anglo-Saxon Chronicle* paints a picture of disaster, and gives the clear impression that even the victories of Alfred were hard-won and precarious; even Wessex came near to dissolution. Alfred, perforce, was a great warrior; nor was he a reluctant warrior. Asser tells us that he had inherited the tastes of his kind. He listened eagerly to Saxon poetry day and night – though we are not told whether this meant epics of heroic blood-feud, or religious poetry; both kinds were recited in Heorot, and we may guess that both appealed to Alfred. He was also passionately fond of the chase, as were all successful medieval kings: it was the sport of kings; it canalized the energy of warriors in an occupation less harmful (anyway to human victims) than war; it accustomed men to swift, rapid and effective action in the field; it kept them in training.

If this was all we knew of Alfred, we should be excused for thinking that his life was spent in the hunting field, on campaign and in the mead-hall; and so he must have spent a great part of his time. But we also know of a host of other activities into which he entered with equal ardour. He turned his penetrating mind to long-term problems of defence, to improving the fortification of towns, to the design of better warships, to reorganizing the army. He reckoned that a king must have men who pray and men who work as well as soldiers, and he cared much for the Church and tried (not very successfully) to found monasteries. He cared for his estates and for all his subjects; issued a substantial collection of laws; inquired into the activity of law-courts, attempted to raise the standards of his legal officers, constantly interfered. The royal revenue was put on a new footing.

Most remarkable of all, he found time for intellectual adventure: organizing a seminar of learned men to translate key works of instruction and devotion into English, taking an active part himself in the work of translation; longing to rule a kingdom of literate men – a dream as hopeless, yet inspiring, as so many of his schemes. In the hall at Cheddar Alfred may have rested from the chase, and dined with his followers like Hrothgar in Heorot; the great hall is the symbol of a militant and military type of kingship. But much else took place in and out of it. Even though Alfred was exceptional, his life reveals what a king could do, the horizons of royal vision; and the variety of his work reminds us that every king had much to do apart from feasting in the mead-hall.

It is also in Alfred's time that we first hear about the workings of the royal treasury and apparently about the king's seal. Royal treasure consisted of jewels, precious metals and coins. Before the Conquest no written accounts were kept, and precious few records of any kind. But by the standards of the day the English treasury was comparatively highly organized: the king and his officers supervised the minting of coin; the king had a variety of sources of revenue which came in due course to include some forms of direct taxation; and it is clear that he could dispose of considerable sums of money. The treasure was normally too bulky for most of it to be carried round, and the late Saxon kings apparently had permanent treasure houses in more than one place, the chief one, no doubt, in Winchester. In the royal chamber, in whatever place the king was staying on his travels, was kept a chest which contained jewels and money for immediate use. The royal secretaries always travelled with the king. The great charters of King Athelstan's time and later were probably written by royal scribes. These scribes were few, since government was still mainly illiterate, but it is likely that royal scribes normally wrote royal charters in the time of Athelstan and in the later tenth and early eleventh centuries. In the eleventh century the large Latin charter was being replaced by the much smaller writ, in origin a letter written in English, as a means for the king to express his royal will. The writ has a special interest, since it was the first serious attempt to make government partly literate, and the first document to which the great seal was attached. We know that Alfred had a seal, but no examples of English royal seals survive before the time of Edward the Confessor. By then it was not uncommon for a royal grant of land or privileges to be written out in a brief writ in English and sent to the court of the shire which it concerned. There a clerk could read the writ to the assembled folk; and although they could not check that he read it aright, since most were illiterate, they could at least see the large lump of wax with the impress of the great seal: it was this which provided the best means of authenticating documents before most men were literate enough to sign their names. In the shire court of Norman times not everyone understood English – French was the language of Norman lords – and so the writ came to conform to the normal convention of written documents in the period, and was written in Latin, to be interpreted no doubt to its audience in whatever languages they understood. But the writ remained the basis of all documents issued under the great seal after the Conquest; in this and in other ways the Normans simply took over and adapted and developed what they found.

The life of the last Saxon king is described idyllically, and naively, by his first biographer, writing perhaps while he was still alive: 'And so, with the kingdom made safe on all sides by these nobles [Earl Harold and his brother], the most kindly King Edward passed his life in security and peace, and spent much of his time in the glades and woods in the pleasures of hunting. After divine service, which he gladly and devoutly attended every day, he took much pleasure in hawks and birds of that kind which they brought before him, and was really delighted by the baying and scrambling of the hounds. In these and such like activities he sometimes spent the day, and it was in these alone that he seemed naturally inclined to snatch some worldly pleasure.' The author goes on to say how assiduous Edward was in 'practising the Christian religion', and how he delighted in meeting abbots and monks, especially from overseas. 'He used to stand with lamb-like meekness and tranquil mind at the holy offices of the divine mysteries and masses, a worshipper of Christ manifest to all the faithful; and at these times, unless he was addressed, he rarely spoke to anyone' – an unusual virtue apparently; other kings spent the hour of mass in gossip, and Henry I is said to have chosen one of his leading subordinates first of all as his chaplain because he could finish mass in record time. 'Moreover, it was quietly, and only for the occasion – in any case, it should be distinctly said, with no mental pleasure – that he displayed the pomp of royal finery in which the queen obligingly arrayed him. And he would not have cared at all if it had been provided at far less cost. He was, however, grateful for the queen's solicitude in these matters, and with a certain kindness of feeling used to remark on her zeal most appreciatively to his intimates. He stooped with great mercy to the poor and infirm, and fully maintained many of these not only daily in his royal court but also at many places in his kingdom. Finally, his royal consort did not restrain him in those good works in which he prepared to lead the way, but rather urged speedier progress, and often enough seemed even to lead the way herself. For while he would give now and then, she was prodigal, but aimed her bountry to such good purpose as to consider the highest honour of the king as well. Although by custom and law a royal throne was always prepared for her at the king's side, she preferred, except in church and at the royal table, to sit at his feet, unless perchance he should reach out his hand to her, or with a gesture of the hand invite or command her to sit next to him.'[50]

As a picture of a king's life this is clearly one-sided; and although Edward in his later years seems to have been content to leave a part of his work to his subordinates – the army to Harold, the 'under-king' as one writer called him, and the administration of government to earls and bishops and sheriffs – this picture of languid sanctity, broken from time to time by a good day's hunting, is probably overdrawn. None the less, it shows us a medieval king in two characteristic places: in the hunting field and in church. The author goes on to describe Edward's zeal for the rebuilding of Westminster Abbey, which he enlarged and re-endowed as a token of his devotion to God and St Peter, to house his own monument, and, no doubt, to provide a fitting church for the greatest of his palaces. In the second part of the *Life* Edward the king is on the way to becoming Edward the saint – Edward the Confessor: 'chosen by God before the day of his birth, and...consecrated to the kingdom less by men than...by heaven'.[51] God was the real elector; the king was His anointed; and we are told how appropriate this seemed in Edward's case, since God through him performed miracles of healing while he was still alive.

Edward was holy, *sanctus*, in virtue of his office, and also in virtue of his life. The latter claim, first adumbrated in the second part of the *Life*, written shortly after Edward's death, took some time to mature; it was clearly not so obvious to other contemporaries as to the author. Eventually it bore fruit when the monks of Westminster, who possessed the precious relic of his body, with support from Henry II and a throng of leading churchmen, won from Pope Alexander III the bull of canonization in 1161. Alexander canonized a saint; the monks of Westminster raised a shrine behind their high altar; in popular esteem the sanctity of the royal office was proclaimed. At this date men did not easily distinguish between the king and his office – they were of a piece; loyalty was a personal thing, owed to a man. But in the twelfth century it was argued that a king can do holy things even if he is not holy himself, like a priest.

In the time of William Rufus and Henry I a Norman cleric was deploying some of the most extravagant language ever used about a

50 *Edward*, pp. 60–5.
51 *Edward*, pp. 90–3.

king to describe the office and person of royalty. The holy chrism transforms a man; makes him the anointed of the Lord, Christ's vicar, his *alter ego*; the holy occupant of a holy office. The Norman Anonymous, at one time known as the Anonymous of York, here represents old, traditional notions of royal authority, the divinity that doth hedge a king, carried to their logical extreme with the help of the tools of the revived logic of the late eleventh century. He also propounded a doctrine which tended to drive a wedge between king and office: the moral authority he ascribes to the king might have seemed fitting in Alfred or Edgar, or even Edward; scarcely in Rufus or Henry I. None the less, the sacral authority of the royal office was widely accepted in Norman times, although rejected, in its more extreme form, by the papacy. The most interesting of Edward's miracles was the first example in England of 'touching for the king's evil', the cure of scrofula.[52] Soon after, it became a regular royal practice in France and England; and it seems that this was so already in the days of Henry I – perhaps to emphasize the sacral authority which Henry had inherited by being born after his parents were anointed monarchs, and which he had confirmed by marrying into the line of Cerdic.

The Norman kings were sacred persons, like their predecessors, and they took over much of what they found in every department of kingship. The range of their activities was not much different from that of a Saxon king, though the amount of administrative work organized in their court and household steadily increased; but their dress and the buildings they lived in altered somewhat more. Beowulf, like the lost warrior of Sutton Hoo, was distinguished by his costly armour, especially the helmet, 'inlaid with gold, hooped with lordly bands, decorated with effigies of boars'.[53] In the Bayeux Tapestry, William and Harold appear in full armour, but they cannot be distinguished from their followers except by the inscriptions: all wear chain-mail, conical helmet with nose-piece, and kite-shaped shield, and carry sword or mace or axe or spear. The crowned helmet, as distinctive royal wear, seems to have come in with Henry I (1100–35). But the Tapestry also shows us Edward and Harold enthroned as kings, with the special royal insignia. The golden helmet was apparently the earliest headgear of Saxon kings; and a jewelled diadem, of late Roman style, appears on early coins. We do not know when a crown was first worn; it appears on some coins of King Athelstan (924–39), and in a painting of the same king. Royal insignia came of age in the coronation of King Edgar in 973. The sceptre was used as

52   *Edward*, pp. 92–5; cf. Barlow 1980.
53   *Beowulf*, trans. D. Wright, p. 61.

well as the crown as a special symbol of kingship – and to it was added soon after the orb – in imitation of Frankish and German monarchs, especially of Otto the Great of Germany, who had been crowned Roman emperor in 962. Athelstan's crown was a simple ring of metal, with a number of prongs rising from it, plain in shape. By Edgar's time these have blossomed into *fleurs-de-lys*; and the lily-crown is shown in pictures of Edgar, Cnut, Edward the Confessor and Harold. The Conqueror's crown was the work of a Greek crafts-man, covered with Arabian gold (so Guy of Amiens tells us), Egyptian gems and glittering jewels.[54] In form it may have resembled the Hungarian crown of the eleventh century – and perhaps the crown of Otto the Great, which still survives among the imperial treasures in Vienna; it may reveal a conscious imitation by William of the great-ness of the German emperors; he shored up his own doubtful claim by increasing still further the outward panoply of kingship.

It is very difficult to reconstruct the palaces of the early Norman kings. No part of the early palaces of Westminster or of Winchester, the most substantial of their many homes, now survives. So far as we know, their palaces were not at first much different: a large complex of buildings with a great hall in the centre. The Normans had a passion for raising large buildings of stone; and as time passed, the great aisled hall of timber was replaced by a stone hall, like the beautiful great hall of the castle at Winchester; but this is of the thirteenth century, and is on the site of the castle, not of the old palace.[55]

The stone castle was the characteristic novelty of the Normans. In every large town the Normans built a castle – many of them held by or in the name of the king; and every Norman baron had his head-quarters in one, sometimes several castles. At first these were not usually of stone. But the Conqueror himself set the fashion, which was increasingly followed in the twelfth and thirteenth centuries by leading barons, of building a large castle of stone which could serve both as fortress and house. In most large castles, as in the royal palaces, the main domestic buildings were not part of the fortifica-tions, though they might abut on the inside of the castle walls. But in the enormous keep of the Tower of London built by the Conqueror himself, substantial living rooms were incorporated in the central defensive work of the castle. Apart from cellars, guard rooms and small domestic offices, these great stone keeps normally contained two public rooms, either side by side or one above the other, and a

54 Guy of Amiens, pp. 44–7, ll. 753–82.
55 On Saxon and Norman palaces, see Biddle and Keene 1976, pp. 289–302.

chapel. In the chapel the king or great lord heard mass every morning; and if he were exceptionally devout, other services as well. In the great hall his household lived and ate and slept; in the chamber, a room usually as large or nearly as large as the hall, the king took council and lived withdrawn from the throng, with his family and immediate councillors and servants; and with his jewels and such part of his treasure as he carried with him. The chamber may in some sense have been the king's private apartment; but he had little or no privacy in it. It may well be that king and queen could have more privacy in their larger palaces; and great houses certainly came to have more private rooms in the late Middle Ages. The time when lesser folk expected to have rooms to themselves, when anyone could assume that even the most intimate moments of their life would be spent alone, lay far in the future. Halls and castles were designed for splendour and not for comfort. On great occasions Heorot was adorned with golden tapestries and other ornaments, as were many a Norman castle. But its solid furniture consisted merely of benches and tables. When night came the benches were cleared away and 'pillows and bedding spread upon the floor'.[56] Things were probably no different in a Norman castle. Tapestries adorned the wall; but there were probably no carpets on the floor; no upholstery on chairs; no glass in the windows. In the twelfth century glass was coming into fashion. But it remained throughout the late Middle Ages a rare extravagance, and the nobleman who possessed a set of windows carried it with him from house to house. As the hall was normally lit and warmed by a great open fire in its midst, the open windows had their advantages; but the Normans never lived without a draught.

Like Edward the Confessor, the Norman kings were all passionately fond of hunting. They added substantially to the area of forest, which means, not continuous woodland, but space in which special laws operated, special punishments were enforced, intended to ensure the safe-keeping of game, especially deer and boar. In these areas beasts were more precious than men. It is well known that the early Normans created, or rather extended the New Forest; less well known that they could ride from Windsor, through the New Forest, to the sea without leaving territory subject to the forest laws; that the whole county of Essex was a forest; that only three English counties were entirely free from forest law; and that there was probably no part of England more than fifty miles from a forest. William I, says the English chronicler, loved the tall deer as if he were their father.[57]

56   *Beowulf*, trans. D. Wright, pp. 50, 56.
57   ASC E (1087).

The life of Edward the Confessor, in his later years, seems to have been relatively peaceful. The Norman kings were rarely at peace with their neighbours, never at peace with themselves. They lived lives of strenuous and hectic activity: hunting, fighting, begetting children, bargaining for advantageous marriages for their children, receiving petitions, taxing their barons, making and enforcing judgement, struggling to enforce a rudimentary order, to foster the country's wealth, founding monasteries, indulging in conventional, sometimes in sensational piety, and in conventional crimes.

Norman kingship was, in a sense, autocratic: there were no strict and precise limits to royal power. The king was expected to consult his councillors, but who were his councillors? When did he have to consult them? on what issues? who could enforce his duty? To these questions there were no simple answers; yet we should be wrong to imagine him free of all restraint on this account, for two good reasons. First, custom might not be precise, but it was deeply felt, and it was supported by oaths made by a king at his accession (at least as early as 1066), and sometimes (as in the case of Henry I and Stephen) by a solemn charter extracted from a new king in exchange for his subjects' support and allegiance – a charter which Henry was too strong and Stephen too weak to keep; but Henry I's charter could be unearthed and thrust under the nose of King John on the eve of *Magna Carta*. In the second place, autocracy today can have instruments to make its will effective. In days before standing armies or regular police forces, with no means of communication faster than a galloping horse, when roads were at best distant memories of Roman ways, at worst *'l'endroit où on passe'*, a king had to rely on his people's support if his government was to be effective. England was the most governed country in Europe in the central Middle Ages because it had the most highly developed system of local government. In shire court and hundred court royal officials met the local notables, and they agreed, or agreed to differ, about all the problems of a rudimentary administration. The strength of English local government and its continuity are illustrated by the fact that the boundaries of the English shires were established by the great kings of the tenth century, and then not seriously threatened before the boundary commissions of the twentieth. This does not mean that we should read back democracy into the tenth century, or Parliament into the Witan. The men whom the king had to consult were a small proportion of a population perhaps about 3 per cent as large as the country holds today. This is a rough estimate. The only period in the centuries covered by this book for which we can make anything better than wild guesses of the population of England is in the time of Domesday

Book (late 1080s).[58] Even Domesday is no very secure guide. But if we say that there were one and a half million people in England in 1086, and about 200 barons whom the king had to consult, we shall not be far wrong; and we may be fairly sure that in the tenth century the population was smaller, but the Witan somewhat larger. It was only by consulting his leading subjects that the king could hope to rule as well as to reign; only by visiting different parts of the country that he could hope to gain and hold his subjects' loyalty.

Winchester had been the chief city of Wessex for several centuries; London had been the chief city of England even longer – since the Roman conquest, save, perhaps, for an interval after the Romans left. But we should misconceive Saxon or Norman government if we called either the capital of England in this period in a modern sense – though the word was sometimes used.[59] Government travelled with the king round his many residences; the Witan met where he summoned them. William I held solemn councils at Christmas, Easter and Whitsun; when he was in England these were held at Gloucester, Winchester and Westminster, respectively. The kings even carried a proportion of their treasure with them, and the whole of their secretarial staff. It is true that they had permanent treasure-houses here and there; the most important was at Winchester. In the twelfth century it moved, with all the panoply of financial administration, to Westminster. But to the ordinary man kingship meant the person of the king, as he met him on his travels, in the hunting field, in solemn pageant and procession. Where we think of government in terms of Whitehall, Downing Street and the Houses of Parliament, he thought of the royal household.

It is not easy to say precisely in what the royal household consisted in early days; but we are helped by the fact that one of Henry I's clerks drew up a catalogue of the officials of the royal household shortly after his death. This document indicates that the number of household officials was carefully watched, and their wages only paid if they were performing their offices. It is concerned with pay, not with the officers' duties; but it gives the impression that Henry I had had a tight grip on the cost, and on the functions, of his household. None the less, it presupposes a household of at least 100, and possibly far more persons in regular employment, ranging from the heads of the departments, whose wages were 5s. per day, to the laundress, whose wages could not be discovered. The chancellor was head of the chapel and

---

58 The Domesday Inquest took place in 1086. Roffe 2000 deploys convincing arguments for dating the book or books, as we have them, in or after 1089. For the *evidence* they contain we can keep the date 1086.

59 Of the events of 1135: 'totius regni caput', the head or capital of the whole kingdom (*Gesta Stephani*, pp. 12–13).

the writing office (oddly enough, as we see it, the same department); two 'sewers' or stewards, called 'cupbearers', *dapiferi*, were in charge of the pantry and the kitchen; the butler had charge of buttery and cellar; the master chamberlain and treasurer between them controlled the royal chamber, the royal treasury, and the recently formed audit department, the exchequer; the constables looked after the royal army and the king's horses. The chancellor was usually a leading cleric, likely to be rewarded sooner or later with a bishopric; the treasurer was sometimes a cleric, sometimes a layman; the other heads of departments were all leading barons, ministers of state of a rudimentary kind. The butler performed the ceremonial work of his office indeed; but he was in no sense a menial. Each of these great men had a staff of subordinates, who did the real work of their offices. The largest of all the departments, characteristically, was that of the hunting staff: four hornblowers, twenty sergeants, sundry keepers of greyhounds, keepers of the royal pack, knight-huntsmen, ordinary huntsmen, a leader and a feeder of the hounds, huntsmen of the 'trained pack' (hounds kept on a long lead), the keeper of the small hounds, wolf-hunters, archers.[60]

The court was mobile; the household included a tent-keeper for the royal pavilion. It was large, but had to be prepared for frequent and exhausting travel on horse-back, with a train of ox-drawn and horse-drawn wagons and packhorses. It was the centre of government: the chancery, the royal jewels and a part of the royal treasure travelled with it, only the treasury and exchequer were static in Winchester. It was the magnificent household of a great lord whose splendour must impress his visitors; it was also a domestic organization with chamber, pantry, buttery and kitchen. It was the headquarters of a war-lord, with constables and marshals to organize the troops. But as one's eyes wander to and fro through the pages of the catalogue, ever and anon they return to the final item: the hunting staff. It reminds us that the consuming occupation of medieval kings was hunting; it is the monument of a savage sport in which men and animals were sacrificed to delight in an adventure often more destructive than medieval war. It is also the personal monument of a man who won a kingdom from an accident in the hunting field.

60 Richard FitzNigel, pp. 128–32.

5

Queens

At first sight the queens of Anglo-Saxon England seem doomed to live in a twilight world. Of only about thirty do we know more than the name; of all but a handful of these we know nothing more than the names of their fathers and of some of their children. After 1000, and especially after the Norman Conquest, the queens fare better: we have many details and some inkling of the personalities of almost all of them.[61]

Already before the Conquest Queen Emma, wife of Ethelred II and Cnut, and Queen Edith, Edward the Confessor's wife, each had something like a biography written about them. Furthermore, the information which we have, carefully and imaginatively analysed, enables us to see a remarkable variety of status and marriage strategy among them; and an honorary member of the society of English queens, the English St Margaret, queen of the Scots – great-niece of Edward the Confessor, mother-in-law of Henry I, grandmother-in-law of Stephen – was both an outstanding personality and one of the best recorded of all medieval queens.

Of the thirty wives of Anglo-Saxon kings whose fathers are recorded, only three were daughters of foreign potentates: Bertha, queen of Ethelbert of Kent, who came from the region of Paris before 597; Judith, daughter of Charles the Bald, king of the West Franks (that is, of approximately what we call France), who married King Alfred's father, Æthelwulf of Wessex, as his second wife in 856; and Emma, daughter of Duke (or Count) Richard I of Normandy, who first came to England in 1002. The remainder were daughters or sisters of English potentates – in the seventh to ninth centuries, of

61 This field has been opened up – for England and Europe – by many books and articles of the last thirty years. I am especially indebted to Stafford 1983 and 1997; a number of essays in Duggan 1997 and Parsons 1994. The *Handbook of British Chronology*, 3rd edn (see p. 173), pp. 4–36, lists all the known queens of the period.

kings of other kingdoms; in the tenth and eleventh, of the ealdormen and earls who replaced the kings after the Angles became subject to a single king of the English. This might lead us to think that queens and queenship were of local, English, concern, that the customs attaching to them were insular.

This was not so. First of all, it is always a mistake to see the English Channel and the North Sea primarily as frontiers: they were, even more, the great highways of north-western Europe. Across them had come many generations of invaders into this much-invaded island. It was indeed also, in Shakespeare's (or John of Gaunt's) words,

> This fortress built by Nature for herself
> Against infection and the hand of war –

but Gaunt's celebrated rhapsody enshrines a superficial half-truth. England – Britain – was part of Europe; and the English kings from time to time absorbed the customs and traditions of the Continent (see below); queenship, like kingship, dwelt in a large enclosure, which at times stretched as far as the confines of western Europe and even beyond. In the 1090s, for example, Duke Robert of Normandy lost the chance to become king of England by lingering too long in Jerusalem; in the 1140s Eleanor of Aquitaine, estranged wife of the king of France, lost her only chance for a single life in Antioch (where her uncle was prince) – and so had to seek a new husband in the west, and became queen of the English (see pp. 72, 153). The coronation rituals which some queens enjoyed from the ninth century on were – like the kingly rites – part of the common European culture of the time. In particular, Charles the Bald, doubtful, evidently, of the way queens were treated in Wessex, had his daughter Judith consecrated as queen before she left his court. The consecration of Edgar's third wife, Ælfthryth, in 973, was clearly modelled on Judith's: in this respect Judith's brief marriage – her husband died two years later, and she had no children by him – permanently affected the role of the queen in Wessex and England.

It is certainly the case that the overseas marriages, though few, were exceptionally influential. Queen Bertha of Kent was the first Christian, English queen. She was the daughter of the Merovingian King Charibert and his Queen Ingoberg, who ruled in Paris; and Bede tells us that the condition of her marriage to the pagan Ethelbert was that she be allowed to practise her Christian faith, and bring her own personal bishop, Liudhard, with her.[62] It is clear that Bertha and Liudhard prepared the way for the mission of St Augustine – that

---

62 Bede i. 25, pp. 72–5.

her role in the conversion of England was in some senses as significant as those of Pope Gregory and Archbishop Augustine.

Most remarkable of the overseas alliances were those formed by the daughters of Edward the Elder, the sisters of his son Athelstan.[63] In 916–19 Edward sent Eadgifu to marry Charles the Simple, king of the West Franks. After Edward's death another of the same family married Sihtric, a Danish king in Northumbria. In 926 Eadhild married Hugh the Great, Count of Paris, and so became the stepmother of the Capetian kings – for after her death Hugh married Hedwig, sister of Otto the Great of Germany, who was to be Hugh Capet's mother. In 929–30 Ælfgifu (if such was her name) accompanied her sister Edith, the former to marry a Burgundian prince, the latter the young Otto, heir to the throne of Germany, the future Otto the Great. In the museum attached to Essen Cathedral are still to be seen some of the wonders of Ottonian art: crosses and a miniature crown of exquisite metal and paintwork. Some are monuments to the taste of Matilda, granddaughter of Otto and Edith, who was curious to enquire of her cousin the Ealdorman Æthelweard about her English forebears – inspiring a rather uncouth Latin translation of the *Anglo-Saxon Chronicle*.[64] Thus the English and German royal families intermarried, and their genealogies mingled, as did their coronation rites (see pp. 7, 32).

Slender as is the evidence for most of the queens before 1000, they none the less illustrate a variety of aspects of married life. The normal tendency of historians in the twentieth century was to seek common factors in the history of marriage: to exaggerate the differences of human relations in medieval and modern times, and to narrow the range of choice and variety. Very likely most queens sought their vocation above all in the marriage-bed and in bearing children; but human beings are infinitely various, and to some women the marriage-bed is a wholly unattractive feature of the relationship. It was generally believed that Mary herself, Jesus's mother, had remained a virgin; and the marriage of Mary and Joseph (regarded by some as the perfect marriage) could encourage those who were sexually shy – or naturally ascetic – to seek an unconsummated marriage. Such a one was Æthelthryth (Etheldreda), daughter of Anna, one of the first Christian kings of East Anglia, and queen of Northumbria. She was in fact twice married: first to an ealdorman called Tondberht, who died before the marriage was consummated; next to a great potentate,

63   See details in the commentary to William of Malmesbury, *Gesta Regum*, II, 109–10; cf. *Handbook of British Chronology* (p. 173), pp. 24–5.
64   Æthelweard 1962.

Ecgfrith king of Northumbria. For twelve years she was his wife, yet the marriage, we are told, was never consummated. Some, then and now, have doubted the truth of this – 'perhaps she was barren'.[65] To this let Bede respond: 'When I asked Bishop Wilfrid of blessed memory whether this was so, since some had come to doubt it, he said that he himself was the most certain witness of her virgin integrity – to the point that Ecgfrith promised that he would give him broad acres and much money if he could persuade the queen to the marriage-bed, for he knew that she loved no man more than him.'[66] And Bede refers to stories of heroic virgins of earlier days, stories Æthelthryth herself may well have heard, for she was evidently an educated woman, deeply read in spiritual literature. It is in the nature of the case that we can have no other evidence on the matter; but the combination of sexual shyness and saintly idealism is not at all improbable – and Wilfrid loved few things more than money and estates.

However that may be, the queen was released – the marriage was annulled – and after a spell in one family monastery at Coldingham, she set up another at Ely, where her cult has continued (with some interruptions) to this day.

Æthelthryth in the end cut herself off from any political aspirations. In these as in any centuries some queens have tended to be much involved in the political schemes of their kings and their courts. Yet here too we find evidence of much variety in activity and attitude. In 672–3 Seaxburh, queen of the West Saxons, reigned for a year after her husband's death.[67] Nearly two hundred and fifty years later Alfred's able daughter Æthelflæd remained lady of the Mercians – sometimes being accorded the title queen – after her husband's death. The ealdorman Ethelred, her husband, was Edward the Elder's most trusted subordinate, almost an under-king in Mercia and London; and Ethelred and his wife were close allies in government and politics as in the marriage-bed – though she was always loyal to her brother the king. So dominant a figure did Æthelflæd become that there seems to have been some expectation that her daughter Ælfwynn would succeed her as lady or queen in Mercia. On Æthelflæd's death in 918 Edward the Elder took the precaution of depriving his niece of her inheritance and removing her to Wessex.[68]

There are striking examples of queens who held their own with their husbands, from Offa's wife Queen Cynethryth of Mercia, who

---

65 Janet Nelson in *Blackwell Encyclopaedia*, p. 383 – in an otherwise masterly general account of Anglo-Saxon queens.
66 Bede iv. 19 (17), pp. 390–7.
67 *ASC*, trans. Garmonsway, p. 35.
68 See Simon Keynes in *Blackwell Encyclopaedia*, p. 14.

subscribed his charters and issued coins in her own name, to Emma, who stands beside her second husband Cnut, in equal dignity, dedicating a cross in the New Minster at Winchester (Plate 2). In contrast, Cynethryth's daughter Eadburh was alleged to have carried her mother's role into Wessex when she married King Beorhtric, but to have gone too far – even (it was said) to the point of accidentally poisoning her husband – so that Asser assures us that her evil reputation explained the lowly status of a king's wife in Alfred's Wessex, where they were not even given the title queen.[69] Alfred's daughter Æthelflæd and the queens of the eleventh and twelfth centuries were to restore the dignity of Cynethryth.

One could extend the examples of queens who played a leading role in the succession – some by the basic function of bearing royal princes and princesses, some by following the example of Solomon's mother, Bathsheba, in ensuring that it was their son, not a rival's, who succeeded, or in helping them to rule when they did. Thus Edgar's third wife (or so), Ælfthryth, played some part in the succession of her son Ethelred the Unready, and in the early years of his reign; and after a period of retirement she returned to influence at court in 993, two years (by an interesting coincidence) after the death of the regent Empress Theophanu – the former Byzantine princess – in Germany.[70] But Ælfthryth never attempted the dominance achieved by Theophanu, as regent for her son the Emperor Otto III.

Ælfthryth died between 999 and 1001, and in 1002 Ethelred married (as his second wife) the Norman Emma, daughter of Duke Richard I, sister of Richard II.[71] She was the quintessence of a dynastic queen, for she married both Ethelred and his arch-enemy and ultimate successor, Cnut. Her first husband had died in 1016, and in 1017 she married Cnut. This may seem to us a heartless adventure; but she inspired a contemporary to write her *Encomium*, which attributed the good peace that England enjoyed in the 1020s and 1030s (till Cnut's death in 1035) to the influence of Emma. The author protested too much; but there is no doubt that the queen's marriage with Cnut helped to legitimize his reign in England. It is also clear that Emma was tough, and that she needed to be to live with a husband at once violent and unfaithful. But she was after all a Norman princess, and she was not William the Conqueror's aunt for

69 *Asser*, ed. Stevenson, cc. 13–15, pp. 10–14. Cf. the shrewd comment of Janet Nelson: 'This story contains various kinds of truth' (*Blackwell Encyclopaedia*, p. 383).
70 Simon Keynes in *Blackwell Encyclopaedia*, p. 15; for Theophanu, Brooke 2000, pp. 124–5 and refs.
71 On Emma and Edith (below), see *Encomium Emmae Reginae, Edward the Confessor*, and Stafford 1997; cf. Brooke 2000, pp. 126–7.

Plate 2 Queen Emma (Ælfgifu) and King Cnut present a gift to the New Minster, Winchester: British Library, Stowe MS 944, folio 6 recto. In this fine drawing of 1031, the queen's veil and the king's crown are held by angels, each of whom points a finger at Christ, the source of royal power. The centre of the picture is the cross, not the figures, and it is dominated by Christ in judgement, but it is also an unusually lucid portrayal of the role of the queen as partner and collaborator in royal enterprises. See Keynes 1996, pp. 35–9, 79–80.

nothing – nor need we doubt that William in his turn learned from the achievements of Cnut and Emma much that was relevant to making a king by conquest seem legitimate. At the end of her life Emma engaged in political intrigue in favour of her son by Cnut, Harthacnut, and after his death lived to see her son by Ethelred, Edward the Confessor, ascend the throne – and sadly to quarrel with him.

Emma's daughter-in-law, Queen Edith, was also a remarkable woman, if in a different mould. She comes to life in the biography of King Edward, of which she is the heroine.[72] She was the daughter of Earl Godwine and sister of Earl, later King, Harold, and her role as queen depended much on Edward's ambivalent relations with her family. But in his later years there was peace among them, and Edith seems to have won his tolerant affection – though they never had any children. Edward's biographer makes clear that she was a highly educated woman, deeply read, an accomplished linguist, expert in painting and needlework – a pious woman who none the less loved finery and especially enjoyed providing her husband (who was indifferent to dress) with magnificent robes, and a staff decked with gold and gems. She could not influence the political scene in quite the way Emma had done; but the good relations between Edward and her family in his last years very probably owed much to her – as may perhaps Edward's final decision to designate her brother to succeed him. Her learning and piety and love of finery remind us of her husband's great niece, St Margaret.

It was Otto III, in alliance with his fellow-dreamer Pope Sylvester II, who in 1001 provided the Hungarian ruler St Stephen with a crown; and in the cosmopolitan gathering of Stephen's court the Magyar military inheritance was combined with Byzantine and western influences – the event of 1001 gave a decisively western orientation to the Hungarian monarchy. Among the exiles given hospitality by St Stephen was one Edward, son of Edmund Ironside, king of the English, and so grandson of Ethelred the Unready, who came to escape from his father's successor, the Viking King Cnut; and not long after Stephen's death, in the late 1040s, Edward's daughter Margaret was born there.[73] In 1057, when she was still a child, her father and mother, Agatha, 'the emperor's kinswoman', and all their

---

72 *Edward the Confessor*, esp. pp. 72–5, and Frank Barlow's introduction. See also Stafford 1997, esp. pp. 40–52.

73 The date of her birth is not known, though commonly asserted to be 1046. See Baker 1978, esp. p. 134 n. 113. For the mother, see *ASC*, MS D (1057), trans. Garmonsway, p. 188. What follows is based on *ASC* D, under 1067; E, under 1093 (trans. Garmonsway, pp. 201–2, 228); Turgot; John of Worcester, III, 6–7, 66–7 (cf. ibid., pp. xx–xxi). For modern commentaries, see esp. Baker 1978; Huneycutt 1990; Wall 1997.

family, returned to England – doubtless with the idea that he might succeed his uncle Edward as king; but in the same year he died. The uncertain hospitality of the English court finally evaporated in 1066, when her brother Edgar the Ætheling was briefly proclaimed king. Margaret fled to Scotland, where the recently widowed Malcolm III fell in love with her. Some historians, who doubt if love could enter into medieval royal marriages, have sought improbable political motives for Malcolm's courtship: in brutal fact, Margaret was a penniless exile without any obvious value in the marriage market. She apparently hesitated: they came from very different cultures, and she had (like Æthelthryth) a strong urge to the ascetic life. In the event the marriage was amazingly successful, as eight children and the moving testimony of her biographer bear witness. When news came that Malcolm had been killed in a raid into England in 1093, Margaret – already a very sick woman owing (it seems) to her ascetic manner of life – collapsed and died, only three days after him.[74]

For those who seek unusual kinds of historical evidence, Margaret is of quite exceptional interest. Her biographer has been denigrated for excessive hagiography: even so, his picture of a highly educated woman of cosmopolitan culture joined in unequal partnership to a northern barbarian who worshipped her – and of her own remarkable combination of learning, charm, devotion to Parisian fashions and luxury with asceticism – is entirely convincing. But the inescapable evidence of her attitudes and interests lies in the names of her children: Edward, Edgar, Ethelred, Edmund, Edith, Alexander, David and Mary. None of these names is known to have occurred in the Scottish royal family before her day; and if Alexander and David seem natural Scottish names to us, that is her doing. For it cannot be doubted that she chose the names. In this she may have followed her mother, Agatha: Agatha's son was given the English name of Edgar, but the daughters bore the names of virgin saints – Margaret and Christina – like Agatha herself. Margaret's choice, however, followed a somewhat different pattern. The first five are plain English, from her own family – the men representing her ancestors of the previous hundred years. These names tell us of a mother who was the dominant partner in a highly successful marriage – and of a queen who may have reckoned that the Old English kings were on a higher plain than the Scottish, let alone the Normans. Alexander the Great was the central figure in

---

74 Three days, John of Worcester, III, 66–7; on the fourth day, Turgot, p. 322. Malcolm died on St Brice's day, presumably 13 November (but possibly the 14th). As Margaret was later commemorated on 16 November, 13 and 16 November are the likely dates for the two events. The exact place in the list of their children (below) of Edmund, Ethelred and the daughters seems to be uncertain.

a cycle of romances only just surfacing in Margaret's time: the name suggests a knowledge of the classics or a love of worldly vernacular literature.[75] King David the psalmist, the youngest son of Jesse, and Mary the queen of Heaven suggest the growing piety and biblical study of her later years.

In 1093 Malcolm and Margaret died, and the future of the family seemed very uncertain. After an interlude, Edgar, Alexander and David all succeeded; and King David I (1124–53) transformed the face of the Scottish kingdom and became one of the creative figures in Scottish history, as well as an even more notable patron of monasteries than his mother or elder sister.

In 1093 Edith, and very likely Mary too, were sent to the monasteries of Wilton and Romsey, where they were kept under firm discipline by their aunt Christina. To protect Edith from the lust of the Normans, as she herself is reported to have said, she was given a nun's veil. When Henry I became king and instantly sought to bolster his new-found legitimacy by marrying her,[76] it was objected that she was a nun. Edith – shortly to be called Matilda or Maud in a French-speaking court – protested that she had taken no vows; and as for the veil, when Christina's back was turned, she took it off and jumped on it. Eadmer tells us that he was present, and has quoted the 'maiden's words' as they were spoken – though he does also cite witnesses who confirmed that they were true.[77] After due enquiry Edith was married to Henry and took the name Matilda.

It was a hard fate to be married to Henry I, but Matilda seems to have made the best of it. They had two children; and she devoted herself to giving her husband political support – and to the patronage of religious houses. Her husband, with all his faults, founded more monasteries than any other medieval monarch (so far as is known), some of them by remarkably economical methods, some by grand gestures of extravagance. His nearest rival was Matilda's brother, David of Scotland, a notable connoisseur of the different religious orders of the day.[78] Both may have learned much from the

75   Cary and Ross 1956. The earliest surviving secular romance was written shortly after Margaret's death. An oral source for her knowledge of Alexander is likely enough – but she may well have known one or other of the Latin sources, some of which were very popular in the Middle Ages (ibid., chs. 1–4). For Alexander's modest role in surviving Old English literature, see *Blackwell Encyclopaedia*, p. 27.

76   This was the motive attributed to Henry by contemporaries (see Chibnall 1991, p. 7 and nn. 4–5). Others have supposed a Scottish alliance important to him, but this seems very doubtful.

77   Eadmer, *Historia Novorum*, p. 125 – cf. p. 123, and below, p. 153.

78   On Henry, Matilda and David as patrons, see Brooke 1999, chs. 8–9. No continental royal patron of the period is known to have come anywhere near him.

zeal and example of Matilda, who herself founded the house of Austin canons of Holy Trinity, Aldgate, in the City of London, and the leper hospital of St Giles in the Fields beyond the confines of Holborn. The story is told that David, who served his apprenticeship as an Anglo-Normal baron in his brother-in-law's court, was horrified on one occasion to find his sister washing the feet of lepers. Her response was to make him kiss their feet.[79] She was not St Margaret's daughter for nothing.

Matilda died in 1118 and her only surviving son, William, perished in the wreck of the White Ship in 1120. Henry instantly sought a new wife; but his marriage to Adela of Louvain was childless – strangely so, for he had many children by various mothers, and Adela herself bore children to her second husband after Henry's death. Meanwhile, Matilda's younger sister Mary had married Eustace, count of Boulogne, and they had a daughter, Matilda, who became the greatest heiress in Normandy – and so was married under Henry I's benevolent eye to one of his favourite nephews, Stephen of Blois. Thus when Stephen became king of the English in 1135, a granddaughter of St Margaret – Stephen's Matilda – succeeded to the dignity Margaret's daughter – Henry's Matilda – had enjoyed a generation before. But her role was to be challenged by another Matilda, the empress, daughter of Henry's Matilda and cousin of Stephen's. The family of St Margaret thus dominated the English royal family for two generations.

We have encountered queens dominant and submissive, wives who paid the 'marriage debt' with promptitude and one at least who wholly rejected it; we have encountered political marriages and at least one love match – almost all the variety which *la comédie humaine* can offer. Yet the last royal marriage to take place before 1154 introduced a relatively novel theme, that of a queen of France who rejected her husband's bed and sought a divorce, and then became queen of England.[80] Eleanor was the heiress of the duchy of Aquitaine, and when her father was nearing the end of his life, to protect her from the rapacity of other French nobles, he bequeathed her marriage – gave the right to choose her husband – to Louis VI, the French king. Not unnaturally, Louis betrothed her to his son, the future Louis VII. They had one child, a girl, and then no more for

79 Ailred of Rievaulx, *Genealogia*, col. 736, citing David himself in evidence; cf. Huneycutt 1990, p. 92. The substance of it, as it relates to Matilda, is confirmed by William of Malmesbury, *Gesta Regum*, I, 756–7, written very shortly after her death.
80 On Eleanor of Aquitaine, see Brooke 1992, pp. 192–3, and Brooke 2000, p. 129. As a queen seeking divorce, Æthelthryth may seem a parallel to Eleanor – but they had little else in common.

many years; it seems evident that Eleanor was (for some reason)
repelled by her husband, who has otherwise left a good memory
behind him, and refused to sleep with him. She accompanied him on
the Second Crusade in the late 1140s and tried to seek asylum with
her uncle at Antioch. This attempt failed, and on the return journey
they met Pope Eugenius III in Rome. The pope delighted in attempts
to restore broken marriages, and Louis was evidently still fond of her.
Eleanor consented to the pope's insistence that they sleep together in
the same bed, 'adorned with the most precious hangings from his own
store'.[81] Sure enough, a second child was born, also a girl; but by now
both partners were weary of the marriage, and Louis despaired of a
male heir. So in 1152 a French ecclesiastical court declared that as
they were third cousins once removed, they were within the prohibited degrees (as the law of the Church then prescribed them) and
annulled the marriage. Eleanor was at once the most eligible spinster
in Europe, and summoned the Empress Matilda's son, Henry, duke of
Normandy and count of Anjou (her fourth cousin), to Poitiers to
marry her. In 1154 Henry became king of the English, and so by
inheritance, marriage and political intrigue lord of a great empire. By
Eleanor's marriages the fates of England and France were settled, in
ironical fashion. Louis was able to remarry and have a son; but his
divorce helped to raise against him the most formidable rival the
Capetian monarchy ever faced. Yet in the end, domestic quarrels
wrecked the marriage of Henry and Eleanor – and started a process
which enabled Louis's son to dismember the Angevin empire. Eight
children were born to Henry and Eleanor, and the sons rose against
their father in alliance with their mother: Henry's empire had been
won by a series of dynastic marriages – his grandfather's, his mother's
and his own – but his own marriage was as fertile in discord as in
children.

81   John of Salisbury, *Historia Pontificalis*, ed. M. Chibnall, p. 61 (my translation).

6

Origins

Such, in broad outline, were the institutions of Saxon and Norman kingship. Now we can turn and pursue the fascinating problem of its origin. In doing so, we must keep a firm grip on ourselves; pursue real clues, proceed by paths that are, or can be, mapped; avoid the wild speculations to which such subjects are always inviting us.

In this pursuit we can get some guidance from the studies of social anthropologists. They have studied the institutions of modern peoples in a variety of stages from savagery, through barbarism to civilization, many with highly developed ideas of kingship, many with none at all. They warn us that kingship is not a natural or inevitable feature of any type of society, but show that some sort of kingship has been very common in many different parts of the world. Clearly it answers some widely felt needs of human society; precisely how is not easy, in a general way, to say. Most kingships have had a religious and a military significance; we shall do well to look at Anglo-Saxon warfare and religion at an early stage.

The chief lesson of modern anthropology seems to be a warning of our ignorance. When modern, illiterate societies were first examined by scientific methods, attempts were made to deduce the historical evolution of their arrangements, partly by using certain assumptions about how societies work, partly by deductions from the oral trad-itions of the peoples themselves. The technique of deducing history in this way is now discredited: it produced much fascinating speculation, often contradictory. The anthropologist now studies the structure, the functioning of a society as he sees it; and, if he talks history, it is structural history, that is to say he constructs a model, in terms of two or three generations, of how the existing society works. Thus he is able to clarify, and rationalize, the data of present experience; and also to make sense of the people's oral history. Oral history may often contain fragments of genuine tradition going back many centuries; in extreme cases these fragments may hardly alter through the generations; but oral history as we find it today is a compound of old traditions and new; of stories genuine and garbled; and it is intended to explain the present – as a crude attempt in its own right at structural history – not a self-conscious attempt to describe the past for its own sake. By merely inspecting current oral tradition we can never hope to distinguish old from new with any precision; we can only prove the presence of the old if earlier written records or archaeological finds confirm it. This helps to explain why genuine traditions of widely different centuries may become mingled together. The sense of time, as a thing of centuries and decades, is a very sophisticated notion; to most people, especially primitive people, a thousand years are as yesterday, or at least, as the day before yesterday. Students of medieval sources are constantly baffled by the way that plausible history and the wildest fantasy are so often set down side by side, as if of equal credibility. This is partly due to the fact that the medieval world of experience was different from ours – was peopled with devils and monsters and strange, miraculous prodigies, which tend to evade us; partly because only a few men had any concrete notion of the past. A historian like Bede could set seriously to work to piece his materials together into a coherent historical narrative; but he was a rare and startling exception. To most men the past only existed in so far as they or their friends could remember it; and was only recorded in so far as it intrigued them or helped to explain the present.

An extreme example is the practice, common in the modern world as in the medieval, of recording a man's genealogy. The study of genealogy among primitive peoples, as practised by the modern anthropologist, is a highly technical and refined art. The genealogy exists, among other things, to establish a man's title to land, to record his relationship to the tribe or people who own the whole country in which he lives. If it achieves this task, it matters little whether it represents genuine relationships or not. Indeed, in those societies where the rules of inheritance are very complex, and where patrilineal succession is unknown, a genealogy clearly does not represent a family tree of the kind to which we are accustomed. The early Anglo-Saxon genealogies purport to establish the succession to kingdoms, and may contain some genuine king-lists; they may also contain some fiction; they are less likely to give a true account of a man's ancestry. But in some cases, as we shall see, even this is not wholly impossible.

Modern anthropology warns us of our ignorance in another, even more fundamental way. Its students rely on living material; like the psychologist, they can analyse their material, ask it what questions they like, study its reactions to problems of their own choosing. They would not describe a society or a type of kingship which they had not subjected to these tests. The historian has the advantage of studying his victims in depth; but their structure, as the anthropologist understands the term, he cannot study at all. He can find the footprint of Man Friday in the sand; but he cannot meet Man Friday face to face.

'His genealogy', wrote Asser of King Alfred (871–99), 'is woven in this order: Alfred' was the son of Æthelwulf, son of Egbert, son of Ealhmund, son of Eafa, son of Eoppa, son of Ingild; Ingild and Ine were brothers, sons of Cenred, son of Ceolwald, son of Cutha (Cuthwulf), son of Cuthwine, son of Ceawlin, son of Cynric, son of Creoda, son of Cerdic, son of Elesa, son of Gewis, . . . son of Brand, son of Bældæg, son of Woden, son of Frithuwald, son of Frealaf, son of Frithuwulf, son of Finn, son of Godwulf, son of Geat (whom the pagans long venerated as a god), . . . son of Tætwa, son of Beaw, son of Sceldwea, son of Heremod, son of Itermon, son of Hathra, son of Hwala, son of Bedwig, son of Seth, son of Noah, son of Lamech, son of Methuselah, son of Enoch, [son of Jared,] son of Malaleel, son of Canaan, son of Enos, son of Seth, son of Adam.[82]

This list lacks nothing in completeness; the greater part of it, none the less, was the fruit of recent speculation. In the early ninth century it was firmly believed that the West Saxon kings were descended from Cerdic; it was equally firmly believed, needless to say, that they were also descended from Adam. The vital links in the chain between Cerdic and Adam were Woden, Geat and Seth. These links were all forged in the late eighth or ninth century. The kings of almost all Anglian kingdoms claimed to be descended from Woden. Oddly enough, the West Saxons seem in early days not to have looked back beyond Cerdic. This defect was now made good: a section from one of the Northumbrian genealogies, that of Bernicia, was added, and so Cerdic was linked to Woden; and Woden became the common ancestor of the West Saxon, and nearly all the Saxon lines.

Woden had been the high god of the Teutonic pantheon, the leader of the Germanic peoples – though his position had been disputed by Thor. His name survives in place-names like Wednesbury and Wednesfield, and also in the English translation of the Latin *dies Mercurii* 'Mercury's day', Wednesday (French *mercredi*), just as Thursday is Thor's day (Jupiter's day, *jeudi*). The idea that kings ought to be descended from him was very ancient; but originally he himself had no ancestors. It seems to have been the royal minstrels of the obscure kingdom of Lindsey (in Lincolnshire) who bolstered up the decaying

---

82 *Asser*, ed. Stevenson, c. 1, pp. 2–4 (my translation); see also trans. Keynes and Lapidge, p. 67.

authority of their masters by pushing back their ancestry some generations behind Woden, as far as Geat, and this became part of the
accepted lore of English royal descent. The next stage is somewhat
obscure. But it seems that Geat was presently identified with another
legendary figure of the same name, whose ancestors were already
recorded; and this enabled the genealogy of all the Anglo-Saxon
houses to be extended to one Sceaf, perhaps originally the same as
the Sceaf whose son Scyld's ship-burial formed the start of *Beowulf*.
According to *Beowulf* Scyld was put into a ship when he was dead; it
also says, as do other early traditions, that he began his career in a
ship. By what mysterious alchemy his father was made a son of Noah
and brought to birth, as it were, in the Ark, is far from clear; but by
the time we get to Asser he has been given a Hebrew name, Seth, and
is performing the genealogical function of Japhet. From then on, all
was plain sailing.

If we look closely at Alfred's genealogy, we can see that his folk had
no ancient tradition of their ancestry going behind Cerdic. It is striking that the Saxon line which was ultimately to give England her kings
had the shortest and most confused of early traditions. All the kings
from Cerdic to Cenred, Ine's father, begin with C. It may be that this
alliteration was an established tradition: all Ine's successor's to Edgar
the Ætheling began with a vowel. But it is unlikely that the succession
was so orderly as this assumes; it is striking that the change from
initial C to vowels comes just where the line emerges into the plain
light of day; and although some of the line were undoubtedly historical, it is likely that some names have been added from the medieval
equivalent of a telephone directory, and that it is in part fictitious.
Oddest of all, the founder seems not to have been a Saxon at all: his
name, Cerdic, or Ceredig, is Welsh.

Let us put on one side the mystery of Wessex for the time being, and
see why historians, without undue credulity, have greater faith in
others of the genealogies. Most remarkable of all is the list for
Lindsey, which is to all intents and purposes our only evidence for
the history of that kingdom. It lay neglected until Sir Frank Stenton, in
a brilliant article, showed how it could be made to illuminate the
history of its kingdom and of England at large.[83] Ten names take us to
Woden, and not one of them can be certainly identified; nor does
Woden give us any very secure chronological beginning, still less the
mysterious names which carry us beyond him. But Sir Frank noted
four remarkable things about the list: that it is undoubtedly early

83 Stenton 1927. See now the essays in Vince 1993, especially by S. Foot, pp. 128–40, and
B. Yorke, pp. 141–50.

since it contains early Saxon names which later fell out of use – like the name next to Woden, Winta, preserved in no document, but known from early place-names to have existed; that the fourth name from Woden revealed Celtic influence – i.e. belonged to a time when the two races had mingled; that the seventh, Biscop (= Bishop) revealed Christian influence, and must belong after the conversion of Lindsey, that is, to the seventh century at earliest; and that the tenth and latest, (as he supposed), Aldfrith, bore the same name as an unidentified king in a South Saxon charter of the time of Offa of Mercia.[84] By a process of elimination the identification of the two kings is made very probable; and this explains why the genealogy ends with Aldfrith – the minor Anglian dynasties did not for the most part survive the supremacy of Mercia. There is thus every possibility that the genealogy of Lindsey is genuine, or at least a genuine list of kings. We may add that, if one counts the generations back to Winta, it would seem that the dynasty began towards the end of the fifth century. This is a very hazardous means of calculation, but it suggests that Winta may have been the first king of Lindsey, not, like the founder of the Mercian house, a continental Angle.

Various pieces of evidence make the Mercian genealogy seem one of the oldest that survive; and at a point which would seem (by counting generations) to fall approximately in the late fourth century there occurs the name of Offa, who played a part in early legend almost as outstanding as his great namesake of the eighth century played in Mercian and English history. Offa of Mercia seems in fact to have been descended from a continental Angle of the same name who flourished a century before the Saxons came to England.

All discussions of German kingship come back in the end to a terse sentence in the *Germania* of Tacitus (first century AD), a slender foundation on which many large buildings have been erected: 'kings they choose on grounds of noble ancestry; war-leaders for their courage': *reges ex nobilitate, duces ex virtute sumunt*. It is clear that many successful *duces* became kings in course of time; and for some of these noble ancestry was invented. But it may well be that the founders of Lindsey and Mercia were *reges*, just as we can be fairly sure that Cerdic was a *dux* – a Welsh soldier of fortune who became a Saxon war-leader, perhaps; and if this collocation sounds strangely in our ears, let us remember that in the fifth century Romans were

---

84 Alas! – it has been shown that Aldfrith is a misreading in the charter, and we now know less of the dates of the kings of Lindsey even than Stenton did: but Foot, p. 132, still favours a late seventh- or early eighth-century date for Aldfrith.

sometimes found in the employment of Goths and Huns, and a Hun, Odoacer, became effective ruler of Rome.

Beyond this, I doubt if the modern study of genealogy can help us. It warns us to look for fiction in the midst of fact, and fact in the midst of fiction; and it also warns us to look for an explanation of the original form of a genealogy in terms of the social organization of the tribe to which it belongs. But this final warning does us no good: we do not know the form taken by any of these genealogies before the eighth century; and we know too little of the social organization of the Anglo-Saxons to be sure how it would affect their genealogies.

The word 'king' is common to all known Germanic languages, and it seems that all Germanic peoples enjoyed the institution at one time or another. H.M. Chadwick believed that the word meant originally 'son of the family', emphasizing that kings came '*ex nobilitate*'.[85] But surviving evidence does not permit us to discuss the nature of Germanic kingship in general terms at all. When Goths and Vandals and Lombards emerged on to the stage of history, they had strong, unified monarchies; the kings frequently claimed to be derived from the best ancient stock, but in fact, as the conditions of the barbarian invasions dictated, '*virtus*' mattered more to them than '*nobilitas*'; election than heredity. In a new land the absence of nobility was more easily forgotten than in the old. The Byzantine historian Procopius tells a wonderfully absurd story about one small German tribe, the Heruli. They decided to abolish kingship and killed their king; then changed their mind, and sent to Scandinavia in search of a scion of the old royal family; then changed their minds again and asked the Emperor Justinian to provide them with a king; and finally, when the prince from Scandinavia arrived, changed their minds a third time, and accepted him. The Goths looked to the Romans, not for a king, but to provide a genealogy for one already established. These stories illustrate the variety of possibility open to a German tribe; they tell us little of the origin of Germanic kingship, and we shall search for it in vain.

Across the Channel in France, to be more precise in Merovingian Gaul, there flourished a German kingdom which more closely resembled those of the Anglo-Saxons. The Franks invaded Gaul in the fifth century from the Rhineland; and conquered most of what we call France under the first of their great kings, the celebrated Clovis.

---

85 According to the *Oxford English Dictionary* (2nd edn), s.v. king, current interpretations vary between son and scion of the kin or noble lineage. This seems to emphasize '*ex nobilitate*', but the experts may have Tacitus too much in mind when making the interpretations.

Clovis began his career as one petty king among many; the exigencies and opportunities of conquest, and a total absence of scruple which is delightfully portrayed in the pages of Gregory of Tours's *History of the Franks*, enabled Clovis to unite the whole Frankish people under a single rule, for the first time in recorded history. But to the Franks kingship did not traditionally mean monarchy, which literally means the rule of one man. A kingdom was divided between the sons of a ruler, and so the sons of Clovis split Francia between them. They were kings *ex nobilitate*; they were Merovingians, heirs of Clovis and his distant predecessor Meroving, and in later times at least symbolized the special nature of their descent by wearing their hair longer than was fashionable. So efficacious was their long hair, that it kept the last of the Merovings on the throne long after he had ceased to wield any real power; the dynasty did not disappear until 751. Meanwhile there was sometimes one, sometimes a whole committee of kings. In earlier times they may have ruled jointly, like the kings in *The Gondoliers*; in later times they divided the kingdom between them. The early Merovingians were noted for their violence, rapacity and cunning, even in a Europe well acquainted with these qualities; and accident and assassination from time to time left a single king in charge of the whole kingdom. But the principle of family inheritance never disappeared, and election was never more than a formality – the formality of raising a new king on the shield, of acknowledging him as a leader.

In England almost every king from Hengest to Edward the Confessor claimed to be of royal descent. When Northumbria was threatened with destruction by the Danes, its people in despair elected the allegedly non-royal Ælle as the last of their kings; the Mercians probably also took a non-royal king in Ceolwulf II under the same disastrous pressure. The only other example known was Harold II himself. As we have seen, the principle of heredity, and of primogeniture, with certain notable qualifications, was firmly established. But in early days it seems that the English kings, like the Frankish, were not monarchs; it may even be that whole families of sons, brothers and even nephews of kings were called kings. When Edwin of Northumbria invaded Wessex, he killed five West Saxon kings in one battle. In many cases, perhaps in most, the committee had a chairman: the senior king had ultimate authority. But in some, even in the seventh and eighth centuries, the kings were equal, like Sigehere and Sebbe of the East Saxons (Essex). This principle of joint-kingship goes back as far as our records: according to the *Anglo-Saxon Chronicle* the brothers Hengest and Horsa were joint-kings of Kent, and when Horsa died Aesc, Hengest's son, took his place. The same source makes Cerdic and Cynric, his son, joint-kings of the West Saxons; and the examples could be multiplied. In both these cases there may well be an element of anachronism, and even of fiction. But they imply clearly that kingship was not thought of as rule by one man: we have no record of a time when Anglo-Saxon kings had been monarchs.

Even *The Gondoliers* ends with the restoration of monarchy; and in many countries and tribes in the early Middle Ages in which kingship was divided or kings were three a penny, there was some inkling of the possibility of unified monarchy. Ireland had its high king; the Franks commonly regarded one of their kings as the senior; the English had their *Bretwaldas*.

The word *Bretwalda* probably means 'ruler of Britain'.[86] The title was clearly echoed later in the title used on his coins by King Athelstan in the tenth century: '*rex totius Britannie*', king of all Britain. Perhaps we should not take this title too seriously: it was apparently copied shortly after his death by a swashbuckling pirate called Anlaf, the Irish-Norse king of York. Athelstan could only claim effective rule in England, and the title 'king of the English', already used by Alfred on his coins (alternately with 'king of the Saxons'), was the one ultimately adopted by their successors, true kings of a united England. But Athelstan's title was not pure fantasy. Scottish and Welsh kings admitted his overlordship; he was widely respected outside the mainland of Britain. There is some reason to think that he used the title emperor, as did the kings of León in northern Spain in the tenth century, on account of the many peoples he ruled over or might claim to rule. It is unlikely that he had any wish to forestall his brother-in-law, Otto the Great of Germany, who some years after Athelstan's death was crowned Roman emperor in Rome. But he occasionally used the title *basileus*, the official title of the eastern Roman, or Byzantine emperor; and *Anglorum Basileus* is the style of Edward the Confessor on the earliest surviving impressions of the great seal of England.

If we inquire why Athelstan appeared on his coins as king of the whole of Britain, a possible answer is that he was recalling the proud title of his great-great-grandfather Egbert, the last of the *Bretwaldas*. In 829 'King Egbert conquered the kingdom of the Mercians, and all that was south of the Humber, and he was the eighth king to be *Bretwalda*: the first to rule so great a kingdom was Ælle, king of the South Saxons (Sussex); the second was Ceawlin, king of the West

---

86 Wormald 1983 gives an admirably cautious appraisal of the evidence about the *Bretwaldas*. It is not certain (though probable) that *Bretwalda* meant 'ruler of Britain'; but it can emphatically not mean 'ruler of the English'. For Athelstan's coins, see Blunt 1974, p. 55.

Saxons (Wessex); the third was Ethelbert, king of Kent; the fourth was Rædwald, king of the East Angles; the fifth was Edwin, king of the Northumbrians; the sixth was Oswald who reigned after him; the seventh was Oswiu, Oswald's brother; the eighth was Egbert, king of Wessex. This Egbert led his levies to Dore against the Northumbrians, where they offered him submission and peace; thereupon they parted.'[87] The same list, with the omission of Egbert, occurs in Bede over a century earlier. It is a very interesting, and in some ways a very strange, selection. But before we can attempt to understand the selection, or understand what made a man a *Bretwalda*, we must tell in outline the story of the English kingdoms between Hengest and Egbert.

87 *ASC*, trans. Garmonsway, p. 61 (slightly corrected).

7

The Small Kingdoms

The map of England is a palimpsest on which every age has scored its marks; and time, an incompetent eraser, has left much for our inspection. It is a curious fact that the English shire boundaries were fixed before the boundary with Scotland: all the shires we know, with almost exactly their modern boundaries, were established by the end of the tenth century, save only the four northern counties and Rutland. The shires represent the administrative skill of the tenth-century kings; but there is much earlier history incorporated in them. Those of the south-east, Kent and Sussex, Middlesex and Essex, were ancient kingdoms or the like, long since absorbed into larger units;[88] Norfolk and Suffolk had long been joined in East Anglia, a kingdom which had flourished in the seventh century, and survived until the ninth. The shires of the east midlands were carved out of the later kingdoms of the northern Danelaw, the area conquered and settled by the Danes in the ninth and tenth centuries, and they combine Danish elements and earlier groupings. Some shires were grouped round four of the 'five boroughs', the Danish capitals in the east midlands, Derby, Leicester, Lincoln and Nottingham. Lincolnshire still included the old kingdom of Lindsey; but like Yorkshire, based on the ancient kingdom of Deira, it was divided by the Vikings into three ridings (as one might say 'thirdings'). Further north, the later county of Northumberland was to enshrine the name of the English kingdom of Northumbria, which before the coming of the Danes had stretched from the Forth to the Humber, including Deira (modern Yorkshire) and Bernicia (Northumberland and Durham and south-eastern Scotland); it had also included great stretches of north-western England.

The shires of the west midlands were artificially created by the tenth-century kings out of the old kingdom of Mercia. The earlier units are represented not by county boundaries, but by the boundaries

---

88 Middlesex was probably the name of a people, never, so far as we know, of a kingdom.

Map 1 The English kingdoms.
The boundaries are approximately those of the eighth century: by the end of the century only the kingdoms named in capital letters retained any real independence. But kingdoms and their frontiers were always changing – the frontier of Northumbria too frequently for it to be possible to show it on this map. Middlesex became part of Mercia in the mid-eighth century.

of the medieval dioceses of Lichfield-Coventry (Mercia proper), Hereford (the Magonsætan) and Worcester (the Hwicce). The Magonsætan and Hwicce were representatives of the very numerous peoples and small kingdoms which were in due course absorbed into the larger kingdoms of later Saxon times. Many of these, like the Middle Angles, who were among the predecessors of the Mercians, or the Gewissae, who were the predecessors of the West Saxons (or folk of Wessex), have left almost no mark on the map of England. Others, less important in their day, have left as clear an imprint as any so far mentioned; for the counties in the west of Wessex grew out of the little Celtic principalities of Cornwall and Devon, the last Celtic parts of England to be conquered. The other counties of Wessex were divisions made at a date much earlier than the tenth century: Dorset was the shire of the Dorsætan, the folk administered from Dorchester, Somerset of the Somersætan, the folk administered from Somerton; Wiltshire was the shire of the folk administered from Wilton, Hampshire of the folk administered from Southampton. The earlier, pre-West Saxon, groupings have disappeared.

Before the Danish invasions most of the country had been ruled for two hundred years or more by the kings of Northumbria, Mercia and Wessex; and because the kings of East Anglia, Essex, Kent and Sussex were still something more than an antiquarian memory, the seventh and eighth centuries used to be known as the period of the heptarchy, the seven kingdoms, although in the constantly shifting sands there were almost always more or less than seven kings in England. In 450 there were no Saxon kingdoms in this island; in the next 250 years a multiplicity were formed; by 700 the three giants, with a variable group of satellites, were firmly established. Our problem now is to penetrate behind the year 700 and see how these kingdoms had been formed.

Their names fall into two groups: some are Saxon in form, some pre-Saxon. Bernicia and Deira are Celtic words; their history can be traced back to the sixth century, but their origin is a mystery. Kent is also a Celtic name; it was known as *Cantium* in Caesar's time. All these seem to represent earlier units revived by Saxon war-lords. Lindsey is a hybrid: the island surrounding the old Roman town of Lincoln (*Lindum*). In the course of the seventh century a pattern of Saxon names was spread over the other parts of England. These names were based on the assumption that the people of the south were Saxons, the people of the north Angles – that the south was colonized from north-western Germany, the north from southern Denmark and the parts of Germany adjacent to it. Thus the southern divisions were those of the West, Middle, South and East

Saxons – Wessex, Middlesex, Sussex and Essex; the middle kingdoms were those of the East and Middle Angles, and of the Mercians, the Angles of the march, the frontier, presumably (though not quite certainly) of Wales. This division of Saxons and Angles was canonized in a famous passage in Bede, which also speaks of the Jutes from Jutland, who are supposed to have colonized Kent and Hampshire. But the Jutes are a very obscure people. Bede thought that they came from Jutland on account of their name; but some believe they came from Friesland and the Rhineland and not from Jutland; and they have left no clear mark on the map.[89] Bede also adds that all the folk north of the Humber (a part of the area of the Angles) were called Northumbrians. Bede intended his book to be read by others than Englishmen; and so he explains some pieces of geography – such as the situation of Ireland – which would hardly need explaining to an educated Englishman. But he glosses Northumbrians as 'those who live north of the Humber' no less than three times, which seems to establish that the name was novel, and not yet generally familiar, and has even been taken as evidence that Bede himself invented it.[90]

As we move back from Bede's day, the early eighth century, these highly rational tribal names gradually dissolve. Northumbria breaks up into Bernicia and Deira, first united in the late sixth century; Mercia dissolves as we look into the early seventh century; Wessex also changes its name and shape as we look into the seventh century. These names are artificial creations of leading kings of the sixth and seventh centuries, and we cannot tell their story in detail, but in outline it is likely that it went something like this.

In the mid-fifth century, perhaps under the leadership of Hengest and Horsa, the Saxons first established settlements of their own. They encouraged others to follow them, and from all along the littoral of North Germany and Denmark settlers came. They pressed up the navigable rivers, and the Humber, the Wash and the Thames became their chief centres of communication. The method of their settlement – by flotillas of ships – tended to break up the old social and tribal groupings from which they came. Kinship was more easily and rapidly forgotten than among the continental Germans. They remembered the land of their origin; but the various peoples evidently mingled in all parts of conquered England. To outsiders they were known, indifferently, as Angles or Saxons. Some of the leaders were

89 Bede i.15, pp. 50–1, which has inspired a 'vast archaeological debate' (Wormald 1983, p. 100 and n. 6). This debate has enormously enriched our knowledge, without solving all the problems indicated in the text.
90 Bede i.15, pp. 50–1; ii.5, pp. 148–9; ii.9, pp. 162–3.

new men, thrown up by the opportunities of the invasion; leaders of motley bands, they may well have cared little for whether they were Angles, Saxons or Jutes. They were happy to make use of existing names for their kingdoms. But some of the leaders were not new men; and some leaders, from families old or new, no doubt cared much for the history of their race before it crossed the sea, and some maintained communication with the homeland.

In the late fifth century a powerful leader called Ælle established a kingdom in what we call Sussex; and he or one of his successors proudly called his people the South Saxons, having absorbed the earlier unit of Hæsta's folk, *Hæstingas*, whose name survives in Hastings. At the turn of the sixth and seventh centuries a great king arose in Norfolk and Suffolk; and Rædwald was duly acclaimed king of the East Angles. He may have been the first to have the title; it can hardly have existed more than a generation or so before his birth. In the sixth century the Angles of the midlands came to be dominated by the rulers of Middle Anglia and Mercia, and they claimed descent from the mighty Offa, king of the continental Angles, and made quite sure they were Angles and not Saxons; and it may well be to this dynasty that we owe the final imprint of this pattern on English geography. The dynasty of Mercia may have been kings or war-lords from the earliest days of the conquest; but if so it is clear that they did not rule Mercia then, or only a fragment of it. Similarly there may well have been some continuity in other families, but it was a continuity of lordship, not of a kingdom of defined boundaries. Sussex and the kingdoms of Celtic title – Bernicia, Deira, Lindsey, Kent – had long, continuous histories, perhaps going back into the fifth century, though in no case is this certain. Kent may even claim to go right back to the first dawn of conquest; but some scholars now doubt whether Hengest really operated in Kent.

The history of the kingdoms and dynasties is illustrated most clearly from the family of Cerdic. Cerdic was an ealdorman,[91] a *dux* – presumably, in fact, an adventurer – whose military prowess enabled him to found the greatest dynasty of all. His name is Celtic, and it is possible that he was himself of Celtic birth, or the son of a Celt who had joined the English insurgents – an event not uncommon

---

91 'Ealdorman' was the highest title in the Anglo-Saxon nobility under the king, and was later replaced by the Danish 'jarl' or earl. In this case it apparently means a military leader who was not of royal birth. The dates in this part of the *ASC* are not at all reliable, and one wonders in particular whether it is true that Cerdic died in 534 and his great-grandson rose to power in 560. It is possible: but we cannot be sure that either the relationship or Cerdic's dates are correctly recorded; 495 is very probably too early; 534 may be too late. See refs. under Cerdic in *Blackwell Encyclopaedia*.

in the confusion of the barbarian invasions; and it may be significant that he won his successes just at the time when the Britons were staging a revival, and driving the English from much of the midlands. But he appears on the scene as a Saxon leader, and his descendants bore Saxon names. In 495 and later he is said by the *Anglo-Saxon Chronicle* to have conquered parts of the south coast and the Isle of Wight from the Britons. About 500 occurred the famous battle of *Mons Badonicus*, in which a British confederation won a victory over the Saxons; and there is little doubt that for two generations or so the midlands were British once more. This did not prevent Cerdic from carving out his principality in the south. But the greatness of his family probably owed more to Ceawlin, traditionally Cerdic's great-grandson, who about 560 organized a confederation which in the course of the next thirty years drove the Britons out of the south midlands and outbid all Saxon rivals in southern England. His people were known as the Gewissae, and although later speculators invented one Gewis, grandfather to Cerdic, to explain the name, it is highly probable that it really meant 'the confederates'; for confederates they undoubtedly were, as, in origin, were all barbarian tribes and kingdoms large enough to embark on a career of conquest. Sometimes these confederations lasted, and gave their names to later and more stable political units; sometimes they were ephemeral. The Gewissae, in a sense, were both.[92]

In the course of the seventh century the Mercian power in the midlands grew at the expense of all its neighbours; and in due course the Gewissae were driven from the upper Thames valley, the centre of Ceawlin's power, and confined to the south. Meanwhile they were compensating themselves in the south-west, driving the Britons out of Somerset, later conquering Devon and ultimately Cornwall too. The most notable of their kings in this period, Cædwalla (685–8) and Ine (688–726), showed their standards in Kent and Sussex; but their own kingdom was now definitely defined as south-western England; and as the new political geography of the age became established, and the power of Cædwalla and Ine stabilized, they became generally known as kings of the West Saxons. The name Gewissae remained as an antiquarian memory, but thenceforth Cerdic's descendants called themselves kings of the West Saxons; their kingdom lasted until it came to absorb the whole of England, and its memory was canonized by Thomas Hardy. Hardy's Wessex was smaller than Alfred's; but its core was the true core of Ine's power: Dorset, Wiltshire and Hampshire.

92 Walker 1956.

Cædwalla was a member of a cadet branch of the house of Cerdic; or so he claimed. All that we can assert with confidence is that he bore a British name, equivalent to Cadwallon, the name of the greatest Welsh king of the preceding generation, and that he was a successful adventurer. After an abortive attempt to carve out a principality in Sussex, he won the Gewissan throne in 685; spent three years in warfare, loot and arson in Kent, Sussex, Surrey and the Isle of Wight, and then, with dramatic suddenness abandoned his kingdom and went on pilgrimage to Rome. He was still young, but evidently had suffered in the fighting and realized that his end was not far off. He was both a barbarian and a Christian; he knew his career in the first role was drawing to a close, and so he hastily embarked on the second before it was too late; went to Rome; was baptized and given the name Peter by the pope; and died, in the white robes of baptism, on 20 April 689. His dramatic career and edifying end made a deep impression on contemporaries, and Bede devotes more space to Cædwalla's three years than to his successor's thirty-eight – he says little more than that Ine, at the end of his long reign, followed Cædwalla's example, withdrew to Rome and died there. But it is clear that Ine had a far deeper influence on the West Saxon kingdom, and was one of the most distinguished of Alfred's predecessors. The *Chronicle* tells us of occasional outbreaks of violence, and little besides. But his foundation of a new see at Sherborne, whose first bishop was the famous St Aldhelm, and his benefactions to Glastonbury Abbey, reveal a real interest in the Church and an attempt to weld together the Celtic and Saxon elements in his kingdom; Sherborne was the first see specifically for the west of Wessex, in Glastonbury Saxon and Celtic Christianity met and mingled, in Aldhelm was represented the learning both of Ireland and of Europe. Ine's laws, furthermore, are the most substantial early code to survive; significantly, they owe their survival to Alfred, for they show the same passionate concern to establish some semblance of order in an unruly kingdom and the same sense that earthly laws are subject to the divine law which marks Alfred's own.

'I, Ine, by the grace of God, king of the West Saxons,' runs the prologue, 'with the advice and with the instruction of my father Cenred, and my bishop Hædde [of Winchester], and my bishop Eorcenwold [of London], along with all my ealdormen and the chief councillors of my people, and also a great assembly of the servants of God, have been inquiring about the salvation of our souls and about the security of our kingdom, that true law and true statutes might be established and strengthened throughout our people, so that none of the ealdormen or of our subjects might afterwards pervert these our decrees.'[93]

Powerful as Ine was, he was not reckoned among the greatest of English kings by his contemporaries or immediate successors. When the *Chronicle* records the conquest of Mercia by King Egbert of Wessex in 829, it lists the *Bretwaldas* who had preceded him. The list, in fact, is identical with that given by Bede a century earlier: Ælle, king of Sussex, Ceawlin of Wessex, Ethelbert of Kent, Rædwald of East Anglia, Edwin, Oswald and Oswiu of Northumbria. In early days a single kingdom might have several kings; but one was usually recognized as the chief ruler; and, although the whole of England was never united before the tenth or eleventh century, from time to time a ruler arose whose suzerainty was recognized over a great part of England, and sometimes over parts of Wales and Scotland too. His rule was personal, and depended on his prestige as a successful warrior; usually it died with him. He was called *Bretwalda*, ruler, not of England, but of Britain. This title seems to be ancient, is perhaps a memory of titles held by British princes like Vortigern before the coming of the Saxons. It was clearly a title of great prestige; equally clearly, it was not an institution, it carried no formal rights with it.

We owe the list to Bede, and it has many odd features. The title seems to have assumed lordship of some kind over a substantial proportion of England, especially of England south of the Humber; and this would explain why Ine is omitted. But there is no reason to suppose that Ælle ruled any people save the South Saxons; and it is difficult to know how widely spread was the power of Ceawlin, Ethelbert or Rædwald. If these names deserved a place, did not the makers of the Mercian kingdom also, and especially Penda (died 655) and Wulfhere (died 674–5)? Still more, when the list was brought up to date in the ninth century, how did it come to omit the greatest of the Mercians, Ethelbald and Offa, whose rule extended over almost the whole of England? In this we can detect the operation of prejudice. Penda was a pagan, one of the most considerable pagan rulers of the seventh century, and might have been excluded on this score. But Ælle, Ceawlin and Rædwald were also pagans, and Bede may here reflect a Northumbrian prejudice against the Mercians, as the *Chronicle* undoubtedly reflects West Saxon prejudice against the Mercians in omitting Ethelbald and Offa.

One striking feature of Bede's list is that, if one omits the first name, it is almost continuous. One cannot be very precise about this, since a

93   *EHD* I, 399.

man was only regarded as *Bretwalda* while his supremacy was effective, and in several cases we do not know how long this lasted. But if
we reflect that Ceawlin flourished from 560 to 591, that Ethelbert
was king of Kent from 560 or *c.*585 to 616 and presumably *Bretwalda* in the 590s, that Rædwald was already *Bretwalda* before
Ethelbert's death and himself died about 625, and that Edwin,
Oswald and Oswiu were kings of Northumbria over the years 616–
33, 634–42, 642–70 – even though Oswiu's power was only accepted
in Mercia from 655 to 658 – we can see that over the period 560 to
658 it was normal for one or other of the leading kings to be regarded
as *Bretwalda*. The series no doubt had gaps, but they were never long.
It is clear that in the late sixth and seventh centuries, precisely at the
time when the pattern of Angle and Saxon kingdoms was becoming
established, and the mastery of the three giants, Northumbria, Mercia
and Wessex, beginning to emerge, the idea was current that one great
ruler might be lord over most of Britain. He had inherited the position
of earlier British kings, and hence he was called ruler of *Britain*. But
the *Bretwaldas* were masters not of Britain but of England, and in
their succession we witness the first adumbration of English political
unity. (See p. 80.)

The Christian *Bretwaldas*, Ethelbert, Edwin, Oswald and Oswiu,
are the central lay figures of Bede's *History*. Ethelbert, the first Christian king, is treated with considerable respect; but it is clear that St
Augustine had many anxious moments before the king was safely
baptized. Ethelbert was king of Kent, and his kingdom had many
links with Christian Francia; his wife was a Frankish, Christian
princess, and in her train there was a Christian bishop. Ethelbert
could not therefore ignore the Christian claims, but he seems to
have felt the natural suspicion of a husband, liking to imagine
himself the dominant partner, of his wife's private religion. Ethelbert
at first kept Augustine on the Isle of Thanet, safely surrounded
by water; then he went to inspect him – taking due care to sit
always in the open air, since he thought Augustine's magic would be
more potent indoors. To Augustine's preaching he gave a cautious
reply, but established the Christian missionaries in Canterbury,
and allowed them to work among his people. In due course Ethelbert
was himself baptized, and gave the Church important patronage.
But he was in no hurry – the delays made the Christian leaders
very impatient – and refused to enforce Christianity on his
followers. By the time of his baptism his power was waning, so
that the Church under his aegis spread only, and temporarily, as far
as London; and after his death even in Kent there was a pagan
reaction.

Meanwhile Rædwald, the pagan king of East Anglia, had succeeded Ethelbert as *Bretwalda*. We know little about him; but the splendour of Sutton Hoo reflects the glory of his court; and he was responsible for setting the next *Bretwalda*, Edwin, on the throne of Northumbria. Bede tells the story of how Edwin as a young exile from his kingdom took refuge with Rædwald, and how Ethelfrith of Northumbria bribed Rædwald to have him killed. Edwin learned of the plan, and while he was sitting up late at night waiting for a friend to help him to escape, he had a vision of an unknown man (in the form, as it seems, of Paulinus) who told him that he would become a great king, the greatest the English people had known; and asked him if he would in return accept the faith of him who had given Edwin this promise of future greatness. Rædwald meanwhile had been admonished by his queen not to surrender their guest for gold, but rather to win back his kingdom for him. When the vision had disappeared, Edwin learned of Rædwald's change of mind; and soon after, at the battle of the Idle, Ethelfrith was defeated and killed, and Edwin made king of Northumbria. Some years later Paulinus came to preach the Christian faith to Edwin. At first the king did not recognize the man who had come to him in his dream; but presently Paulinus learned by divine revelation that a man in his likeness had given Edwin this prophecy. So he went to the king, laid his right hand on his head, and asked him if he recognized the sign. Edwin was terrified and immediately made preparations to fulfil his promise and accept the Christian faith. This was not, however, the only story told of Edwin's conversion.

Edwin is one of the most attractive characters in Bede's pages: a fine warrior, and a shrewd, kindly, honourable man. He was brought up a pagan. In due course he married Ethelbert's daughter; Ethelbert was dead, but the reigning king of Kent insisted that Edwin's queen be allowed to exercise her Christianity, and was reluctant to let her marry a pagan at all; to this Edwin replied that he would give due consideration to the Christian faith, and allowed the Christian Bishop Paulinus to preach to his people. Next year, on Easter night, King Edwin narrowly escaped death at the hands of an assassin; and the same night the queen gave birth to their first child, a daughter. The king, according to the story passed on by Bede, offered thanks to his gods; but Paulinus, at the same moment, began to offer thanks to Christ, and to assure the king that it was his prayers to Christ which had enabled the queen to have a safe and not too painful delivery.

The assassin was an emissary from the king of the West Saxons, and Edwin had already planned an expedition of revenge. He promised Paulinus that, if he was successful, he would give up his own gods and

become a Christian. He won a notable victory, and on his return to
Northumbria gave up worshipping his idols. But he was still cautious
about accepting Christianity. 'He was by nature the shrewdest of men,
and sat often alone in silence, discussing with himself in the depths of
his heart what he should do, to which religion he should adhere.'[94]

The baptism of Edwin was a great event in Northumbrian history,
and many stories were circulated about it. Bede tells three, all of
which imply a period of hesitation; but it may be that the hesitation
was increased by his attempt to fit all three tales into his narrative;
and he has wholly omitted a fourth (if he knew it at all), by which not
Paulinus but a leading Celtic churchman actually performed the rite
of baptism.[95] The story we have already told is a kind of tale common
in the stories of royal conversion in the early Middle Ages; the king is
forced to admit Christ's superior power. The second is also of a
common type – the dream he had in youth which we have already
described. The third is *sui generis*; the famous story of the debate in
the royal council. 'The life of men on earth,' one of the leading
warriors is reported as saying, 'when compared to that which is
beyond our knowledge, is as if you were sitting in your hall at dinner
with your ealdormen and thegns in winter, with a fire in the midst and
the hall aglow with warmth, but outside winter storms of rain or
snow, and a sparrow flew very swiftly through the hall – in at one
door, out at the other in a flash. While it is within, winter weather
touches it not; but in a second its moment of peace is gone, and it is
lost to your view. So the life of man is seen for a short while: what
follows, what has gone before, we know not at all. If this new
teaching has brought some firmer knowledge, it seems worth following.'[96] The debate ends with the high priest in person rushing off to
deface his altars; and Edwin and all his people are baptized.

If Edwin was indeed baptized by a Celt (which is perhaps unlikely),
the cold truth is that these stories are mythical because two at least
assume he was baptized by Paulinus; and one cannot help feeling that
in Bede's pages, Edwin was converted not once but three times over.
But whether any of them is precisely true matters little: the story of
the sparrow was told in the eighth century if not in the seventh; it
warms the cold earth of Yeavering in either case; and the sparrow is as
secure of immortality as King Edwin. Furthermore, these stories show
that Edwin was a character: a man about whom stories passed from
hand to hand, who entered into legend. No other early English king

94   Bede ii.9, pp. 166–7 (my translation).
95   *Historia Brittonum* in *EHD* I, 262.
96   Bede ii. 13, pp. 182–5 (my translation).

had so good a press as Edwin; and to find a comparable group of stories one has to turn to Clovis, the maker of the Frankish kingdom, whose legendary image is vividly revealed to us in the first book of Gregory of Tours's *History of the Franks*. Clovis was a bloodthirsty ruffian who built up a great empire; and he did it, we are told, as much by fraud as by force. In Gregory's pages he wins kingdoms by practical jokes; he is for ever expressing naive surprise that new territories, new opportunities for plunder, keep turning up – although he had been plotting hard for them. Clovis is an inverted Micawber. The personality revealed has only three points of contact with Edwin: each was a highly successful warrior-king; each was (so the story goes) converted to Christianity because the Christian God won a victory for him; and because of his conversion, in the eyes of Gregory and Bede, each had God's support. Edwin is portrayed as the intellectual warrior; for ever hesitating, thinking up new tests. The portrait is as attractive as that of Clovis (however entertaining) is unattractive; and Bede rounds it off with a picture of the peace and prosperity of Edwin's later years. We cannot tell if the portrait is true; but we learn much of Bede's ideal of a great Christian king.

The golden age of Edwin's later years was shattered in 633, when an alliance between the pagan Penda of Mercia and the Christian Cadwallon, king of North Wales, defeated Edwin's army. Edwin himself was killed; Paulinus fled; his Church collapsed. But Christianity was not entirely forgotten. At least one of the mission stayed on; a new Christian king presently arose in Oswald, who was to become the martyr of the Northumbrian Church; and from the north and west the influence of the Celtic missionaries was being increasingly felt.

Oswald was a Christian from the start of his reign; he built up the largest empire yet seen in England, and was acknowledged overlord (so Bede tells us) by people talking all the languages of Britain: Welsh, Pictish, Gaelic and English. He restored the Northumbrian Church by summoning a bishop from Iona to Lindisfarne. Of the saintly Aidan Bede paints one of his most celebrated clerical portraits; it is wholly sympathetic, enthusiastic indeed, and wholly attractive. Aidan, in fact, would have been without blemish in Bede's eyes but for one extraordinary failing. He celebrated Easter on the wrong day.

Behind this dispute lay a long tradition: the Celtic churches had had for many generations scant contact with the churches of the Continent, and retained ancient customs (like the method of deciding the date for Easter) and developed customs of their own. These differences led to conflict when the churches once more came into close contact. The conflict was not one of doctrine; nor was there any formal schism. The two churches met and mingled in various parts

of Britain in the seventh century, sometimes with more friction, sometimes with less. Aidan, the Celt, was always Oswald's bishop; yet this
did not detract from Oswald's sanctity in Bede's eyes. Oswald died in
battle, as Edwin had done; the victim once again of an alliance formed
by the Mercian Penda. The place of his death became a centre of
pilgrimage; miracles were performed in his name. Oswald became the
saint and martyr, *par excellence*, of the Northumbrians; he was the
'most Christian king'.[97]

Oswald was succeeded by his brother Oswiu, who in due course
revived his brother's power; and in 655 avenged his predecessors
by destroying Penda's last alliance in the battle of the *Winwæd*,
where great numbers of English leaders were killed. Some were
swept away by the river, which was in flood. For a short time
Oswiu ruled Mercia; even after its independence had revived, he
was the leading monarch in England until his death in 670. But his
troubles were not over.

The powerful figure of St Wilfrid had already appeared on the
scene. He was then at the beginning of his long career, but already
trained in Roman ways at Rome itself. Oswiu's wife, who was a
daughter of King Edwin, had been brought up in Kent, and so was
accustomed to the Roman Easter; and his son King Alchfrith was a
pupil of St Wilfrid. 'Whence it sometimes is said to have happened in
those days that Easter was celebrated twice in one year, and when the
king had forgotten his fast and was celebrating Easter, the queen was
still deep in Lent celebrating Palm Sunday.'[98] The Easter controversy
may seem to us trivial, but its results were extremely conspicuous and
awkward. It was not only the catering staff who would suffer in a
household in which the queen fasted while the king caroused; small
wonder that Oswiu determined to resolve the issue. Bede gives an
elaborate account of the controversy between learned men on both
sides. Rome and Wilfrid, and the queen, were victorious. The Synod
of Whitby, in which the decision was taken, was a crucial step in the
reabsorption of the Celtic churches into western Christendom. Both
parties were the gainers; each had much to contribute to the other;
and it is no coincidence that Northumbria, and England at large, in
the generations following Whitby, in the age of Theodore and the age
of Bede, saw a Christian civilization with Roman and Celtic roots
such as could hardly be paralleled on the Continent in this period.

97 'Osuald Christianissimus rex', Bede, p. 208.
98 Bede iii.25, pp. 296–7 (my translation).

8

Interlude: 670–871

After Oswiu's death no Northumbrian king ever stood so high, or was remembered as *Bretwalda*. They were not nonentities; several make their bow in the pages of Bede, as fine warriors, as men of learning, even sometimes as monks; but none seemed to be of the stature of the three *Bretwaldas*, who had made Northumbria Christian, and helped to set a stamp on the English Church at large. The frontier of England and the Scottish kingdoms was not fixed for many centuries to come – save that it lay well to the north of its present line in the estimation of the rulers of Northumbria. The frontier with Wales was now coming into prominence: the frontier which was giving its name (so it seems) to Mercia, which was shortly to be the greatest of the English kingdoms. This reveals that the line was beginning to be stabilized. In the seventh century the march gave its name to an English kingdom; in the eighth the rulers of that kingdom gave definition to the march. The dykes of Wat (or Wade) and Offa are the most formidable monuments now surviving to any pre-Conquest kings. Wat's dyke may belong to the mid-eighth century, to the time of Ethelbald (716–57).[99] The dyke, like the reign of Ethelbald, was a dress rehearsal for the work of Offa; without it Offa's achievement would hardly have been possible. But it is no chance that the author of the earlier dyke was soon forgotten, and that it was associated with the legendary Wade, an antique figure from the days of Teutonic paganism, while the dyke which followed it has always been Offa's dyke; and even though it by no means follows the present political boundary, it is in a deep sense the frontier of Wales. For a Welshman to live a few yards the wrong side of Offa's dyke is still a disgrace, even though Offa's warriors no longer patrol it to keep the Welsh out of England.

---

99 But M. Worthington in *Blackwell Encyclopaedia*, p. 468, reckons that Wat's dyke cannot be securely dated before or after Offa's.

If patrol it they ever did. The dykes are essentially boundaries, not defensive works. They made the frontier clear, made it easy to check that the Welsh tribes were not infiltrating; in some sectors they provided magnificent views into Wales; but they were not designed, like Hadrian's wall, for permanent observation. Even Offa could not hope to garrison an earthwork running the whole length of the Welsh frontier. Wat's dyke ran from the Dee estuary down into Shropshire; Offa's from the Dee estuary (a little to the west of Wat's) to the Bristol Channel. A part of the way it followed the line of the river Wye, so that nature provided the boundary. In a few other places, especially in the north, it was never completed. But it remains a magnificent achievement. It was surveyed in detail by Sir Cyril Fox, and his results are laid out in his book *Offa's Dyke* (1955);[100] with the aid of his text, his maps and plans and photographs it is possible to explore Offa's dyke and enjoy at the same time the fascination of observing the techniques of field archaeology at their most refined, and of seeing one of the great engineering achievements of the Dark Ages reconstructed. The concentration of effort, the vast labour force needed over so wide an area, reveals the energy and determination of Offa; the skilled alignment of the dyke, the use made of natural features, reveal the experience and skill of the engineer who designed it. Over the whole a single mind presided; but local differences in technique show that various sections were organized by local officials, as we should expect. Their failure in the north to complete the work allotted to them may be due to inefficiency in this sector, or to inadequate resources in a part of England in all probability very sparsely populated; or it may reveal that Offa was less anxious about this part of his frontier.[101]

Offa bore an unusual name: technically, it is a shortened form of a longer name. Whether on his parents' initiative, or (as is quite possible) on his own, he was the one ruler of Mercia to bear the name of the great king of continental 'Angel' from whom the Mercian kings claimed to be descended. Of the first Offa we know little; but in the mysterious ragbag of legendary references known as *Widsith*, we are told: 'Offa ruled Angel, Alewih the Danes: he was the bravest of all these men, yet he did not perform mighty deeds beyond Offa; but Offa, first of men, while still a youth, gained the greatest of kingdoms; no one of the same age achieved greater deeds of valour in battle: with

---

100   Fox 1955: for later revisions, see M. Worthington in *Blackwell Encyclopaedia*, pp. 341–2, 468; Hill 2000.
101   Hill 2000 suggests that Offa's principal interest lay in the central section, the frontier with Powys.

his single sword he fixed the boundary against the Myrgings at Fifeldor.'[102] We do not know if Offa knew *Widsith*, but we cannot doubt that he knew the legends of his great namesake; nor that they stirred him to fix the boundary against the Welsh.

It is perfectly clear that Ethelbald and Offa regarded themselves as successors of the earlier *Bretwaldas*, and with reason. But the little that we know of Ethelbald strongly suggests that he was by nature a ruthless barbarian. Towards the end of his career he drew on himself a stern rebuke from St Boniface and other bishops of English birth working in Germany: his sins were having an evil effect on his people; the place for nuns was within their convents; the privileges of churches must be respected. Boniface acknowledged that Ethelbald kept the country at peace and was generous in almsgiving; but his rebuke and other hints prepare us for the dénouement: in 757 Ethelbald was murdered by his followers.

Offa, like Ethelbald, was strong and ruthless; also like Ethelbald, we know very little about him as a person. But what we do know reveals a width of interest and capacity which sets him quite apart from any of his predecessors. We have no coherent narrative of his reign; but from the evidence of charters it has been possible to reconstruct in outline the stages by which he spread his power over much of the south of England, often, it is clear, against stiff local opposition, sometimes suffering reverses. He was the only western monarch of the age treated as an equal by Charlemagne – the two great men cultivated each other's friendship, at least in a formal way. His reign saw the first substantial English silver currency, the effective start of the silver 'penny', which was to provide England with the basis of a money economy from the eighth to the fourteenth century, when a gold coinage was added to it. He took an interest in England's foreign trade. He was the patron of several monasteries, and showed his power by making Mercia the seat (for a brief time) of an archbishopric.

In 787 he had his son Ecgfrith anointed king of the Mercians to secure an orderly succession. But the plan miscarried. Ecgfrith survived his father only by a few months; the kingdom passed to a distant kinsman, and the Mercians never again wielded the authority of Offa. They were the leading power for another quarter of a century; but in 825 Egbert of Wessex defeated the Mercian king at the battle of *Ellendun*, and supremacy passed to Wessex. For a time Egbert was master of all the south of England, and so earned (at least in his subjects' eyes) the title *Bretwalda*. From 830 Mercia was independent

---

102   Gordon 1954, p. 68.

once again; but Egbert continued to be overlord of the rest of southern England. The kingdom of East Anglia still had a native dynasty, commonly under West Saxon suzerainty, until 869, when it was finally destroyed by the Danes. Kent, Sussex and Essex were kingships dependent on the West Saxon house; and were handed out from time to time by Egbert and his son and successor Æthelwulf as 'kingdoms' for one or other of their sons. In effect, there were now three English kingdoms, Wessex, Mercia and Northumbria.

The future lay with Wessex; and this was due, partly to the dynasty of Egbert, partly to the Danes. Already, in Egbert's time, the first serious Danish raid had occurred. Through the middle of the century they grew fiercer and more frequent; in 865 a major invasion was staged; the Danes had come to settle. East Anglia, Northumbria and Mercia became their victims; only Wessex survived; and even Wessex it seems would not have outlived the 870s but for the heroic defence organized by Egbert's grandson Alfred.

9

Alfred

The accession of Alfred was a very singular event. In the first place, it was surprising that he should ever have become king at all. His father Æthelwulf is known to have had six children: Athelstan, Ethelbald, Ethelbert, Ethelred, Æthelswith (his one known daughter) and Alfred.[103] His eldest brother died before his father; the three others ruled Wessex in turn. When Ethelred died in 871, he left two sons; but both were minors, and only an experienced leader could hope to save Wessex from the Danes. Alfred's succession was undisputed, although one of his nephews tried to win the throne after his death.

In the second place it was singular that at the crucial moment Wessex should fall into the hands of the most inspiring king of his line; a man with the determination and imagination to plan a really successful defence, to leave his kingdom with some hope of future security. Even more surprising, Alfred found time to let his imagination roam in other fields; to think of monasteries and libraries and books which even laymen could read.

There is much about Alfred's life which would be wholly dark to us if we lacked Asser's biography. But it must be admitted that Asser often informs us only to tantalize: the curtain is lifted, only to be dropped again; Asser is devoted, wordy and clumsy.

It is clear that Alfred's life was even more difficult than we should expect. He was brought up to be pious and ignorant; he suffered constantly from fear of his own failings and shortcomings; and from physical disorders of a grotesque kind partly perhaps the result of mental anxiety. His career and writing were those of a man fundamentally healthy and sane; but Asser's marvellously confused account of his illnesses and anxieties shows that this sanity was won at a price.

---

103 The names were originally even more alliterative than they appear in the text, since all began with the diphthong Æ.

The worst affliction struck him on his wedding day, and this, Asser plainly implies, was no coincidence. We are given a vision of a man of strong imagination, anxious and temperamental; always afraid of himself, afraid of illness and incapacity to the point of hypochondria, aware of a larger world than he himself lived in, desperately keen to live in it, and to enable others to live in it.

Here is Asser's summary of his career. 'Though established in royal power, the king was wounded by the nails of many tribulations. From his twentieth to his forty-fifth year (in which he now is) he has been troubled incessantly by the severe visitation of an unknown disease; never an hour passes but he either suffers from it, or is nearly desperate from fear of it. He was troubled too (not without cause) by the constant attacks of foreign peoples by land and sea which he bears without intermission. What shall I say of his numerous campaigns and battles against the heathen, of the ceaseless problems of government? Of his daily concern for the peoples who live from the Tyrrhenian Sea (the Adriatic) to the far side of Ireland? We have seen and read letters and gifts sent him from Jerusalem by the patriarch Elias. What of the cities and towns he has restored and the new ones he has built where none were before? What of the buildings incomparably adorned with gold and silver on his instructions? What of the royal halls and chambers wonderfully built of stone and wood at his command? What of the royal manor houses of stone moved from their ancient sites and splendidly built in more suitable places by royal edict? His illness apart, his worst trouble was the obstructiveness of his own people, who would not willingly submit to any, or very little, toil for the common need of the kingdom. But he stood alone, dependent on divine assistance; like a skilful helmsman struggling to bring his vessel, loaded with much riches, to the longed-for, safe harbour of his own land; though all his sailors were nearly worn out, he did not permit the helm of government, once he had taken it over, to quiver or turn, though sailing amid the diverse raging whirlpools of this present life. He took every pains gently to teach, flatter, exhort, command, finally, after long patience, sharply to punish the disobedient, and to abhor in every way common foolishness and obstinacy; and so he wisely grasped and bound to his will and the common good of his whole kingdom his bishops, ealdormen and nobles, his dearest thegns, and also his reeves, to whom after God and the king the kingdom's power is seen to be subject, as is right. Sometimes through the people's laziness royal commands were not carried out; or tasks begun late were not finished and so of no use – I could mention fortifications ordered by him but not yet begun, or begun too late to be finished. Then the enemy's troops attacked by land or sea, or (as often) by both together; and the folk who had obstructed the royal commands were filled with shame and useless penitence.'[104]

As a boy Alfred twice visited Rome. In 853, at the age of four, his father sent him to stay at the court of Pope Leo IV, who robed him as a consul and treated him as his son. Two years later Alfred visited Rome again, this time in his father's company. King Æthelwulf was following in the footsteps of Cædwalla and Ine; but death did not come, and so, after lingering a twelvemonth, he returned home, to find his eldest surviving son in rebellion. The kingdom was divided between them, until the death of Æthelwulf two years later. Meanwhile Alfred had had a vision of Rome, ancient and modern, and had visited the Frankish court. But Latin literature was still a closed book to him; nor could he read and write. He was brought up, a favourite younger son, to love hunting, to love the Saxon poems he heard recited in his father's court; to dream, perhaps, of the kingdom to which he thought Pope Leo had anointed him; but with little prospect of achieving it. He grew up conscientious to a fault, but also imaginative and ambitious.

One of his gifts was an exceptional memory. His mother showed his brothers and himself one day a manuscript of Saxon poetry, and promised to give it to whichever learned it by heart the quickest. Alfred was stirred by the opportunity to outdo his elder brothers; also, Asser tells us, by the beauty of the initial letter on the first page. He took the book to his master, who read it to him; and he went back to his mother and recited what he had heard. Later he learned the daily office, and certain psalms and prayers, and had them written in a book which he always carried with him 'as I have seen myself'. But he was still unable to read for himself. In later life he complained that there were no good scholars in Wessex. There was some truth in this; but it hardly excuses his failure to read and write. These were not accomplishments normal in royal children; but one cannot help feeling the mature Alfred excused the failings of his earlier years somewhat too readily. None the less he grew up with some understanding of Latin; able to follow the services of the Church – to attend daily office, observe the day and night hours, hear daily mass with comprehension; and his piety was not conventional; he used also, in later life, to visit churches to pray – by night, so that his followers should not know that he did it.

We first hear of Alfred engaged in campaigning early in 868, when he was second-in-command to his brother King Ethelred against the

104 *Asser*, ed. Stevenson, c. 91, pp. 76–8 (my translation); see also trans. Keynes and Lapidge, pp. 101–2.

Danes. He was then eighteen (or nineteen), which seems to us an early age to command an army; but many medieval warriors were veterans by the time they reached twenty, and we may be reasonably sure that this was not Alfred's first taste of warfare. In 868 the brothers were fighting in Mercia, in a vain attempt to save the Mercian kingdom from collapse. In 871 they were fighting in Wessex itself. In the same year Ethelred died, and Alfred was left in sole command. Year after year he fought inconclusive engagements with the Danes, gradually gaining experience but losing territory. In 878 the Danish army made a surprise attack in the middle of winter, when the West Saxon army was scattered about the country, on its manors and farms and small holdings.

'In this year the host went secretly in midwinter after Twelfth Night to Chippenham', says the *Chronicle*, 'and rode over Wessex and occupied it, and drove a great part of the inhabitants oversea, and of the rest the greater part they reduced to submission, except Alfred the king; and he with a small company moved under difficulties through woods and into inaccessible places in marshes.... And the Easter after, King Alfred with a small company built a fortification at Athelney, and from that fortification, with the men of that part of Somerset nearest to it, he continued fighting against the host. Then in the seventh week after Easter he rode to *Ecgbryhtesstan* [Egbert's stone], to the east of Selwood, and came to meet him there all the men of Somerset and Wiltshire and that part of Hampshire which was on this side of the sea,[105] and they received him warmly. And one day later he went from those camps to Iley Oak, and one day later to Edington; and there he fought against the entire host, and put it to flight, and pursued it up to the fortification, and laid siege there a fortnight; and then the host gave him preliminary hostages and solemn oaths that they would leave his kingdom, and promised him in addition that their king would receive baptism.'

To this Asser adds nothing of moment; but a twelfth-century chronicle largely based on Asser, the *Annals of St Neot's*, has added to this famous story one yet more famous. 'As we read in the *Life* of the holy father Neot, Alfred long lay hid in the home of a cowherd. It happened one day that a peasant woman, the cowherd's wife, was preparing to cook some loaves, and the king was sitting by the fire preparing bow and arrows and other weapons. Presently the unfortunate woman saw the loaves set by the fire burning; she rushed

---

105   This means either 'those to the west of Southampton Water', and indicates that the author lived in the south-west of England, or (more probably) 'those who were still in England' as opposed to those who had fled overseas when the Danes invaded Wessex.

up and removed them, upbraiding the most unconquered king, and saying [in Latin hexameters]: "You wretch, you're only too fond of them when they're nicely done; why can't you turn them when you see them burning?" The unfortunate woman had no idea that he was King Alfred, who fought so many battles, won so many victories against the heathen.'[106]

We cannot tell whether the story has any basis of truth, but we can be sure it lost nothing in the telling. The earliest known version is a sermon about St Neot, a Cornish saint, which was probably written in the mid-eleventh century.[107] In this version the king is in no way at fault: he actually turns the loaves (or cakes). The better-known story given above is an embroidered version, written in the priory of St Neots in Huntingdonshire later in the twelfth century. Clearly Alfred's memory was not held in respect there: in this later version St Neot reproves the king in early life for tyrannical behaviour, and prophesies disaster; and the loaves are badly scorched.

Disaster was averted, and the six weeks on the isle of Athelney proved the turning point of Alfred's career. One would dearly like to know more of the secrets of King Alfred's underground movement; of the means by which he summoned the militia to Egbert's stone. About this we can only make guesses; but we can make something more than guesses about the reflections which this crisis stirred in Alfred's mind. It is clear that it revealed to him, in a new way, the weakness of Wessex in face of the Danish menace. The Danes were mobile; could attack both by land and by sea; they could achieve surprise, and overwhelm Wessex before the English militia could be summoned. The Danes formed the practice of fortifying a camp, or rather taking over an old fortification and using it as a base. In 878, while the Danes were operating in this way from Chippenham, Alfred took a leaf out of their book, and organized Athelney, hidden in the Somerset marshes, as a base for counter-attacks. The battle of Edington was decisive, not because it ended the Danish threat to Wessex – that was not lifted until after Alfred's death – but because it showed that it was possible for the Danish host to be heavily defeated, and because of the measures which Alfred took to follow up his victory.

His first action, to insist on the baptism of King Guthrum and other leaders, seems to us both high-handed and utopian; it looks as if he thought that forcible baptism would civilize the barbarian. High-handed I think it was, an act of ruthless, conventional piety; but it

---

106 *Annals of St Neot's*, ed. Dumville and Lapidge, p. 76; also in *Asser*, ed. Stevenson, p. 136 (my translation).
107 *Annals of St Neot's*, ed. Dumville and Lapidge, p. 126; for the date, see p. xcvi.

also seems to show another side of King Alfred. Already he reckoned himself responsible for the well-being of English folk under Danish rule; and he clearly hoped by this step to save them from religious persecution by the pagan Danes.

In the years which followed Edington he set in motion a fundamental reorganization of the defences of Wessex. The army consisted in the main of the king's followers or thegns and the peasant militia or fyrd. Each was divided, so that a part of the total force could serve as something approaching a standing army, ready under arms in case of attack; while the rest were tilling the soil or running their estates. Each part took their turn, so that the duty was fairly distributed. Next Alfred arranged for the fortresses of Wessex to be restored and occupied, and for new ones to be built. When this was finished, early in the next reign, a network of fortresses was spread all over southern England. They were large enclosures, surrounding areas some of which were already beginning to grow into towns. The word borough indeed is derived from the Old English *burh*, a fortress; and it was from the marriage of market places and walls to protect them that many English boroughs were formed. The two centuries after Alfred's death saw striking growth in English towns; and one of the reasons for this was the security which their walls gave to them, and the larger security which Alfred's fortresses gave to the country at large. Their immediate purpose was mainly military. When the Danes attacked, the folk of the neighbourhood could take shelter behind their walls; and their garrisons could use them as bases from which to attack the Danes. They formed a defence in depth, and for the first time made it possible for the defenders of Wessex to look forward to raids with some degree of confidence, and take rapid initiative against the raiders when they came.

The Danes were still, however, more mobile than the English; and Alfred's third plan was designed to meet them before they landed. He had large, speedy ships built, according to the *Chronicle*, to his own specification.

These measures did not abolish the Danish menace. Few of Alfred's later years were free from wars, none from rumours of wars. Between 878 and 890 he made a further truce with Guthrum, and settled the frontier between their kingdoms; but in the 890s another large Danish army battened on England and raided into Alfred's territory, and the Danes in the north were a permanent menace. None the less, it was possible for Wessex to breathe again; to imagine a future in which she would be secure; and this she owed to Alfred's imaginative plans of defence. They were widely admired at the time; and his *burhs* and his reorganization of the militia were copied by the most powerful European monarch of the next generation, Henry the Fowler, the first Saxon king of Germany (919–36), in planning the defences of Saxony against the Magyars or Hungarians. But as one looks closely at Alfred's measures, and at all the striking innovations which have made him famous, one is struck not only by their novelty, but by how slow he was to devise them. He had been king nearly seven years when the crisis of 878 struck him, and a general longer than that. In this period he seems to have done nothing to improve the defences of Wessex, but to have been content with continuing the methods of his brothers, which had already proved at best indecisive, and at worst disastrous. Suddenly, on the verge of thirty, a new dimension was added to his mind. He was a man whose powers matured slowly, who became increasingly capable of absorbing new interests and learning from new experience.

This comes out most clearly in his intellectual pursuits. Alfred was brought up illiterate, though not wholly ignorant. As he grew to maturity, the ambition to have learned men about him grew too; and Asser likens him to a bee in his pursuit of scholars, flying away from home, alighting on diverse blossoms, taking what it fancies, and carrying it home. Alfred's store of honey contained four Mercians, including Werferth, bishop of Worcester (*c.* 872–*c.*915), Plegmund, archbishop of Canterbury (890–923); one native of northern France, called Grimbald, and one continental Saxon, called John; and one Welshman, Asser himself. Their work developed slowly, and Alfred's efforts to revive monastic life, with John and Grimbald's help, achieved relatively little. At a fairly early stage Alfred seems to have had the idea of making the riches of Christian literature available to more of his people by having them translated. But it was only slowly that he came to join in the work himself.

Asser tells us at length the story of how he came to join Alfred's seminar of learned men. There is something almost pathetic about the king's anxiety to have the company of this tedious, pedantic and naive man; but Asser served him well. In the mid-880s, when Asser was first installed at the royal court, they used to sit together in the royal chamber, discussing subjects of common interest. One day Asser read to Alfred a passage which particularly struck him; and he produced the book of offices and prayers which he always carried with him, for Asser to copy the passage into it. But the book was full; so with the king's agreement, Asser prepared a new quire; and this was soon filled with passages chosen by the king.

When a passage had been written in the book, Alfred had the urge to read it, to turn it into English and pass it on to others. And so he determined to learn to read, and to read Latin; and in both these projects he took his first steps on the festival of St Martin, 11 November 887, when he was thirty-eight years old.[108] It may be that Asser was a good teacher; it is even more likely that Asser was somewhat lumbering in his methods, and made Alfred impatient; no doubt the winter evenings gave him leisure for his lessons. How rapidly he advanced we cannot tell; he never dispensed with his seminar; we can never be entirely sure how much he did himself, how much he left to them; but between *c.* 890 and 899 five major works were translated into English, and of this operation Alfred himself was the director.[109]

Alfred had visited Rome twice as a child; and had been devoted to the exercises of religion, at times neurotically devoted, at least from his teens. But his piety was conventional at root; and we cannot expect from a man who was illiterate till nearly forty deep or original understanding of ancient texts. In taking to letters late in life he was following in the footsteps of Charlemagne; and we know that Asser was acquainted with Einhard's famous *Life of Charlemagne* and can assume that Alfred was too. Literacy enabled both of them to take a sympathetic interest in the work of the scholars of their court – much more than the external patronage affected by many medieval kings. Neither contributed anything original to the history of thought. But both have an honourable place in the history of learning and letters. Charlemagne personally inspired and directed a formidable revival of learning, and attempted to have his own sons and leading laymen as well as the clergy of his empire brought up to be literate and speak Latin. The intellectual revival cast long shadows before it and had many consequences; the palace school foundered after a brief life. Alfred worked on slighter foundations, with a less ambitious aim. He tried to spread the fruits of ancient wisdom by translating them into the vernacular. He directed the enterprise, as did Charlemagne; but imprinted his personality, not only on the enterprise, but also on the written word.

The books produced under Alfred's direction, or inspired by him, strongly suggest the lines of his interests. Early on Bishop Werferth translated Gregory the Great's *Dialogues* for him; and the next product of his seminar was Gregory's *Pastoral Care*. They enshrined for Alfred the wisdom of a great teacher: they taught by example – in the miracle stories of which the *Dialogues* are composed – and by precept, in the *Pastoral Care*, which laid emphasis on the bishop's duty to

---

108   *Asser*, ed. Stevenson, cc. 87–90, pp. 73–6; also trans. Keynes and Lapidge, pp. 99–100.
109   For the chronology, see ibid., p. 35.

instruct, and to instruct laymen as well as clergy. In a special way, Alfred and Gregory had the same sources of inspiration; Gregory was one of the finest of the popes, a symbol of Roman greatness, and he was the pope who had sent Augustine to convert the English, the author of English Christianity. Gregory was also one of the main characters of Bede's *History*, another of the works translated. The *Dialogues*, Bede and the universal history of Orosius (written in the early fifth century) all reflect an interest in the past; and in Alfred's time the traditions of his own people, and to a lesser extent of Rome and the Church at large, were collected in the *Anglo-Saxon Chronicle*, which he may have inspired, and almost certainly, like Asser, perused. But Alfred's interest in history was part of a wider interest in the world about him. To several of the translations he made his own characteristic additions. To the Orosius he added his own practical comments on the campaigns and political affairs of ancient history, and, above all, an original account of the geography of northern and central Europe, that part of Europe which had not been included in the Roman empire. His searching curiosity was never more clearly revealed than in the way he tells the story of travellers who came to his court, and uses the information they could give him.

In his last two works he struck the personal note even more clearly. The Roman Boethius had written the *Consolations of Philosophy* while awaiting execution at the hands of the Goth Theodoric the Great. Alfred had lived to see his own world shattered by the Danes, and lived in constant expectation of disaster. Not infrequently he draws his readers from the heights of Roman philosophy to the concrete world in which they were living; and though there is a certain naivety in his procedure, these asides are of great interest, and few men could have treated texts so cavalierly and got away with it. A passage from the Boethius illustrates his interests and his outlook to perfection. The words in italics bear some relation to what Boethius wrote; the rest are Alfred's own, though suggested apparently in part by an earlier commentary.

'*You know that covetousness and greed for worldly dominion never pleased me over much, and that I did not all too greatly desire this earthly rule,* but yet I desired tools and material for the work that I was charged to perform, namely that I might worthily and fittingly steer and rule the dominion that was entrusted to me. You know that no man can reveal any talent or rule and steer any dominion without tools and material. That without which one cannot carry on that craft is the material of every craft. This, then, is a king's material and his tools for ruling with, that he have his land fully manned. He must have men who pray, and soldiers and workmen. Lo, you know that without these tools no king can reveal his skill. Also, this is his material, which he must have for those tools – sustenance for those three orders; and their sustenance consists in land to live on, and gifts, and weapons, and food, and ale, and clothes, and whatever else those three orders require. And without these things he cannot hold those tools, nor without these tools do any of the things that he is charged to do. *For that reason I desired material to rule that dominion with, that my powers and dominion would not be forgotten and concealed.* For every talent and every dominion is soon worn out and silently passed over, if it is without wisdom; because no man can bring forth any craft without wisdom, for whatever is done in folly can never be accounted as a craft. In brief, I desired to live worthily as long as I lived, and leave after my life, to the men who should come after, my memory in good works.'[110]

In the last of the translations, Alfred's version of the first book of St Augustine's *Soliloquies*, his thoughts turn from the uncertainties of the present life to the hope of future peace; the main theme is immortality. In the preface he explained his attitude to ancient learning, in the famous metaphor of the wood, from which he gathered 'staves and props and tie-shafts...and crossbars and beams' and carried them home and built himself a house. 'It is not to be marvelled at that one expends labour on such material both in the carriage and in the building; but every man, when he has built a village on land leased to him by his lord, with his help, likes to stay in it sometimes, and to go hunting and fowling and fishing, and to support himself in every way on that leased land, both on sea and land, until the time when through his lord's mercy he may acquire bookland and a perpetual inheritance. So shall the rich giver act, who rules both these transitory habitations and the eternal mansions. May He who created both, and rules both, grant me that it may be in my power both to be useful here and to attain thither.'[111]

The purpose of his translations was to give others a chance to enjoy the wonderful products of his wood; and his methods can be seen in other of his activities. In his laws he started from the characteristic assumption that English law was somehow closely linked with divine law. The sources range from the Book of Exodus to the laws of his predecessors, kings of Wessex, Mercia and Kent; they are gathered together, and a selection made, freely made at the king's own choice, and then promulgated with the consent of the Witan.

110   *EHD* I, 919–20.
111   *EHD* I, 917–18.

Alfred was only fifty when he died; yet he had altered and developed rapidly in his later years; and his last books read like the reflections of an old man. He had certainly travelled a long way. The shrewd, mature, sophisticated simplicity of the *Soliloquies* is a far cry from the sensitive, neurotic enthusiasm of the boy who had learned Saxon poems by heart. His career shows how far a man could travel on the road to civilization in a single lifetime; and how difficult it was to go thus far, even for a man with the talents and opportunities of Alfred. So wide was the range of his achievements, so attractive is the voice which speaks from his writings, so rare is it to be able to listen to the voice of a medieval king, that we are in danger of idealizing him. He was after all human; in some respects, intensely human. But in a world falling into ruins he had the courage to plan for a happier future; not only to plan defence, but to plan for a fuller and richer life for his subjects. In this there is something heroic. The achievement is impressive; the vision astonishing.

10

The Tenth Century

Many of Alfred's talents were distributed among his descendants, who ruled Wessex and England from 899 to 1016. None achieved quite his width of interest. None was an author in his own right, and none had an Asser to tell us of his private life. They are shadowy figures compared with their distinguished forebear; but they were clearly not shadowy figures in their own day. Edward and Athelstan were distinguished soldiers, who greatly extended the area of Alfred's kingdom. From a purely military point of view the formation of the English kingdom owes as much to Edward as to Alfred; and no Saxon king save perhaps Offa was so widely known and respected in western Christendom as Athelstan. Edgar's reign was peaceful, but his grip on the country was as tight as, perhaps tighter than, Athelstan's; and he was patron to a monastic and intellectual revival such as Alfred and Athelstan had dreamed of, but could not live to see. These were outstanding men; and although the kingdom was subjected again to Danish attack under Ethelred II, the Unready, its achievements had been very notable. But it is not easy to get any real glimpse of these kings as persons. If we wish to do so, we must concentrate on Athelstan and Edgar.

Edward the Elder had succeeded Alfred as king of Wessex. With the aid of his sister Æthelflæd, lady, later queen of the Mercians, he set about the reconquest of the midlands and the south-east. When he died he was effective ruler of all England south of Trent; but the Mercian folk remembered that he was a West Saxon. He was succeeded by his son Athelstan, the natural heir of the West Saxon line, who had been brought up in Mercia, and so commanded the allegiance of the Mercians in a way which had been denied his father. Athelstan, indeed, was acknowledged king by the Mercians before he was acknowledged by the West Saxons.

Athelstan won recognition of his kingship over northern England and southern Scotland. He was king, *basileus*, even perhaps emperor of Britain. He substantially enhanced the notion of English kingship.

The centre of Athelstan's life was in his court, in his hall, where his warriors gathered round him and he dispensed gifts. When the *Chronicle* suddenly breaks into heroic verse, in the famous piece on the battle of *Brunanburh*, it calls the king 'lord of warriors, ring-giver of men'. He was the heir of Hrothgar and Beowulf; but he was much more than that. The clerks who gathered round him and wrote his charters tried to impose upon the long-suffering Latin tongue their sense of his majesty by inflating the language in which they couched his solemn grants with strange outlandish words, often remotely derived from Greek, and portentous obscurity. On 28 May 934 one of his clerks inscribed a document granting an estate in Kent or Sussex to a thegn. It is a masterpiece of hideous absurdity; and warns anyone who infringes it that he will burn with Judas the committer of impious treachery, a sentiment which does not suggest complete confidence in the effectiveness of human punishment.[112] But in fact Athelstan's power was growing steadily more effective and more confident; and the list of the Witan gathered at Winchester who attached their crosses to this document is very impressive. On 7 June the same scribe wrote another charter, in similar terms, but of more ambitious purpose: the grant of Amounderness in Lancashire to the archbishop of York – a grant whose authenticity has often been questioned, especially in Lancashire, but has on the whole been successfully defended. Almost exactly the same impressive list of signatories put their crosses to this instrument. They start with Athelstan himself, who in the body of the document calls himself 'king of the English, elevated by the right hand of the Almighty, which is Christ, to the throne of the whole kingdom of Britain'; it continues with two archbishops, three sub-kings – Welsh princes – sixteen bishops, seven ealdormen, six Viking earls, eleven king's thegns, and thirteen other folk.[113] The court was now at Nottingham, and the *Chronicle* explains rather tersely why this large gathering was moving rapidly north from Winchester: 'In this year King Athelstan invaded Scotland both with a land and a naval force, and harried much of the country'.[114] The leading Welsh princes were already in his train; he now set to work to subdue the Scots. In this, however, he was not immediately successful. Three years later an Irish-Norse leader, in alliance with the kings of Scotland and Strathclyde, staged a major invasion of England itself. At a place called *Brunanburh*, whose situation we do not know, they were met by Athelstan and Edmund his brother; Athelstan's great victory is

---

112   Sawyer 1968, no. 425, with refs.
113   Sawyer 1968, no. 407, translated with commentary in *EHD* I, 548–51, at 549.
114   *ASC*, trans. Garmonsway, p. 107.

recorded in the stirring verse of a contemporary poet. No doubt the *Battle of Brunanburh* was recited before Athelstan in his equivalent of Heorot. On his way north he stopped at Chester-le-Street, where St Cuthbert's relics lay, and his cathedral, later to be moved to Durham. To St Cuthbert he presented a copy of Bede's *Lives* of the saint, made, perhaps, at Glastonbury, and at the beginning is a picture of the king presenting the book to the saint. Then he passed on to subdue Scotland, and for the remaining two years of his life his prestige was unquestioned, his power unchallenged.

Athelstan was the Pierpont Morgan of his age. As the clergy of Chester-le-Street saw the great army pass on into Scotland, and turned to enjoy their new acquisition, they may well have wondered whether the king would be remembered in future ages mainly as a great conqueror or as a princely collector. Like Pierpont Morgan, Athelstan collected books and works of art. Unlike the American millionaire, he also collected relics of saints, and was himself a connoisseur of all that he collected. He was a great giver of gifts; but the gifts in Athelstan's Heorot were more varied than in Hrothgar's; and so were the men who received them. Gold and silver ornaments, land, weapons, pieces of craftsmanship of every kind flowed through his hands; and also rare and beautiful books, interesting for their content as well as their appearance; and, above all, relics. He received gifts from all over Europe, gave richly in return, and gave especially to his followers, to his bishops and to churches in his own land. To Canterbury Cathedral he gave a Gospel Book which had belonged to the coarb (or abbot) of Armagh; and another Gospel Book which Athelstan had received from his brother-in-law, Otto the Great of Germany, on Otto's accession to the throne in 936. It is now in the Cotton collection in the British Library, and it carries an inscription which opens with these words: 'This volume of the gospels Athelstan emperor of the English and ruler of the whole of Britain (*Anglorum basyleos et curagulus totius Bryttannie*) with devout mind granted to the cathedral church dedicated to Christ, the first in the land, at Canterbury.'[115]

Otto the Great was the most eminent of Athelstan's continental friends; but he was one among many. William of Malmesbury, writing in the twelfth century, but (as some scholars think) using a much earlier Latin poem, lists a number of these: Harold, king of Norway, who sent an embassy to Athelstan at York, including among his gifts a ship with 'a golden beak and purple sail, hung around within a dense rank of gilded shields'; Henry I of Germany, who asked for Athel-

115 Robinson 1923, p. 60.

stan's sister as wife to his son Otto; Hugh the Great, duke of the Franks, and Conrad, duke of Burgundy, who married two other sisters of the king. To these we could add the Carolingian Louis, later king of the Franks, called Louis d'Outremer because he was brought up in Athelstan's court. When Duke Hugh sent his request for an English princess, he chose his embassy and his gifts with canny skill. The leader of the party was the son of Baldwin, count of Flanders, whose wife was Athelstan's aunt. 'He expounded his requests in a meeting of nobles at Abingdon, offered the most ample gifts, calculated instantly to satisfy the most rapacious greed: fragrance of spices never seen before in England; princely gems, emeralds especially – in whose wonderful green the sun dazzled the eyes of the beholders with a gracious light; very many swift horses with their harness, "champing", as Virgil says, "on bits of tawny gold"; a vase of onyx so subtly sculpted that the corn seemed truly to wave, the vines truly to bud, the images of men truly to move – so clear and polished, it reflected faces as in a mirror; the sword of Constantine the Great, on which the name of its ancient owner was to be read in letters of gold, and on its scabbard over thick golden plates you could see an iron nail fixed – one of four which the Jewish faction had prepared for the torture of Our Lord's body; the lance of Charlemagne, which – if the unconquered emperor raised it against the enemy when leading his army against the Saracens – never failed to make him victor (it was said to be the same which the centurion's hand drove into Our Lord's side, opening Paradise to wretched mortals by this precious wound); the banner of the most blessed martyr Maurice, leader of the Theban legion...; a crown of gold, yet more precious for its gems, whose splendour sent flashes of light' to dazzle the beholders; 'a tiny fragment of the holy and adorable cross enclosed in crystal...; a small part also, similarly enclosed, of the crown of thorns – which the madness of the soldiers set upon His most sacred head, mocking his kingship.'

The gems sparkled; the king was delighted; his sister was shipped off with presents of like quality. The chronicler sees in his mind's eye the glory of the gifts; and for this he had a special reason. His own monastery, Malmesbury Abbey, was enriched with part of the Cross and Crown of Thorns 'by whose support, so I believe, the house still thrives' in spite of all the storms it has been through.[116]

So much of the tenth century is gathered in this extraordinary accumulation of genuine works of art and bogus relics, that it is

---

116   William of Malmesbury, *Gesta Regum*, I, 216–21 (my translation). On the authenticity of this account, see ibid., II, 116–18; Wood 1983, pp. 265ff.

worth dwelling for a moment on it. How did it come about that Athelstan, and the monks of Malmesbury, thought so much of pieces of wood and bone, of antique and decrepit weapons; valued them both as earthly treasure with an earthly price, and heavenly treasure beyond payment? The logic is quite simple. The saints are in Heaven; but they care for men as much as ever, and where there is a fragment of their earthly body, there they will agree to have an earthly habitation; they will even see to it that God performs miracles there. By how much the more will not Christ himself perform miracles for those who have relics of his earthly life? They cannot have pieces of his earthly body, which rose from the dead and ascended into Heaven, but Cross and Crown of Thorns and lance and garments were divided and redivided and spread over the world, and a new kind of celestial currency formed from relics of Christ and his saints. Granted the premise, the logic is clear enough. But the chain has a weak link. It assumes that we can be sure that the relics are genuine. No one now doubts that the majority of medieval relics were spurious; they were not what they claimed to be; and for this reason the cult has fallen into some disrepute. It is fortunate that no one ever tried to reassemble the Cross or the Crown of Thorns or the garments of the Blessed Virgin. It has been estimated that the fragments of the 'True Cross' circulating in the Middle Ages would have built a battleship; the Crown of Thorns would have hedged many acres; and no doubt St Mary's wardrobe would have cast doubts on the notion that Our Lord came of poor family.

The story is told of an eminent painter who was shown what purported to be one of his own paintings by a friend. He knew perfectly well that it was not his; but to save his friend's feelings he immediately signed it. Innumerable saints were honoured by having bones of other people, and sometimes of animals, encrusted in silver and gold and gems, enclosed in altars, carried in processions, in their name. Perhaps they honoured the intention; allowed faith to conquer fiction; perhaps the weak link in the chain was by-passed. When St Teilo died, so we are told by his biographer, three communities fought for his body; their troubles were resolved by the saint obligingly providing three bodies of himself. The saint died in the seventh century; the story was told in the twelfth. To us it is an example of how logic could be applied to explain the inexplicable – since three bodies were known to exist; to most of its readers it must have seemed a happy example of celestial diplomacy and tact.

Athelstan's elder contemporary, Henry I of Germany, is supposed to have been as hard-bitten a ruler as one could find in Europe in his age.

But late in life he bartered a large slice of territory – a portion of modern Switzerland – for another holy lance, a particularly potent talisman of victory, and an object supposed, like Athelstan's sword, to have belonged to Constantine, and to be a necessary possession for anyone aspiring to be Roman emperor. Henry died soon after; but with the lance Otto his son conquered the Magyar hordes on the Lechfeld in 955, and with it he rode to Rome to be crowned emperor in 962.[117]

Faith in the potency of relics was universal. What marked Athelstan out was the scale of his collection and the refinement of its contents. He was not a miser: he gave away much of what he collected; but he never ceased to gather, from all over Europe, what he could find, what his agents could buy. The church of Dol in Brittany wished to thank him for a favour, and wrote a letter to him. They promised to pray for him, and the prior wrote: 'I send you relics, which we know you value more than earthly treasure – bones of St Senator, and of St Paternus and his master St Scabillion, who died on the same day as he. These two lay right and left of St Paternus: their solemnities like his are on 23 September.'[118] Athelstan was well acquainted with some of the churches of Devon and Cornwall, and had good relations with Wales, so he may well have known about some of the the Celtic saints. The prior evidently assumes that he knows about Paternus; but that Senator and Scabillion will be new additions to Athelstan's collection. The relics of Paternus went to Malmesbury; his companions to the new church at Milton Abbas, founded by Athelstan himself, along with the letter to authenticate them; and there the letter was found 150 years or more later. Also to Milton went another fragment of Athelstan's part of the Cross, an arm and bones and the crozier of St Samson, bishop of Dol, an arm of St Branwalader, other relics sealed in five boxes 'still closed' – which he had brought from Rome and from Brittany.

No inventory has survived of the relics which passed through Athelstan's hands, and any attempt to reconstruct a catalogue faces two serious difficulties. For the bulk of the collection we have no list at all; for a substantial part of it we have a list, but pious fraud has so enlarged it that we cannot tell what it originally contained. A century later Exeter Cathedral claimed to have a third of all the relics that King Athelstan brought from abroad. Westminster and Glastonbury Abbeys and other churches also claimed very substantial gifts, which have probably been inflated in the course of time. In handling relics

---

117 Brooke 2000, p. 211 and n. 16.
118 Robinson 1923, p. 73.

special rules of morality applied. Lying may be sinful, but a lie about relics was very white, for those who benefited. Theft, however, was neither good nor bad; it was only possible if the saint himself wished to be moved, and the thief was thus merely the passive instrument of the saint's intentions. Kleptomania, to which avid collectors can be liable, could be regarded as pious zeal. When St Hugh of Lincoln took a piece off their best relic with his teeth, the monks of Fécamp Abbey in Normandy were furiously indignant, but his biographer tells the story without a blush. The monks of Abingdon read the story of Duke Hugh's embassy to Athelstan, read the list of relics, and their mouths watered. Then they noted that the court took place at Abingdon. So pious a king could not possibly have stayed there without giving a notable present to the abbey. It was clear indeed, that he had given them a part of the Crown of Thorns, part of one of the nails, St Maurice's standard and a finger of St Denis, all in a silver chest. 'Of this', wrote Dr Armitage Robinson, 'we need only remark that it was a bold claim.'[119]

In 939 Athelstan died, still in the prime of life, at the height of his power. By extending his sway over Wales and Scotland and by his relations with the rulers of western Europe, he had added a dimension to the royal power of his predecessors. His princely accumulation of relics, however much it owed to the crank and the charlatan, added an extra dimension to the treasures of ancient Heorot. Like Alfred, he was literate, and he was evidently a man of considerable artistic taste; it is no coincidence that he was a patron of the artistic St Dunstan. But we read about him through the haze of the foggiest court-Latin any country or any age produced; and as we pause for breath amid the interminable, grotesque periods of his charters, we cannot help feeling that he was something of a parvenu emperor. They remind us of the famous gloss in a preacher's sermon notes: 'argument weak, shout like mad', and it has been suggested that they protest so much simply because he could not be sure of obedience. This, in Athelstan's case, may not be the whole truth; clearly he loved baroque splendour of every kind. But the protestation serves to remind us that only his prestige and success as a warrior kept the Vikings at bay; that the time was not far off when they would strike again.

Athelstan was succeeded by his brother Edmund, and he by his brother Eadred; both were conscientious monarchs about whom comparatively little is known; neither lived long. Then the kingdom passed, in quick succession, to Edmund's two sons, Eadwig and Edgar. Edgar was the last great king of Alfred's line; and, as Edgar

119 Robinson 1923, p. 80.

started his career in rebellion against his elder brother, Eadwig has had a bad press. He quarrelled with St Dunstan. We are told that the reason for the quarrel was that Eadwig left the banquet on his coronation day to engage in idle conversation with two ladies of doubtful virtue; that Dunstan was one of those who reproved him, and that he took it ill. Subsequently his misgovernment brought its due reward; Edgar was proclaimed king of Mercia in 957, and in 959 the dissolute Eadwig died. But Eadwig may only have been thirteen when he was crowned, and is unlikely to have been much older; and he was probably under twenty, perhaps well under twenty when he died. It is difficult to take any of this very seriously; and it is perfectly clear that Edgar also sowed his wild oats.

Edgar died in 975, aged thirty-two. By then his childhood was long forgotten, and he had achieved enough to leave an indelible mark on English kingship. He was a friend of leading churchmen, and no doubt they saw to it that he received a good write-up; but it is clear that his achievement, for his age, was substantial. It is also clear that he owed much to his eminent clerical advisers, Dunstan of Canterbury, Oswald of York and Ethelwold of Winchester; how much, it is hard to say. He ruled England with a strong hand; he was known as Edgar the Peaceful, but his peace was a sign of strength, not of weakness. He pushed the union of Danes and English a stage further; like Athelstan, his power was acknowledged by the other kings of the island. In 973 he was anointed and crowned with great solemnity; in the same year eight Welsh and Scottish kings submitted to him at Chester – though whether they really rowed him on the river Dee as legend has it, we cannot tell. He was the patron of a great monastic revival.

Not unnaturally, the last item was the best recorded. The revival of monastic life, and with it of many types of learning, of art and architecture, is one of the most exciting events of the tenth century. Alfred and Athelstan had had comparatively little success in their attempts to patronize such a movement. Under Athelstan's immediate successors, the triumvirate of saints began their work. Under Edgar it came to fruition. What is of special interest to us is that they attributed their success to him. It shows how lofty a sense men had of the royal office that they should do this. The language they used has a familiar ring today, when we are used to hear dictators adulated as authors of all good things, including scientific discoveries. But there is this difference. It is doubtful if Edgar could read Latin; and it is doubtful therefore whether his courtiers needed to flatter him to this extent in the text of their treatise on monastic customs. This treatise, the *Regularis Concordia*, the *Monastic Agreement*, was probably

written by St Ethelwold; it clearly reflects both his views and Dunstan's. By invoking royal authority it attempts to weaken the grip of
secular lords on monastic property and to plaster over cracks of
disagreement between the monasteries. But it is perfectly clear that
its author really believed, as did most churchmen in northern Europe
in the tenth century, that the king was Christ's vicar on earth, chief
repository of divine authority, mediator of divine blessings – not of
the eucharist, for a king was not a priest – but mediator of the scarcely
less efficacious blessing of divine order and good government.

'Edgar the glorious, by the grace of Christ illustrious king of the
English and of the other peoples dwelling within the bounds of
the island of Britain, from his earliest years began to fear, love and
worship God with all his heart. For while he engaged in the various
pursuits that befit boyhood, he was nevertheless touched by the divine
regard, being diligently admonished by a certain abbot who explained
to him the royal way of the Catholic faith. Wherefore, lest the spark
of faith, which was beginning gradually to brighten, should be extinguished by sloth and idleness, he began carefully and earnestly to
consider by what holy and deserving works it could be made to burn
with the brilliance and ardour of perfection.' The preface goes on to
describe, and exaggerate, the low state of monasticism at his accession, his labours and his wife's for its revival.

'When therefore the Rule of the holy father Benedict had been
accepted with the greatest goodwill, very many of the abbots and
abbesses with their communities of monks and nuns vied with one
another in following in the footsteps of the saints; for they were
united in one faith, though not in one manner of monastic usage.
Exceedingly delighted with such great zeal the aforesaid king, after
deep and careful study of the matter, commanded a Synodal Council
to be held at Winchester. To this assembly he most humbly sent a
letter, set forth magnificently on parchment and couched in encouraging and peaceable terms, in which, moved by the grace of Christ, he
urged all to be of one mind as regards monastic usage, to follow the
holy and approved fathers and so, with their minds anchored firmly
on the ordinances of the Rule, to avoid all dissension, lest differing
ways of observing the customs of one Rule and one country should
bring their holy conversation into disrepute. Deeply moved by the
wise advice of this excellent king, the bishops, abbots and abbesses
were not slow in raising their hands to heaven in hearty thanksgiving
to the throne above for that they were thought worthy to have so
good and so great a teacher.'[120]

---

120 *Regularis Concordia*, ed. and trans. T. Symons, pp. 1–3.

To a modern reader this adulation of Edgar is not attractive. But it seems likely that this strong, capable, wilful young man was in many ways an attractive person; at any rate his piety was genuine, for Ethelwold and his associates would not have written like this if it had been wholly absurd. This ideal of the religious king was to appear later in the German kingdom, in Henry II and Henry III; and the Emperor Henry III, in 1046, carried it to the length of disposing of three popes, who were trying to occupy the Holy See at the same time, and instituting reform at the heart of western Christendom. From this reform in due course arose the doctrine – not a new one, but one very commonly ignored in the centuries immediately preceding – that it was for pope and bishops to regulate the Church, not for kings; and out of the powerful doctrines of the papal reformers came the conflicts which we commonly call the investiture disputes. This lay far in the future in 970, when the *Concordia* was probably published. But already there were not wanting folk who observed that too close a lien of king and Church was not altogether healthy for the Church; that if the king was able to treat bishoprics and monasteries as pieces of personal property, he might use them for unsuitable ends. In Edgar's integrity Dunstan and Ethelwold trusted, and Edgar was not yet thirty. But five years later, in 975, he suddenly died, and his young sons, and the factions who supported them, squabbled for his kingdom.

The party of Edward (who was about thirteen) argued that he was the elder and better candidate, and should be king. The party of Ethelred (who may not have been more than six or seven) had serious doubts about Edward's character. It was alleged much later that they also argued that Ethelred was born when his father was king and his mother queen; was *porphyrogenitus*, 'born in the purple'. (See pp. 153, 159.) It is very doubtful if they really argued so at the time, though not wholly impossible in a Europe still dominated by Otto the Great, whose succession to the throne of Germany had been challenged by his younger brother, on account of such a claim. But it is more likely that this suggestion belongs to the world of Henry I's early manhood, not the childhood of Ethelred.

Whatever their grounds, the followers of Ethelred were not content to let Edward rule. On 18 March 978 Edward came to visit his brother at Corfe (Dorset). As he approached the hall where his brother was living, Ethelred's retainers came out and gathered round the king's horse, as if to greet him. But they greeted him with blows, stabbed him, and buried his body in Wareham, near by, with maimed rites or no rites at all; and the English people learned that violence and treachery had made Ethelred their king.

Edward was dead, but his career was by no means over. A year later the ealdorman of Mercia unearthed his remains, and had them solemnly translated to Shaftesbury. The story was told that they were marvellously uncorrupted; a whisper of miracles began to gather round the tomb. The young man's bones became holy relics; his brother was inspired to acknowledge him a saint, and to pronounce the day of his death a solemn festival. Thus was made King Edward the Martyr. When the ealdorman translated the body to Shaftesbury, he seems to have been performing an act of reconciliation; by doing honour to the murdered king, he seems to have hoped to rally Edward's supporters to Ethelred. If this explanation (hinted at by one contemporary) is correct, one may doubt if he was successful. The growing cult of Edward must have been a constant reminder to Ethelred of the manner of his accession. The murder was performed by Ethelred's retainers, so he could not escape some measure of responsibility. Since he may not have been more than nine or ten at the time, we find it difficult to take this charge very seriously. But it cast a gloom over Ethelred's accession, and in a measure over his whole reign. Yet he reigned for thirty-eight years, and in his later years was constantly threatened by Viking attacks; that he held his own till near the end deserves some credit.[121] In the 980s, however, Ethelred failed to win or hold the allegiance of several of his leading thegns. The ealdorman of Mercia died in 983; in 985 his son and successor Ælfric was sent into exile, presumably for rebellion; in 992 one of the other leading ealdormen of Ethelred's early years, Ælfric of Hampshire, turned traitor; in 993 Ethelred tried to check his activities by blinding his son; yet ten years later Ælfric was in a position to turn traitor again. This illustrates the way in which some of Ethelred's leading supporters sat lightly to their allegiance. In Ethelred's code of 1008 it is specially noted that 'the councillors have decreed that Edward's festival is to be celebrated all over England on 18 March.'[122] I used to think that they wrung this decree from a reluctant king; but the indications are that Ethelred welcomed this recognition of his brother.

Dissidence and half-suppressed revolt had never been uncommon in Anglo-Saxon England. In Ethelred's time they came to walk openly. A thirteenth-century chronicler records that he was known as Ethelred *Un-ræd*; from which the modern corruption 'the Unready' is derived. The chronicler is late,[123] but he had access to information now lost,

---

121 See the revisions by Simon Keynes – Keynes 1978, 1980 – and S. Miller in *Blackwell Encyclopaedia*, pp. 15–16.
122 *Councils and Synods*, I, 1, 353–4.
123 But the nickname was almost certainly known to Walter Map, writing in the late twelfth century (*De nugis*, p. 412 and n. 2).

and the pun is so clever that it seems not at all unlikely that it was given to Ethelred by a contemporary wit. 'Ethelred' is a compound of two Old English words, *æthel* and *ræd*, meaning noble counsel. *Unræd* meant 'no counsel'. But it had overtones and alternative meanings; and these included 'evil counsel' and 'a treacherous plot'. Ethelred was king, according to his charters, 'by the grace of God', or, more precisely, 'with the divine approval pre-ordained by the grace of the same our God and Lord'. This may have comforted him; but there were other words which could be used to describe the manner of his accession. He could never wholly escape the curse of Cain.

Unræd could imply that Ethelred was given bad counsel by his followers; or that he did not take the advice they gave; or that he had no followers to give advice; or simply that he was unwise. There would be some truth in all of these statements. He could never count on the obedience of many of his subjects; there were always some whose allegiance would be doubtful in case of war. It was a mixture of this and his own temperament that made him an indecisive and ineffective general. At times he was deserted by most of his followers; and the Witan elected two kings to replace him before he was dead.

Yet we have no reason to attribute his misfortunes entirely to his incapacity. A medieval king had to be feared and admired if he were to be successful; he also needed good luck. Ethelred was very unlucky: unlucky to have become king in the way he did; unlucky that the Danes should be ready for further attacks on the country within two years of his becoming king; even more unlucky in the strength and skill of the Danish leaders who attacked him. The Danish armies and fleets were particularly well armed and trained and led in the last quarter of the tenth and the first quarter of the eleventh centuries. Even so, the English could have resisted them if they had been united and led by an able soldier. Even if Ethelred had been a brilliant soldier, he could not have resisted the Danes without a greater degree of loyalty than he could command. The battle of Maldon in 991, when an English ealdorman fell heroically defending the coast in the name of King Ethelred, showed that some ealdormen were loyal; but they were not sufficient.

In these circumstances Ethelred adopted a policy which belies his name. The Danes came to plunder; that was the basis of their way of life. If he fought them, he might lose, and a part of England be laid waste; if he won, the Danes were bound to come again or their leaders would be impoverished or lose face. But England was still a comparatively rich country; silver was in good supply; the currency was the most highly organized in Europe. Even if England was in some disorder, the basic organs of government could be made to work;

the mints could produce large quantities of highly desirable coins. If one bought off the Danes, they would sail away without committing further destruction. True, they would come again; but so long as silver was more plentiful than reliable troops, it was sound policy to use silver to protect England. And by its use, and by the use of such thegns as were loyal, Ethelred kept the country from total collapse for thirty years. For this he and his advisers deserve some credit: in counsel and in readiness he fell short of his distinguished forebears, but he kept his throne till near the very end of his life.

At length, in 1009, the Danish King Swein determined to make an end of Ethelred, and to be king of the English himself. First, he sent his best lieutenants, who raided the country with remarkable thoroughness for three years. In 1012 an immense payment of 'Danegeld' was made; but before the Danes left they had treacherously murdered Ælfheah, the archbishop of Canterbury. This seems to have upset one of their leaders, Thorkell the Tall, so much that he deserted to Ethelred's side. But Thorkell's desertion brought the English king no comfort; on the contrary it brought on him a visitation from King Swein in person. In 1013 Swein landed in England at 'Sandwich, and very soon after went round East Anglia into the mouth of the Humber, and so up along the Trent until he came to Gainsborough. Then Earl Uhtred and all Northumbria straightway submitted to him, and all the people of Lindsey, and then the people belonging to the Five Boroughs, and soon afterwards all the Danes to the north of Watling Street; and he was given hostages from every shire. After he realised that all the people had submitted to him, he gave orders that his host should be provisioned and supplied with horses; he then turned southward with his whole force, committing his ships and the hostages into the charge of Cnut, his son. After he crossed Watling Street, they did the greatest mischief that any host was capable of, and made their way then to Oxford, and the citizens immediately surrendered and gave hostages; and from there to Winchester where they did the same. Thence they went east to London, and a great part of his host was drowned in the Thames, because they did not bother to look for any bridge. When they came to the borough, the citizens would not submit, but held out against them with the utmost valour, because King Ethelred was inside, and Thorkell with him. Then Swein turned thence to Wallingford, and so over the Thames westward to Bath, and encamped there with his levies. Thither came Ealdorman Æthelmær and the thegns from the west, and they all submitted to Swein and gave him hostages. Having made his way thus far, he turned northward to his ships, and the whole nation accepted him as their undisputed king. Thereafter the citizens of London submitted and gave hostages, because they were afraid he would destroy them. Then Swein demanded tribute in full and supplies for his host during the winter... yet despite this they went harrying as often as they pleased. At this time nothing went right for this nation, neither in the south nor in the north.'[124]

In due course Ethelred abandoned the struggle and joined his queen, Emma, who had already fled to Normandy, where her brother was duke. But Swein's triumph was short-lived. On 3 February 1014 the savage Viking suddenly died, and confusion reigned in his stead.

124 *ASC*, trans. Garmonsway, pp. 143–4.

11

Cnut and Edward the Confessor

For the English throne there were now three contenders: Swein's second son, Cnut, who was barely twenty; Ethelred's son Edmund Ironside, who was probably in his mid-twenties; and Ethelred himself, who in spite of his long reign and many misfortunes was still under fifty. At first Cnut, opposed only by Ethelred, seemed the most likely candidate; but he threw over his immediate chances by withdrawing to Denmark. It seems that he was too young, too inexperienced to deal with the situation. But he went in order to return, and was back in greater strength in 1015. Meanwhile Ethelred had been restored, but not to everyone's satisfaction; and his eldest surviving son Edmund Ironside was determined to make the best use he could of Cnut's absence. The details of the quarrel of father and son are somewhat obscure; but the effect was that when Cnut returned, English royal authority was divided. Edmund acted with great determination, and his path was made easier by his father's death in April 1016. But like his father he never won the undivided allegiance of the English ealdormen; some elected Edmund, more elected Cnut in April 1016. Then the two kings marched and counter-marched against each other; and for a time it seemed as if Edmund's power was growing. But in October Cnut won the battle of Ashingdon, and in November Edmund suddenly died.

From 1016 till his death in 1035, when he was aged about forty, Cnut was undisputed master of England; for most of the time he was king of Denmark too, for some of it king of Norway and lord of part of Sweden. He was the greatest figure of the northern world, and he entered into legend in his lifetime. After the emperor he was the most formidable monarch in western Europe. This was partly due to his inheritance; but also to his personal qualities, since he combined in an extraordinary way the qualities needed by a successful medieval king.

Cnut was not a man to trifle with. Before leaving England in 1014 he dispensed with the hostages his father had collected; but he mutilated them in the process. A contemporary Norse poet, singing a song with the refrain 'Cnut is the foremost suzerain under heaven', observed in passing 'Cnut slew or exiled one and all of Ethelred's sons.'[125] In the early months of his reign Cnut listened to the advice, we are told, of Ealdorman Eadric, who recommended that Edmund Ironside's brother and children be removed. The brother, Eadwig, was duly killed at Cnut's command, and Edmund's two small children sent into exile – according to one version, with instructions that they be slain; but this may not be true, and it was certainly not performed. Edmund's sons went to Hungary; and the two boys of Ethelred's second marriage, to Emma of Normandy, went to Normandy. Cnut was free to turn his attention to lesser fry; and in the course of the Christmas festivities the perfidious ealdorman himself was murdered in the palace by royal command, and with him fell three other leading Englishmen. Shortly before, Cnut had solemnly married Ethelred's widow, Emma of Normandy. But he was a Viking, and among the Vikings monogamy had not as yet a firm hold. So he did not dismiss his 'temporary wife', as Ælfgifu of Northampton has been neatly called, but sent her into Denmark, where she ruled with him as queen. And so, in the north, Cnut was remembered as a splendid Viking: 'Gracious giver of mighty gifts, you made corselets red in Norwich. You will lose your life before your courage fails. Still you pressed on, blunting swords upon weapons; they could not defend their strongholds when you attacked. The bow screamed loud. You won no less renown, driver of the leaping steed of the roller, on Thames's bank. The wolf's jaw knew this well. King bold in attack, you smote the Swedes in the place called Holy River [we have moved on to 1026], and there the she-wolf got much wolf's food. Terrible staff of battle, you held the land against two princes, and the raven did not go hungry there. You are swift to deal with the race of men.'[126] Swift indeed he was; he failed in his purpose at the Holy River, and the Viking earl whose double-dealing had frustrated his plans was soon murdered. Cnut had a short way with his enemies; and the result was that he never suffered in England from the divisions and disloyalties which marred the milder rule of Ethelred.

Cnut, then, was feared. But he was also respected and admired as a just king who ruled equitably, as a man who strove to emphasize his position as the successor to the dynasty of Alfred, and especially to

---

125 Vigfusson and York Powell 1883, pp. 135–6; cf. *EHD* I, 337–8.
126 Ashdown 1930, p. 139.

King Edgar the peaceful, and as a pious man who fostered the Church. We find it very difficult now to reconcile the two Cnuts. Yet if we can try to gain imaginative insight and sympathy into the mind of the savage Viking who was also the Lord's anointed, we shall see in vivid focus much that is characteristic of medieval kingship. We cannot entirely acquit Cnut of hypocrisy. But he was a Christian of the second generation only; his father had hardly been a Christian at all, even in name; Cnut was brought up in a world very unused to Christian standards. Nor could the medieval Church exact much more than formal exercises of piety from most monarchs. The moral standards of lay courts were not high; medieval kings were spoilt children, and never ceased to be. But what is striking in Cnut's case is that the edicts issued in his name contain much more than the formal statement of pious intentions. No doubt they were written for him; but there is strong reason to suppose that he approved the language in which they were phrased. 'King Cnut greets in friendship', ran a letter written in 1019 or 1020, 'his archbishops and his diocesan bishops, and Earl Thorkell and all his earls, and all his people.... And I inform you that I will be a gracious lord and a faithful observer of God's rights and just secular law. I have borne in mind the letters and messages which Archbishop Lyfing brought me from Rome from the pope, that I should everywhere exalt God's praise and suppress wrong and establish full security, by that power which it has pleased God to give me.... Now I thank Almighty God for his help and his mercy, that I have so settled the great dangers which were approaching us that we need fear no danger to us.... Now it is my will, that we all thank Almighty God humbly for the mercy which he has shown for our help.'[127] He goes on to establish certain rules for the maintenance of good order in Church and realm; and although English law was still very rough and ready, we may be sure that Cnut and his officers enforced some degree of law and order as it had not been enforced since the death of Edgar. To the Church he was a devoted and lavish patron; and under his rule the organs of English government steadily developed. In 1027 he went on pilgrimage to Rome, walking in the footsteps of Cædwalla and Ine and Alfred. He was able to be present at the coronation of the Emperor Conrad II by the pope; he enjoyed being received by them as a great monarch; with the emperor he could discuss the frontier of Germany and Denmark; with the emperor and other princes the rights of English traders and pilgrims on the path to Rome; with the pope he could arrange some privileges for the English clergy. But we need not doubt that his main purpose was 'to pray for

127 *Councils and Synods*, I, 1, 435–7.

the redeeming of my sins and for the safety of the kingdoms and peoples subject to my rule', to visit the holy apostles Peter and Paul, and the other sacred places of Rome, and 'especially... because I learned from wise men that St Peter the apostle had received from the Lord the great power of binding and loosing, and was the keeper of the keys of the heavenly kingdom, and I thought it very profitable diligently to seek his special patronage before God'.[128] This confirms what we should otherwise strongly suspect, that the young king listened assiduously to what his clerical advisers said to him; and especially to Wulfstan, archbishop of York, whose pen wrote many of Cnut's *Laws*, and whose mind directed Cnut's notions of English kingship. We can see a broad conception of his role emerging in Cnut's mind and acts; but monarchy still depended on fear as well as on loyalty and good government, and the Viking in Cnut never disappeared.

Nor was the element of disorder in England fully suppressed; indeed it found in Cnut's method of government new opportunities. Cnut had ruled England with the aid of a small group of leading earls, English as well as Danes. At the end of his life a great area of England was ruled by Siward of Northumbria (famous today for the part he plays in *Macbeth*), Leofric of Mercia and Godwine of Wessex; and his family was ruled by the two queens. These potentates were under firm control so long as Cnut lived; but his kingdoms and his family fell a prey to faction and conflict as soon as he died (1035).

He left one son by Emma, Harthacnut, who was already ruler of Denmark; but he was involved in a major conflict with Magnus of Norway, and was not free to attend to English affairs for some time after his father's death. Emma and Earl Godwine wished him none the less to succeed; but Ælfgifu and Earl Leofric, supported by most of the English thegns, arranged for Ælfgifu's son Harold (who was technically illegitimate, being son of the 'temporary queen') to be first regent, then king. There were other candidates in the surviving members of Ethelred's family; and Alfred, elder son of Ethelred by Emma, came over from Normandy soon after Cnut's death. But he was treacherously murdered; and the responsibility for his murder was fastened on Godwine – a fact which Alfred's younger brother, Edward the Confessor, was unlikely to forget. Meanwhile, in 1040 Harold I died, and Harthacnut succeeded to an undisputed throne. As we have seen, Harthacnut had made an arrangement with Magnus of Norway that each should succeed to the other's kingdom if the other died without an heir. Magnus and his successor, Harold Hardrada, argued

---

128 *Councils and Synods*, I, 1, 508–9 (my translation).

that this applied to England too, and so laid claim to the whole inheritance of Cnut. But this was not accepted by Harthacnut. In 1041 he summoned Ethelred's one surviving son, Edward, to join his household, and probably designated him his heir. He was taking somewhat elaborate precautions, in view of the fact that he was probably about twenty-four; but the precautions were necessary, for in June 1042 he collapsed in his cups at a wedding-banquet, and immediately died.

In Edward the Confessor (1042–66) we see a very different side of English kingship from that revealed by Cnut. Cnut had ruled by fear; and made his authority legitimate by removing native rivals, by marrying his predecessor's queen, by acting the part of king in every way and stressing the continuity of government; and so he won the allegiance both of the Danes and the English, and was, in a sense, the first king of a united England. Edward had all the trappings of legitimacy born in him. He was son of Ethelred, grandson of Edgar, great-great-great-grandson of Alfred. His mother had been queen both to Ethelred and to Cnut. At the same time, he had few rivals. The line of Cnut was extinct; the line of Ethelred consisted of himself and two young nephews far away in Hungary. So far as England was concerned he was undisputed king, and this gave him almost complete freedom from the danger of deposition by his own subjects. At the same time there was the threat of usurpation by the king of Norway, which rallied the English and Danes alike to their allegiance to Edward.

English kingship survived the Confessor's reign undamaged. Yet this is a tribute rather to the strength of the institution and to the historical circumstances than to Edward himself. He was a king neither by temperament nor by upbringing. He had been brought up a prince in exile, without expectation of a throne; he was bred, therefore, to hunting and idleness, and these tastes stayed with him all his days. In later years he acquired a new hobby: he devoted more and more of his slender energies to the building of Westminster Abbey, and to works of piety. Piety seems to have grown on him. It is probably wrong to view him as a would-be monk. He liked to have learned men about him; above all he enjoyed the company of Lotharingian and French and Norman ecclesiastics. They reminded him of the cosmopolitan world in which he had been brought up. But there is not much to suggest that he was himself a man of learning or an intellectual. The piety of his closing years and of his biographer, and the strange transformation of his posthumous career, have marked him indelibly in English legend as Edward *the Confessor*. This notion has been fostered by the story of his chastity. He was married to Earl

Godwine's daughter, Edith. It is probable enough that he cared little for her in his early days; and it is certain that they were childless. But it seems likely that the story that the marriage was never consummated grew up in Edward's closing years as a part of the legend of royal piety (strange as this may seem), and as a delicate compliment to a queen who suffered from the common misfortune of failing to bear children. The story first appears in the biography written at about the time of Edward's death, which was intended to honour Edith as much as Edward. This biography is an exceptionally good example of the way a single source may colour the traditional view of a person. The Tudor legend of Richard III grew out of Sir Thomas More's biography, which was a brilliant historical novel, not perhaps deliberately falsified, but certainly tendentious. In the first part of Edward's *Life*, written while he was alive, his piety is already stressed, but so are his worldly interests, and he shows some notable human failings when he does things detrimental to the house of Godwine, the real heroes of the book. In the second part, written shortly after Edward's death, the author describes the king's miracles, and evidently has already conceived the idea that Edward ought to be venerated as a saint. From this developed the cult which eventually bore fruit in the canonization of Edward in 1161. The piety stressed by the author was doubtless genuine; but it was only one stream in a personality that flowed through many channels; and if we accept the testimony written in Edward's lifetime, we must substitute in our mind's eye for Edward the Confessor Edward the huntsman.

From time to time Edward showed serious evidence of wishing to rule as well as to reign. For some years he had to submit to the tutelage of Earl Godwine, the king-maker. But he could never forget that Godwine was responsible for his brother's murder; and he knew that in the long run his own position was more secure than Godwine's; and that Godwine could be brought to heel if the other great earls would unite against him. Edward was secure largely because there seemed to be no alternative to him save the king of Norway. By marrying Edward to his daughter, Godwine clearly hoped to arrange that his descendants would reign in England. As time passed, it became clear that this plan was going to miscarry. Edward and Edith married in 1045. By 1051 gossip was already rife, no doubt, as to who should succeed if the queen stayed childless. Godwine had perhaps already thought of his own claims, or of his sons'. Cnut had legitimized his rule by marrying the queen; might not one of Godwine's sons succeed as Edward's brother-in-law?

But the success of any such plan depended on the king, and Edward had other notions. He wished his cousin of Normandy to succeed; and he wished above all to be free of Godwine's tutelage. In 1051 he struck. Godwine was exiled; William pronounced the heir (see p. 28); a Norman made archbishop of Canterbury; the queen removed from court. But this success was too swift and too sweeping. In 1052 Godwine returned, and Edward was forced to receive him back to favour. The archbishop of Canterbury went into exile; the Norman courtiers were dismissed. Godwine did not live to enjoy his triumph. He died in 1053, and it seems that after his death Edward and Harold, Godwine's most eminent son, agreed to more moderate courses. Queen Edith had been restored in 1052, and in Edward's later years their relations seem to have been good. Harold never held the full extent of Godwine's power, but he and his brothers were clearly the most powerful men in England under the king. In 1055 Siward of Northumbria died and Harold's brother Tostig succeeded. One chronicler calls Harold the under-king, and in Edward's later years he led the army, and fought major campaigns in Wales. He knew how to humour the king; he organized hunting parties for his entertainment, and always deferred to his regality. He also respected the power of Leofric of Mercia.

In the mid-1050s Edward summoned his nephew and namesake from Hungary, doubtless with a view to making him his heir. But the nephew died before he could see his uncle, under somewhat mysterious circumstances; and his son, Edgar the Ætheling, was evidently felt to be too young to defend England against Harold Hardrada of Norway, the most famous warrior of the Viking world. For the time, it seems, Edward made no arrangement; but William of Normandy did not forget that he had once been designated heir.

12

The Conqueror and the Conquest

The Norman dukes were Vikings by origin, and still in the late tenth and early eleventh centuries Vikings in many of their habits. Their matrimonial affairs were considerably more irregular than Cnut's; and they only practised monogamy when they happened to fall wholly under the influence of one of their mistresses. Duke Robert I (1027–35) was monogamous. But he lived at a time when the normal marriage customs of western Europe were beginning to impinge on Normandy. The marriage of princes was commonly an arranged affair, a political bargain which brought a prince or a king children, and also lands, money and enhanced prestige. This made it difficult for Duke Robert to acknowledge the lady with whom he lived; but he was faithful to her to near the end of his days. Small wonder that romantic legends gathered round this remarkable liaison. An early story tells how Robert spied Herleva at a dance and promptly fell in love with her. In the twelfth century it was said that he first saw her doing the washing in the stream which passed her father's tannery at the foot of Falaise Castle. Local legend still points out the window (which is somewhat later in construction, it must be admitted) from which Robert caught sight of her. But we may doubt if Herleva washed her own linen. Her father, William the Tanner, was evidently a substantial citizen, and he was subsequently made chamberlain to the duke; and after Robert's death Herleva was married to a Norman baron, Herluin de Conteville, by whom she had two sons, Robert and Odo. Robert, as count of Mortain, was the most powerful of Anglo-Norman barons in the Conqueror's later years; and Odo, as bishop of Bayeux, combined the roles of Norman prelate and English earl. Odo became a brilliant, ostentatious man of the world. He endowed his diocese lavishly, but neglected it except when driven out of England by the disfavour of his royal brother or nephew. At the time of his death he was engaged in pursuing the singular ambition to become pope; one can hardly imagine a more incongruous successor to the prophet-reformer Gregory VII. On the whole, and especially in his later years, the Conqueror liked to surround himself with reforming bishops and abbots. Odo was a survival of the warrior-bishop of earlier days; it is even possible that the author of the *Song of Roland* had him in mind when he drew his portrait of the warrior Archbishop Turpin. But we owe Bishop Odo unstinted gratitude on one account: he was the patron of the Bayeux Tapestry.

William the Conqueror was the only son, perhaps the only child, of a happy 'marriage'; but as the marriage was never made formal, he was technically illegitimate. When he was still a small child, his father went on pilgrimage to Jerusalem (1035) and never returned. One of the wildest and most turbulent principalities in Europe fell to the lot of a boy of seven or eight. William's upbringing was tough in the extreme; and his illegitimacy added to his many difficulties. It also influenced the pattern of his own domestic life. In later years he was to marry Matilda, daughter of the count of Flanders, a descendant of King Alfred. The Church prohibited the marriage, but William persisted, and was in the end given dispensation. To Matilda William was a faithful husband. He was in fact the only one of his line to have one wife acknowledged by the Church and to be faithful to her. It is very doubtful if it was a love-match. But its success may have been due in part to his father's example; it may also have been due to a desire to avoid illegitimate children: William's early difficulties, and the nickname of bastard which always clung to him, may well have determined him to be a faithful husband. The history of medieval marriage is like a maze, with many twisting paths and unexpected corners.[129] The Church could only enforce its moral teaching on the great if it found allies in their midst. If we look at William and Odo, we cannot doubt that their mother was a remarkable woman; and it may well have been Herleva who taught William how to be a good husband.

William's early years as duke were passed in an atmosphere of savage violence and intrigue. 'The bowl and the dagger', wrote Freeman, 'soon deprived the young Prince of the support of his wisest and truest counsellors.'[130] He was protected at first by Count Alan of Brittany, Count Gilbert of Brionne and Osbern the Seneschal. Alan was poisoned, Gilbert and Osbern were murdered. Osbern was assassinated by a member of the violent house of Bellême-Montgomery, later to produce earls of Shrewsbury and Pembroke, and to be

129 See Brooke 1989.
130 Freeman 1867–79, II, 191.

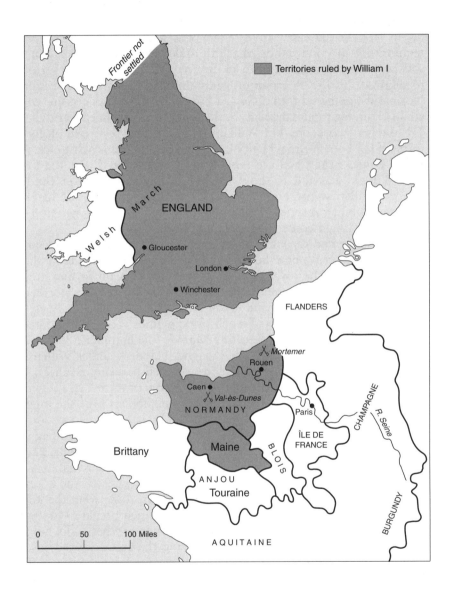

Map 2 The Norman empire.

extinguished by Henry I in the last of their many rebellions. William of Montgomery attempted to kill Duke William himself, and succeeded in killing Osbern; one of Osbern's servants presently avenged his master. In the early 1040s there was a pause. The duchy was temporarily in good hands, the little duke was growing up. But it was only the calm before a storm. In 1047 he faced the most serious rebellion of his life. A group of leading nobles, especially of western Normandy, gathered round Guy of Burgundy, William's cousin, who could claim legitimate descent, in the female line, from earlier dukes. The danger was acute, but William had one notable stroke of good fortune: the French King, Henry I, came in person to his assistance. At Val-ès-Dunes near Caen the rebel army was scattered. For the first time William was able to show his skill on the field of battle. But he was still under twenty, and he was still not able entirely to subdue the Norman nobility. A series of rebellions culminated in the formation of another, far larger confederacy against William in 1053.

King Henry had repented of his support of William in 1047, and wished now to crush him; he seems to have hoped to add a large slice of Normandy to the royal domain. It was not difficult to find other princes jealous of Normandy. In the mid-eleventh century northern France was full of counts and dukes enlarging their principalities; it was the age when the great French principalities were consolidated. Anjou was growing under Geoffrey Martel, 'the hammer'; Blois was united, for the time being, to Champagne; Flanders, under William's father-in-law, was expanding. This process led to many rivalries. In the end Normandy was to outstrip all competitors by swallowing England; but in 1053–4 it seemed to her neighbours as if she might be conveniently dismembered. In 1054 the French king led an army into Normandy which included the contingents of Blois-Champagne, with the moral support of Anjou. The royal and ducal capitals, Paris and Rouen, both lie on the Seine; and the royal army marched in two contingents, one to the north of the river, the other to the south, towards the heart of the duchy. By the southern route went the king himself, and the duke led the Norman force which prepared to meet him. In the north the French leader was the king's brother, Odo. Odo's army marched deep into Normandy, laying the country waste as it came. The Normans bided their time, and awaited their opportunity. Presently their spies told them that the French were in the small town of Mortemer, feasting too well on the fruits of their plunder. At dawn the Normans set fire to the town and fell on the French; they achieved, so it seems, complete surprise, and the army was decisively beaten. The story is told that when Duke William heard the news, he sent a leading vassal secretly to the king's camp; and that from a tree or a rock his voice was heard proclaiming to the French the disaster at Mortemer. In any event, the disaster inspired the king with panic, or prudence, and he hastily withdrew. The story is one of many which the Normans told to illustrate the mixture of force and cunning which they felt were the special marks of their duke.

Some of William's qualities were matured and hardened early in the tough school in which he grew up. He learned to be forceful, and firm; to be ruthless, but to avoid needless violence; he learned that he could only trust the Norman barons when they feared him. Skill at arms, a taste for the hunting field, an interest in military techniques, all came young. But some of his most striking qualities and interests grew slowly to maturity. He was certainly a man of imagination; but his ideas did not come by swift intuition. They came slowly, by experience carefully reflected on; they bore fruit, because William, for all his prudence, was lavishly endowed with moral courage. His political arrangements in England can be shown to have grown out of both English and Norman experience, to have been a development from the inchoate organization of Normandy, as well as from the more sophisticated traditions of England. One can observe his changing outlook very clearly in his relations with the Church. William was a pious churchman, according to his lights, and is remembered as a keen reformer, whose activities won the approbation of Pope Gregory VII himself. It is clear that he always expected his bishops and abbots to be efficient servants and counsellors to himself as well as churchmen; but there was a marked change in the early 1050s in the kind of person he chose for high office. His uncle Malger became archbishop of Rouen in 1037, when William was under ten, so William can hardly be blamed; but for the warrior-bishops Geoffrey of Coutances and Odo of Bayeux, appointed in 1049–50, he must take responsibility; and the other Norman bishops of this period seem all to have been worldly noblemen.

The eleventh century was an age of change and movement, especially in the Church. In 1049 Pope Leo IX, the first pope of the great movement of papal reform, came north of the Alps and announced the principles of reform at the council of Reims. The office of bishop was to be regarded first and foremost as a spiritual office, not that of a secular prince; it was not to be bought; the clergy were to live up to their profession, which included (in the law of the medieval Church) a life of celibacy; the papacy was to be the effective instrument for enforcing the Church's laws. Among other worldly bishops, Geoffrey of Coutances surrendered his see but was allowed to receive it back after penance; and news of this may have had some effect on William. But it is more likely that it was his growing friendship with a group of ardent churchmen which changed his outlook. In 1054 his unsuitable uncle was removed from Rouen and replaced by a reforming monk of cosmopolitan background called Maurilius. Other, similar appointments followed; and even if a number of the Conqueror's ecclesiastics, to the end of his days, were great men of the world, the closest to him, from the 1050s on, was the Italian scholar Lanfranc of Pavia, monk and 'father of monks', a brilliant scholar and a fearless upholder of spiritual standards in the Church. Lanfranc fully approved the standards of clerical behaviour and clerical reform preached by Leo IX, although he did not accept the fully developed claims of papal supremacy put forward by the papal reformers, and especially by Gregory VII (1073–85). Thus there was no inconsistency in Lanfranc taking the role, when he became archbishop of Canterbury (1070–89), which St Dunstan had performed in the court of Edgar: he guided, advised the king, led the reformers in the Anglo-Norman Church; but governance lay still in William's hands, and Lanfranc did not dispute William's right to choose bishops and abbots, so long as he chose men who were suitable. When they first met, Lanfranc was prior of the fervent, recently founded abbey of Bec; in 1063 William made him abbot of St Étienne, Caen, a house he had himself founded; in 1070 he made him archbishop of Canterbury. The friendship lasted beyond the grave; it was Lanfranc who put into force the Conqueror's dying wish and anointed and crowned William Rufus. Their association reveals the characters of both men. They were strong, clear-headed, masterful, loved efficiency and good order; they trusted in themselves, were born to rule. In addition Lanfranc was an Italian, a scholar, a monk, a man of sophisticated education and outlook; William was a soldier, illiterate, a man of the camp, used to hunting and burning and plundering. In their temperaments two very different worlds met in a strange, but firm alliance.

In early days this friendship had suffered a dramatic shock; Lanfranc denounced William's marriage as a sin. The duke expelled him from Normandy, and laid waste some of Bec's estates. But as he was setting out to leave the duchy, Lanfranc met the duke by accident, won a hearing from him, and was reconciled; in return he helped to plead William's cause to the pope, and eventually the pope confirmed the marriage.

The marriage was forbidden by the pope as early as 1049; it was solemnized none the less by 1051; it was eventually confirmed in 1059, on condition that husband and wife joined to found two abbeys, the Abbaye-aux-hommes for monks and the Abbaye-aux-dames for nuns, St Étienne and La Trinité at Caen. The two abbeys still stand, splendid monuments of their founders, at either end of the town; they even survived the devastation of the Second World War, which swept the town clear between them. But we do not know precisely why the pope forbade the marriage or exacted so heavy a price; nor do we know why William was so persistent, so loyal to his betrothed against such odds. The medieval Church forbade third cousins (and sometimes sixth) to marry, and this produced many tangles, sometimes overcome by dispensation, sometimes by defiance of authority. It was not difficult to break the law out of ignorance; nor to invoke the law to end an unwanted marriage. In the early eleventh century the French royal family were involved in a sensational difficulty on this account, and it has been alleged that it was for this reason that Henry I of France, to avoid all danger of consanguinity, married a Russian princess. So far as we know, William and Matilda were not blood relations; but the prohibition extended to certain types of affinity, that is to relationships by marriage. The tangled skein of their affinity is best avoided. What is clear is that it was not so much the technical objection as William's flagrant disobedience which incensed the papacy and Lanfranc; and it was this which made the path of reconciliation so difficult and the penance so heavy.

The marriage was celebrated by 1051. It is highly improbable that any romantic motive had led William, or his father-in-law, to take the step, although it is quite probable that real affection quickly grew between the parties and stiffened William's obstinacy in the years which followed. The whole story illustrates William's firmness: once he made up his mind, he could not be shifted. He was the most obstinate of men. But there was also policy in his marriage, as in everything he did. He needed a firm and reliable ally; and although Count Baldwin of Flanders does not seem to have given him much military aid in the 1050s, the alliance greatly strengthened the position of both parties. It was to be a vital condition of William's success in 1066. It is possible, too, that it had a closer connection with William's English ambition, since Matilda, unlike William himself, was descended from King Alfred.

When did William first think of winning the English crown? How did he come to conceive that it was a practical possibility? These are the central problems of his career. If Matilda was desirable as a princess of English royal descent, then he had conceived the idea before 1049; and there may be some truth in the stories which tell how Edward the Confessor as an exile had promised the succession to his throne to the young duke. But it is not likely that Edward himself took any such notion at all seriously; he had no strong expectation of the English throne, so far as we can tell, before 1042, and William was then fifteen at the most. In 1051, however, Edward evidently took the idea very seriously. He placed a Norman in the key position as archbishop and himself (it seems) designated William as his successor (see pp. 27–8); and William paid his cousin a state visit. Political events in England rapidly transformed the project; the Norman influence was ousted; the house of Godwine was restored. Edward gave thought to his English relations. But it is abundantly clear that William never forgot what he regarded as his right to the English throne. He had many difficulties; France and Anjou continued to attack him; he faced the papal ban on his marriage; Edward, to all appearance, had changed his mind. In due course some of the difficulties disappeared. In 1057 Henry I's last invasion was decisively beaten at Varaville; in 1060 both Henry I and Geoffrey of Anjou died; Baldwin of Flanders became regent; in 1063 William completed the conquest of Maine. The situation in France was now extraordinarily favourable. In 1064, by a stroke of fortune still wholly inexplicable, his chief rival for the English throne fell into his hands. Harold set sail from Chichester harbour; the wind blew him to the coast of Ponthieu. The count of Ponthieu captured him, but surrendered him to William, who treated him as an honoured guest. The whole story is most vividly portrayed in the Bayeux Tapestry, and it culminates in the famous scene in which Harold is made to swear an oath to William on the relics of Bayeux Cathedral. This story is full of difficulties; not least because the Tapestry does not explain the motive for Harold's embarkation nor the nature of the oath he swore. Other sources say that he was sent by Edward on embassy to William and blown out of course. If so, Harold acted very imprudently, or else William took excessive advantage of him. An alternative story, that he set out on a pleasure cruise, seems even more improbable. There can be little doubt that William exacted an oath that Harold would help him to the English crown; and it seems highly likely that in exacting this oath William was taking unscrupulous advantage of having Harold in his power. (See pp. 27–8).

It is possible, but not certain, that Edward himself still wished William to be his successor. It is clear that William had few if any other supporters among the English leaders. At the end of 1065 Harold's brother Tostig lost his earldom of Northumbria and went into exile. Although this was a blow to the house of Godwine, it seems to have strengthened Harold's chances of the throne. England was in dangerous confusion; Harold of Norway and William of Normandy threatened it from without; King Edward was dying. It is scarcely to be wondered at that the earls and thegns felt that Harold, the under-king, must succeed; and that they overruled any scruples Harold may have felt and the personal feelings of the king. In January 1066

Harold succeeded, and an able warrior and an anointed king held England in a strong grip. William's chances seemed slender, definitely inferior to those of both the Harolds. Nor does even his devoted chaplain and biographer, William of Poitiers, hide the fact that many Normans thought 'the enterprise too difficult, far beyond the strength of Normandy'. But William swept all difficulties aside. The Bayeux Tapestry pictures the preparations for the campaign: cutting trees, making boats, gathering weapons. Equally vital were the preparations it does not show us: the diplomacy which left William free to desert his duchy, and gave him in addition very substantial reinforcements and mercenaries from many parts of northern France, in particular from Brittany and Flanders. His immense energy bore wonderful fruit: a great army was collected, with a sufficient fleet of transports; his French neighbours were quiescent, Germany and Denmark squared; the pope was prevailed on to send a banner to bless the enterprise. William went to oust a perjured usurper, to free the see of Canterbury from the intruder Stigand, condemned by successive popes for holding the archbishopric while his predecessor, the Norman removed in 1052, still lived. His leading counsellors continued to argue with him, pointing out the wealth and military and naval resources of Harold. They might as well have argued with the Matterhorn.

William's strangest ally was the weather. A contrary wind kept him in Normandy throughout the late summer of 1066, seeming to frustrate his designs. Meanwhile, Harold's resources were being steadily spent in watching the Channel for an attack. In September he was forced to disband his forces; in the same month Harold Hardrada swooped down on the Yorkshire coast, landed a large army and defeated the northern earls and the northern militia. Harold of England was drawn away from the south. On 25 September Harold and his army destroyed the Norwegians and killed Harold Hardrada and Tostig at the battle of Stamford Bridge. On 27 September the wind changed, and William was able to land his army, or at least a substantial part of it, in England. Like Agamemnon avenging the insult to Helen, so William of Poitiers tells us, he came to claim the crown that was his; like Xerxes, he built a bridge of ships which united Normandy and England. Or, if we prefer Freeman's vision of the event, the mighty Norman came to destroy the noblest of the English, 'the hero and the martyr of our native freedom'. When he leapt out of his ship at Pevensey, he slipped and covered his hands with English sand or mud. 'You've got a grip on the soil of England, duke,' said the knight next to him, 'and will soon be king.'

William was king sooner than anyone could reasonably have expected. On 14 October the Norman army, marching north from

Hastings, came on the English on the edge of the great forest known as the Weald. Harold had come south with great speed, and marched to meet William with only a small army. It was a very rare event for a king to be killed in battle in the eleventh or twelfth centuries. Yet Harold of Norway fell at Stamford Bridge and Harold of England at Hastings. It is hard to understand why Harold offered battle so soon, before he had had time to collect his full forces; equally hard to understand why he allowed himself to be killed. William's strokes of fortune continued. Even so, the battle was very hard-fought, and the campaign by no means over at its end. The English occupied a small hill, with the forest covering their rear, and dismounted (as was perhaps their normal practice) to face the attack of William's archers and cavalry. All day long the Normans mounted one attack after another. For some hours the English front stood firm. Then the Normans, retreating from an attack, fell into confusion, and some of the English broke ranks to attack them. The Normans rallied and cut down their pursuers; then attacked, and twice feigned a confused retreat, on both occasions drawing the English to follow them. By now the English front was seriously weakened, and soon after, in another major attack, Harold himself was killed. As the sun went down the English fled; and although the Normans did themselves much damage in pursuing the English down a steep slope in gathering dusk, this sudden change of fortune could not help the beaten English.

The English leaders were still not inclined to submit. They thought of making Edgar the Ætheling king. William meanwhile marched slowly on London, sweeping through Sussex, Surrey and Hertfordshire in a great figure-of-eight. He laid the countryside waste as he went, to leave no one in any doubt what it meant to cross him. After a few weeks, the English leaders submitted; and on Christmas Day 1066 he was anointed and crowned in Westminster Abbey.

The adventure was complete; and an astonishing adventure it was. One might think that William's childhood would have taught him caution, as it taught him to be firm and ruthless. But as in the case of his marriage, a desperate obstinacy, mingled perhaps with a kind of imaginative vision, overcame everything else. This is surprising enough; what is even more surprising is the adaptability with which he grew into the job of being king of England. We cannot pause to study this process. He conquered England, and gave the lands of the thegns who fell at Hastings or rebelled against him, and above all the personal possessions of the house of Godwine, to his Norman supporters. In 1069–70 there was a great rebellion in the midlands and the north; William put it down by the familiar methods, with much firmness and devastation. Yet more land fell into his hands. By the end of his reign all but a handful of the Saxon thegns had been replaced by Norman lords; only the greater churches remained in possession of the lands they had held in 1066. No doubt there was much rough justice, and plain injustice, in this vast rearrangement. But it was put through; and at the very end of his reign, in the Domesday Survey, he took stock of what had been achieved, what was still to be done, how England was peopled, what its manors were worth. So large, so complete a survey was unparalleled at this time. It issued in two stout volumes still preserved in the Public Record Office. The first, which covers most of England, is mainly written in a single hand, probably English, corrected by another hand, probably Norman. Perhaps we may see in the corrector the hand of the mastermind, the man who worked out the detailed organization of this elaborate and impressive book. In 2001, it now seems likely that, though the survey was set on foot in 1086, the two volumes were composed after the accession of William II in 1087 – and that volume I, covering all but East Anglia, was the work of a northern scribe of English origin linked to Durham, working under the direction of William II's favourite servant, Ranulf Flambard, later duly rewarded with the bishopric of Durham.[131] But it is still abundantly clear that the survey was the work of William I. He planned it at the Christmas Court at Gloucester at the end of 1085; and we can imagine the ageing king portrayed for us by William of Malmesbury, tall, immensely stout, with a fine presence, a head going bald in front, and a stern, almost ferocious expression, presiding and directing the discussion of the project. Even if written after his death, the book is a monument to him as eloquent as the Abbaye-aux-hommes. On 9 September 1087, aged about sixty, the king died. In his later years his relations with his French neighbours had deteriorated. The French royal commanders had been plundering Normandy from Mantes. The Conqueror fell on Mantes and burned it; but as the flames rose his horse stumbled, he was thrown heavily against the iron pommel of his saddle, and he received an injury from which he never recovered.

Of most great medieval kings we have a variety of conflicting portraits: their enemies reviled them, their friends flattered them. The conflicting views which surrounded, and still surround the mercurial personality of William's younger contemporary, the Emperor Henry IV, are a dramatic example of this. But from friend and foe alike there emerges much the same portrait of William: massive, impressive, with the strength and gauntness of a great Alpine crag, and almost as inhuman. We can indeed penetrate to many human traits: his passionate

131 For the most recent studies, see Roffe 2000, esp. pp. 73–4 and nn.

desire to be king of England, his devotion to his wife, his warm alliance with Lanfranc, his love of hunting, his fondness for building large stone abbeys and castles. 'But he was too relentless', wrote an English chronicler, 'to care though all might hate him.'[132] Relentless he undoubtedly was; he conquered by fire and sword, and ruled by fear. He was just and discerning, and the punishments he meted out were not savage by the standards of the day, save to those who interfered with his hunting. But he was a hard man, a stark man; and although he was far more predictable, more honest, more honourable than Henry IV of Germany, Henry still has the power to bewitch us by his charm, while William still inspires us only with fear. No doubt this sense of inhuman remoteness is partly due to the accidents of time, partly to the kind of face William felt bound to present to the world. A strong ruler often makes himself appear more fearless, more granite-like, than he really is. One certainly sees a little behind the screen in the obituary notice interpolated into an early copy of William of Jumièges, *Acts of the Norman Dukes*. The author (writing about 1100) took passages from Einhard's *Life of Charlemagne* and the 'Astronomer's' *Life of Louis the Pious*, and adapted them to William and to 1087 – not always accurately. He tells of William's deathbed, of his worries about the future, his floods of tears as he prayed for divine mercy, of the immense effort needed to soften his heart against his eldest son, Robert, who had rebelled against him, how he made an inventory of his treasures and arranged their disposal to churches, to the poor, to his sons – and in particular his crown, sword and gilt and bejewelled sceptre to William, his second son; finally the author looks back over the great man's career, notes his wisdom, his inflexibility of purpose, his fearlessness. He then gives a famous description of William, which is, however, based in almost every detail on Einhard's description of Charlemagne, so that we cannot be sure how much of it was really appropriate to William. And the monk goes on to describe how William was buried in the Abbaye-aux-hommes at Caen, and how his son William raised a tomb covered with silver and gold over his grave.[133]

Very often a man's true face is reflected in his family. The Conqueror's fidelity to his wife, and the loyalty and devotion of his second son, speak to his credit; but one is bound to say that on the whole his children present the least attractive side of him. England has had few kings as unprepossessing as William Rufus and Henry I.

---

132 *ASC*, trans. Garmonsway, p. 221.
133 *William of Jumièges*, ed. E. Van Houts, I, pp. lxiii–v, II, 184–91; Engels 1973. One has most confidence in his descriptions when he departs from his models.

13

The Conqueror's Sons

On 9 September 1087 the Conqueror died, leaving three sons to dispute his inheritance. It was generally assumed that the eldest, Robert, would become duke of Normandy; the second, William, was already at the coast waiting to cross to England to seize his father's crown; the youngest, Henry, had silver but no land, yet wit and luck were in the end to make him the most powerful of the three.

The younger William, shorter than his father, but equally stout, red-faced (hence his name), with piercing eyes and stammering speech, carried with him to England a letter to Lanfranc from his father saying that William was the Conqueror's choice for the English throne. Within three weeks he had been crowned in Westminster Abbey by Archbishop Lanfranc, the primate of All Britain, his father's most trusted counsellor. The speed of his accession and the support of Lanfranc did not make his passage entirely clear; twice he had to face a major rebellion, and relations with his elder brother, who was not wholly reconciled to the loss of the better part of his father's dominions, were never easy. But Rufus had the strength and the ruthlessness of a successful monarch, and as the years passed, his grip on the throne tightened and his taste for adventure on the Continent increased. In 1096 Duke Robert went on the First Crusade, and mortgaged what was left of his duchy to King William. William's ambitions grew. In 1100 he boasted that he would spend Christmas in Poitiers. But on 2 August, while hunting in the New Forest, he was struck by an arrow, and died forthwith.

'A few of the peasants carried his corpse to the cathedral at Winchester on a horse-drawn wagon, with blood dripping from it the whole way', writes William of Malmesbury. 'There in the cathedral crossing, under the tower, he was interred, in the presence of many great men, mourned by few. Next year there followed the tower's collapse. I forbear to tell the opinions which were held on this event, lest I seem to believe in trifles – especially since it would have collapsed in any case, even if he had not been buried there, because it was badly built.'[134]

William Rufus, in popular esteem, was not the sort of man a self-respecting cathedral would wish to house. He was not popular with the Church, and he has rarely been popular with modern historians. Recently he has received more kindly, and more discerning, treatment from Professor Barlow; but commonly he has been castigated with a ferocity akin to his own: 'A foul incarnation of selfishness in its most abhorrent form, the enemy of God and man' is how he appeared in Stubbs's *Constitutional History* (1874); to Dr A.L. Poole (1951) he was 'from the moral standpoint... probably the worst king that has occupied the throne of England'.[135]

Rufus thus takes his place as one of the three or four villainous kings of medieval English history; and it is curious that no one so far has taken the trouble to whitewash him. Societies have sprung up to protect the memory of Richard III; grave doubts have been cast on the traditional view of King John; but William Rufus, though not friendless, has not caught the popular imagination – the rubble still buries him.[136] We shall see in a moment that Rufus's character was not all black, and that his better side has been observed by a number of historians, as it was hinted at by some of his contemporaries. But the comparison with Richard III is worth a moment's thought. Popular attention has been attracted to Richard III, first by the sensational mystery surrounding the death of his nephews, and then by the discovery that some professional historians have been a little incautious in accepting the Tudor legend of the last of the Yorkists. The excitement of the detective story is enhanced by the sport of shooting at the experts. The experts have been forced to admit (what many of them had been saying for years in any case) that he was not as bad as he has been painted. They have also made clear that many of the mysteries surrounding Richard are mysteries still. This is not to say that he could have been a saint. No one doubts (so far as I know) that he declared his brother's children bastards and seized their throne. To his extreme defenders this merely illustrates his single-minded devotion in the pursuit of truth; to most of us it seems as vile as any of the charges which cannot be proved.

William Rufus was brought to public notice in 1931 in rather a different way. It is not alleged that he was a Christian saint, but it was

---

134   William of Malmesbury, *Gesta Regum*, I, 574 (MSS CB) (my translation).
135   Stubbs 1874, p. 328; Poole 1951, p. 154. For all that follows relating to the manner of William II's death, see Hollister 1986 and above, p. 2.
136   But he has had much more sympathetic treatment in Barlow 1983.

asserted that he was not a Christian at all; and Dr Margaret Murray argued that he adhered to an exciting underground religion of the witches, that his death was the ritual murder of the king by fellow devil-worshippers. 'Walter, do thou justice, according to these things which thou hast heard.' 'So I will, my lord', Walter Tirel answered, took an arrow from the king, and subsequently shot him with it.[137]

If the line of revision is different from that of Richard III, some of the ingredients of the case are nevertheless remarkably similar. Ingenious minds are attracted to Richard by the mystery of the princes in the Tower; to Rufus by the mystery of his death. The attempt to whitewash Richard involves contradicting a quantity of the evidence about his reign. The attempt to attach Rufus to an underground sect forces us to explain why this sect is never mentioned by the chroniclers – in other words it forces us to rewrite all the contemporary accounts of Rufus. There are two mysteries here, the mystery of his faith and the mystery of his death. Both are worth pursuing.

'The spirit of God takes up its abode in a human being, usually the king, who thereby becomes the giver of fertility to all his kingdom. When the divine man begins to show signs of age he is put to death lest the spirit of God should also grow old and weaken like its human container.... In some places the time of death was indicated by signs of approaching age, such as grey hair or loss of teeth; in other places a term of years was fixed, usually seven or nine.... That the sacrifice was repeatedly consummated within the historic period of our own country and of France depends upon evidence which would be accepted if it were offered in respect of an Oriental or African religion.' The study of comparative religion has had its aberrations, but for my part I do not believe that its modern students accept such evidence as this.

Dr Murray's account of Rufus's character – 'a dutiful son,... a faithful friend,... recklessly courageous, lavishly openhanded...' – has much truth in it; and she is right to say that his savagery was of the period, that his character alone does not explain the enmity of the chroniclers. She is right, too, in attributing this enmity to his anti-clericalism, his oppression of the Church, and to his blasphemies. But her explanations of the roots of his attitude to the Church and of his death dwell in fantasy.

A new historical theory very frequently originates in a puzzle. A scholar reading the given account of an event or course of events finds some elements in the story which worry him; the effort to resolve his

---

137   This and the quotations which follow are from Murray 1931, pp. 160–1, 162, 165, 167–8.

perplexity leads him to revise the accepted account. If we wish to understand the roots of an original theory, we shall be well advised to look for the perplexities which started the new train of thought. Before Frank Barlow's *William Rufus* (1983), most substantial study of William II was E.A. Freeman's *Reign of William Rufus* (1882). 'Freeman, having no anthropological knowledge,' writes Dr Murray, 'is entirely biased by the ecclesiastical point of view, and acknowledges himself totally unable to understand the character of Rufus or to explain many of the events of his reign.' It is true that an atmosphere of mystery is made to shroud some of the events of the reign, and that there is a certain hesitancy in his portrait of the king. Partly this was due to his technique of writing: he liked drama, mingled with a touch of mystery; and at the same time he never suppressed any of the evidence, however worthless, so that the sharp edges of contemporary narratives were sometimes blunted by accounts from later and even legendary sources. He was determined never to waver in the pursuit of truth; he was equally determined not to be untrue to the moral standards of his Church and his age. Stubbs was still an Oxford Professor when Freeman wrote, and his own version of Rufus was less than ten years old. They were close friends, and Freeman, a deeply sensitive man, hung on Stubbs's approbation. One suspects that Freeman felt bound to live up to his friend's denunciation; and yet he felt – as Stubbs himself had indicated – that there was a better side to William. In one respect only did Freeman go beyond the evidence. Rufus never married, and apparently had no children; and yet his private life is said to have shocked even his younger brother. This has led to the view that Rufus was homosexual. There is no precise evidence in support of it; conditions of his age and his life make it perfectly possible. But only under special conditions would this explain the absence of children, and historians who have followed Freeman in saying 'that no mistresses ... are mentioned or hinted at' are in error. It is true that most descriptions of Rufus's private life are generalized. But they all accuse him of licence. If no children are recorded the probable explanation is either that the king could not beget children or that none grew up.

This final touch makes Freeman's Rufus a remote, untouchable man, difficult to fathom; fundamentally depraved, and yet not lacking in good qualities. He struts in a canvas from the days of Freeman's youth: dark, stormy, impenetrable. Similarly with the accident which led to Rufus's death. Freeman quite rightly saw that there is conflict in the sources; that we cannot reconstruct precisely what happened. By gathering all the rumours which floated round the event, Freeman has immensely increased the atmosphere of mystery; and in doing so, unwittingly, invited other historians to further speculation and Dr Murray to declare that the accepted story made no sense.

The two fullest accounts name the same human agent. William of Malmesbury's version (c.1125) goes like this. After dinner on 2 August 1100 the king rode into the New Forest with a few companions to hunt. The party split up in search of deer, and the king was left alone with Walter Tirel. As evening was drawing in, a stag passed near them, and the king shot an arrow at it, but failed to kill; it fled westward, the king shielding his eyes to watch it disappearing into the setting sun. Then another stag passed by, and in a flash Walter had loosed another arrow. The arrow struck the king, who died immediately, without a word.

Orderic Vitalis (c.1135) tells a similar story. After recording portents, he takes the king swiftly to his doom. 'He got up, mounted his horse and sped into the wood. Count Henry (his brother) and William de Breteuil and other great men were there; they went into the woodland, and the huntsmen were scattered in their various positions. The king and Walter de Poix [i.e. Tirel] established themselves with a few companions in the wood, and waited eagerly for the prey, with weapons ready. Suddenly a beast ran between them; the king jumped back from his place, and Walter let an arrow fly. The arrow shaved the hair on the animal's back, sped on and wounded the king standing beyond. He soon fell to the ground, and died – *proh dolor!* – instantly.'[138]

In its main lines, both chroniclers tell the same story; and it is clear that this was the story most widely believed, although other versions give minor variants of it. But the eminent Abbot Suger of St Denis, in his *Life* of King Louis VI of France (c.1144), says that he had himself often heard Walter Tirel deny that he was in the same part of the wood as the king that day, or saw him at all during the hunt; this denial is also mentioned as a solemn protestation by Tirel on his deathbed in John of Salisbury's *Life of St Anselm* (mid–late twelfth century).[139] John adds that many thought William had shot the arrow himself. At the end of the twelfth century Gerald of Wales tells a similar story of accidental shooting, but names a different bowman. No early source attributes his end specifically to human malice; Eadmer says that there was dispute how he actually died – whether the arrow struck him, or he stumbled and fell on it. The *Anglo-Saxon Chronicle* (not later than 1121, and perhaps much earlier) says simply

138 Orderic, VI, 290 (my translation).
139 Suger, p. 12; John of Salisbury, *Vita S. Anselmi*, col. 1031.

that he 'was killed with an arrow while hunting by one of his men. . . . He was hated by almost all his people and abhorrent to God. This his end testified, for he died in the midst of his sins without repentance or any atonement for his evil deeds.'[140] This might be taken to imply assassination; but it is plain that what his end testified in the author's mind was God's judgement; the human agent was of little consequence.

If William of Malmesbury was right in saying that the king and Walter were alone, only Walter could have told the story. Yet Walter firmly and frequently denied it. The contradiction is baffling. Regicide has always been a serious matter; but in this case one might have expected that if the common story was true, Tirel would have been tolerably happy to be (in general estimation) God's instrument in the removal of a wicked man. If it was an accident, we should be inclined to believe that Tirel was not the agent. But what if it was deliberate? We must not jump too hastily to this conclusion; no contemporary accuses Tirel of murder; accident was the official story, widely believed.

Hunting accidents have been frequent in every century, and an accident it may have been. But we have to consider two alternative possibilities, witchcraft and murder. First, let us look at Dr Murray's remarkable version of the story. 'It is clear that his death was expected, and the account of his last hours indicates that he knew his time had come. He could not sleep during the previous night, and he ordered lights to be brought into his bed-chamber and made his chamberlains enter and talk with him. . . .' Quite a saga surrounds the event. The earliest source tells us that it was known immediately (by angelic messenger) to St Anselm in France. William of Malmesbury describes a dream the king had had that night, and then how a monk's dream was related to him: 'He is a monk,' said William, 'monklike he dreams for money; give him a hundred shillings.' And so the legend of strange portents grew.

To the modern reader all this sounds very suspicious; he wishes to rationalize, to explain. The cunning of Dr Murray's explanation is that it does, indeed, explain the warnings and prognostications, even the king's dreams. Everybody knew he was going to die! Unfortunately, her explanation involves a number of assumptions for which there is no evidence, and which are wildly improbable.

First of all, let us see what precisely needs to be explained. The stories are told as marvels, as portents of divine grace and divine judgement: St Anselm knew because St Anselm was the sort of man to whom angels brought messages. William had dreams because God

140 ASC, trans. Garmonsway, pp. 235–6.

does not leave the victims of his judgement wholly without warning. William's death made a tremendous impression, not because of any suspicion of human foul play, nor of any suspicion of human sacrifice; but because it was seen as God's judgement on a wicked man. It made all the more impression because it was generally thought to be an accident, at the human level. In the prime of life, at the height of his power, the great man was struck down.

It is not the aura of mystery but the plain fact of the king's death which needs explaining. The stories which surrounded Rufus's death were the normal currency of the time. Similar tales grew up round other notable events in a similar fashion. Prognostications of this kind are common in the literature of the age. The legends which surround Thomas Becket's end are even more remarkable, because we know how swiftly they grew and how widely they were accepted. This parallel did not escape Dr Murray; Becket, too, was a divine victim. But so much has to be explained away to make a case about Becket, that it would be tedious to pursue its contortions.

The stories which surrounded Rufus's death underline the fact that men regarded his end as a divine judgement, and this is a part of the explanation for the unfavourable treatment he immediately received from the chroniclers. The Church was mainly hostile to Rufus before 1100, and with good reason.

To this hostility among ecclesiastical chroniclers there is one exception. The monks of Battle Abbey (founded by his father on the site of the battle of Hastings) remembered him as a benefactor; and it is highly probable that he put on a sound foundation endowments which his father had left somewhat precarious.[141] He was also a benefactor of St Étienne at Caen, his father's other great foundation. A monastic chronicler was inclined to base his judgement of a king on his treatment of his own house and its revenues, and this is certainly reflected in the attitude of Eadmer, historian and biographer of St Anselm, archbishop of Canterbury, and of a version of the *Anglo-Saxon Chronicle* which also comes from Canterbury. For most of his reign, on one pretext or another, Rufus was enjoying the income of the see and of the monks of Canterbury, and keeping the monks themselves on a shoe-string. This was characteristic of him. Like many feudal leaders, he regarded churches primarily as pieces of property. Anselm begged him to allow abbots to be elected to the vacant abbeys which he was 'despoiling'. 'What is that to you? Are the abbeys not mine?' was the king's retort.[142]

---

141 Brooke 1999, pp. 148–50.
142 Eadmer, *Historia Novorum*, pp. 49–50; see Brooke 1999, pp. 139–40.

Rufus owed his crown to the support of Archbishop Lanfranc, and we are told that he behaved himself, and kept his promises of good government, while Lanfranc lived. In 1089 Lanfranc died, and William settled down to enjoy his revenues. Lanfranc had spent a number of his best years as monk and prior of Bec; and after his death there was no one in the Anglo-Norman Church of higher prestige than his friend and disciple Anselm, abbot of Bec. Anselm was one of those rare personalities who was admired and loved, even by his enemies. He was tricked into visiting England in 1092–3, even though he knew that his name was on everyone's lips as the next archbishop. Very opportunely the king fell ill, and thought he was dying. Immediately he offered Anselm the archbishopric, and pressed him very urgently to take it. He had conceived the idea that his illness was a judgement for keeping the archbishopric vacant, and would only pass if he could fill the vacant see with the saintly Anselm. Anselm had no wish for the office, nor was he superstitious; he told the king he would recover in any case. 'Do you know what you are at?' he is reported to have said to the bishops who were urging him to accept. 'You plan to place an untamed bull and a feeble old sheep in the same plough under a single yoke. And what will come of it? The untameable ferocity of the bull will haul it through thorns and thickets, and so lacerate it that it will become utterly useless. . . .'[143]

The king recovered, but kept his word to Anselm, and insisted on making him archbishop. The arrangement, however, was satisfactory to neither. The king seems to have felt that he had been tricked into the appointment, and saddled with a saint; Anselm found it impossible to keep on peaceful terms with William without impossible compromises on matters of principle. Eventually Anselm asked for leave to go to the pope for his pallium, the symbol of his office as archbishop. There were at the time two men claiming to be pope in Europe, owing to the circumstances of the dispute between Pope Gregory VII and the Emperor Henry IV in the previous decade. Officially, no pope was recognized in England, a situation evidently satisfactory to William II. From which pope, he asked, was Anselm demanding his pallium? – to which Anselm, who had been at Bec when the schism arose, and had already made his choice with the rest of the Norman Church, replied 'from Urban'. The king objected that he had made no decision, and that the custom of himself and his father was that no one in his realm might accept a man as pope without his permission; and whoever wished to take this prerogative from him was trying to snatch off his crown.

143   Eadmer, *Historia Novorum*, p. 36.

In the end Anselm won, and Urban was recognized; but the disputes between them grew, and when he realized that William intended to persecute him come what might, he withdrew from the country and spent the rest of the reign between the hospitality of the papal court and of the archbishop of Lyon. Rufus's excommunication was threatened, but put off at Anselm's request; then Urban died. When Rufus asked what his successor was like, he was told that in some ways he was like Anselm. With an oath the king burst out 'his paparchy won't get on top of me this time; I've won my liberty and I shall do what I like'. 'But he did not live long to enjoy it; before a year had passed he was struck down by death....'[144]

There is sufficient in this to explain the attitude of the chroniclers, and especially of those who admired or served St Anselm. They hated the king, but they enjoyed telling stories about him. His quick temper, his ready wit, and his characteristic oaths, 'God's face!', 'By the face of Lucca' (a representation of Christ's face), made his exploits and utterances pass from mouth to mouth. We can see the picture of Rufus as a character growing even in Eadmer's history, the first edition of which was written within a dozen years of Rufus's death. Some of the stories may be apocryphal, but the picture they reveal is probably true enough. Rufus was blasphemous, grasping and avaricious; cared not a rap for the Church save when he thought he was dying; thoroughly enjoyed shocking his clerical associates – though perhaps not much more than they enjoyed retailing his depravities; in sum, an engaging scoundrel.

There is no case here for whitewash. In his dealings with the Church Rufus was violent and unscrupulous. The question thus arises whether he was a Christian at all. To Dr Murray he was a devil-worshipper, as we have seen; but her positive evidence is of the most scrappy and circumstantial kind. It is very likely that there were devil-worshippers in the eleventh century: we have evidence of various kinds of witchcraft, and the Luciferians, whose rites were described in detail in the late twelfth century, may well have existed a century earlier. But the Luciferians lived in Germany, and we have no detailed evidence of black magic or devil-worship in the countries in which William Rufus spent his days. To fill this gap, Dr Murray draws on sixteenth- and seventeenth-century evidence. It is from much later sources that she produces the evidence of doctrine and ritual on which her reconstruction is based.

Her theory, in fact, can be dismissed as fantasy; but we are still left with the problem of Rufus's beliefs. It is extremely unlikely that he

144 Eadmer, *Historia Novorum*, p. 116.

was an intellectual agnostic. Under pressure of illness, he immediately tried to propitiate God. He treated God as he treated his elder brother, with disrespect, as often as he dared. Every age of faith has its blasphemers, and Rufus was an extreme example of a phenomenon probably commoner than we realize: the man who accepted the basic tenets of the Church, but with distaste; who enjoyed shrewd hits at its more intolerant, priggish or portentous aspects; who enjoyed blasphemy in open court as well as in the comparative privacy of the camp and the hunting field.

Late in his reign, William spent some time in the capital of Normandy, Rouen. Eadmer tells the story of how the Jews of Rouen bribed the king to order some of their number, who had recently been converted to Christianity, to return to their native Judaism. He tells the moving story of how one Jewish boy was converted by a vision of St Stephen the Protomartyr. His father went to the king and offered him 60 marks (£40 in the currency of the day) if he would compel him to return to his old allegiance. The king gladly embarked on this enterprise, and summoned the boy to him. 'Your father complains that you became a Christian without his licence. If so, I command you to obey his will without any prevarication and return to Judaism at once.' The young man replied: 'Lord king, I think you are joking.' William was angry: 'Would I joke with you, son of the dung? Go back and do as I say double quick, or, by the Face of Lucca, I'll have your eyes put out.' The young man stood his ground, rebuked the king for his sentiments, and was thrown out of the court. The king was rewarded for his efforts with half the promised fee.[145]

The trappings of the story are partly comic, partly repulsive. It is meant to illustrate the king's cynicism and blasphemies, and very probably does so. But it also seems to indicate something else: a sense that the Church was not just or honourable in its treatment of the Jews. William was not an advanced free thinker, still less a student of comparative religion. But behind the cynical and blasphemous exterior lay a shrewd mind, a ready wit, even a code of some sort – to the narrow circle of his knights he was generous and honourable; and also (as he showed in his illness) a deep vein of superstition.

In the eyes of many contemporaries, the death of William Rufus was a divine judgement. This explains the portentous atmosphere, the prodigies, some of the mystery which surrounded it. For these we need no esoteric solution. But at a more mundane level the mystery remains: how did he die? He died in a hunting accident, and an

145   Eadmer, *Historia Novorum*, pp. 100–1.

accident it probably was – though some modern historians (myself included) have suspected a conspiracy in which William's younger brother and successor was involved. Henry was present at the hunting expedition. As soon as he heard of his brother's death, without waiting to see the body removed for burial, he turned his horse's head and galloped to Winchester, to secure the royal treasure. After a wrangle with William de Breteuil, a leading Norman baron, who pointed out that Henry's eldest brother was still alive, Henry was allowed to take over the treasure, and pass on to London. To those who objected that Robert was the rightful heir, he may have given the specious answer that he was 'born in the purple', born after his father had become king, and so had a better title.[146] This perhaps served some purpose for the moment, and he himself may well have believed in it; but essentially Henry became king by strong and forceful action. William II died on 2 August, on the 5th Henry was anointed and crowned king in Westminster Abbey by the bishop of London – Archbishop Anselm was still in exile. By this means he established himself as king *de facto*; he was the Lord's anointed, and would not be easy to unseat. In November he strengthened his title by marrying the Princess Edith or Matilda, daughter of St Margaret of Scotland, niece of Edgar the Ætheling, a descendant of Alfred and Cerdic.

The speed of Henry's seizure of the throne is very striking: it provokes the question whether all this could have been accomplished – in particular, whether he could have been crowned in Westminster three days after his brother died in Hampshire – if there had been no preparation, no nucleus of supporters formed. The question can hardly be answered; but Henry certainly had need of haste. Rufus died in the nick of time. In September their elder brother Robert returned from the Crusade; worse still, he brought a wife with him, and might reasonably be expected to have a legitimate heir. When Robert set off for the First Crusade, he made an arrangement with Rufus whereby each was the other's heir; of Henry no mention was made. If Robert had returned from the First Crusade before Rufus died, he might well have succeeded to the English throne. As it was, he made a nearly successful invasion, and retained strong support for

---

146   The doctrine was applied to Ethelred II by Eadmer in his *Life of St Dunstan*, written between 1095 and 1109 – that is, close to the date of Henry I's accession (*Dunstan*, p. 214); for the date see Southern 1963, p. 281 n. 2. William of Malmesbury, *Gesta Regum*, I, 708–9, written *c*.1125, makes it plain that the point had been applied (he seems to say, widely applied) to Henry I: 'while still an infant he was splendidly educated as everyone wished, because he alone of all William [I's] sons had been royally born, and the kingdom might seem to belong to him' (my translation: *ei regnum uideretur competere* is translated 'the throne seemed destined to be his' by Michael Winterbottom).

some years in the English kingdom. Henry might have hoped in earlier years that his brothers would die without legitimate heirs; but Robert's marriage seemed to make this somewhat remote. August 1100 might well seem his last real chance of securing the English throne; and it was singularly fortunate that the king should die not far from Winchester. This made it possible for Henry to seize the royal treasure and hurry straight on to Westminster accompanied by those barons and bishops who were prepared to support him. It is a strange coincidence that Rufus died in that month, and in that part of England.

Tirel's wife Alice was a Clare; his mother-in-law Rohesia was a Giffard. The leading figures of the great house of Clare, his brothers-in-law and overlords, were well patronized by Henry; one of them was made abbot of Ely this same year; a sister-in-law married Eudo *dapifer* (the Steward), one of Henry's firmest friends. One of Rohesia's brothers (so it seems) was instantly made earl of Buckingham; another of her brothers bishop of Winchester, the richest of all the English sees. Tirel himself immediately fled – even if not guilty, he was clearly suspected by Rufus's devoted knights. He did not suffer in the long run, and his family clearly benefited from the change of king. Tirel's gains appear to have been mainly, if not entirely, vicarious; and hardly suggest that he himself was at the heart of a conspiracy. But they may well suggest that he was the tool of his grand relations. Some of these family details were pointed out by J.H. Round.[147] They add little to the circumstantial evidence suggesting conspiracy for others were equally rewarded. Henry filled many bishoprics and abbeys in and after 1100: Rufus had made a practice of keeping them vacant and enjoying their revenues. Henry was naturally a good patron to barons who helped him: he needed supporters in 1100. Nor should one make too much of relationship by marriage as a factor in politics. The English baronage had a solid core of no more than 200 tenants-in-chief. The Church forbade any man to marry his third (and sometimes his sixth) cousin; and although this rule was often broken, it meant that marriage among the barons was widely spread; since it was not rare for a man to have two wives or a woman three husbands, a fair proportion of the baronage would inevitably have been connected by blood or by marriage to any baron suspected of shooting the fatal arrow. It need not necessarily be surprising, therefore, that clerks or barons so connected should be among those favoured by the king. But the Clares and Giffards were favoured, and favoured early, none the less.

147 Round 1895, pp. 468ff.

Six years later, after many anxieties, Henry met his elder brother Robert in pitched battle at Tinchebrai in Normandy, defeated him, took over his duchy and imprisoned him for life. A decisive battle was a rare event in this period; but even Tinchebrai could hardly have been decisive if Henry had behaved according to the normal code of the time. To imprison a great noble for life was rarely done; to imprison an elder brother almost never.

The nearest to a parallel comes from the north of Spain at the time when Henry was a child. We do not know how well informed a Norman count would be of the affairs of Christian Spain; but there are special reasons for thinking that this story would have been well known to Henry. A great part of Spain was still in Muslim hands, though the movement of reconquest was already under way. The leading Christian power was the kingdom, or empire, of León, which at one time or another included most of northern Spain. In 1065 Ferdinand I died, and according to custom his kingdom was divided between his three sons; Sancho took Castile, Alphonso León, Garcia Galicia. Presently the brothers fell out among themselves. In 1071 Sancho and Alphonso deposed Garcia and divided Galicia between them; in 1072 Alphonso was deposed and sent into exile to Toledo. Fortune's wheel, however, had not ceased turning, and on 7 October 1072 (when Henry was about four years old) Sancho was murdered. With the aid of his sister Urraca Alphonso was now able to return and become sole ruler of the empire; Garcia was temporarily removed to Muslim Seville. But Alphonso VI's accession was not free from difficulty. He was suspected of complicity in Sancho's murder, and made to swear an oath in solemn form by the nobles, led by the famous Rodrigo Diaz, the Cid. For this, it may be, Alphonso never forgave the Cid; their relations were never good thereafter, and the king-emperor refused to make use of the remarkable military talents of his famous subject. But Alphonso's throne was tolerably secure. To make all safe, Alphonso summoned Garcia to a conference in 1073 and then imprisoned him for life in the castle of Luna in León, where he died seventeen years later. Alphonso was free from competition by his brothers, and able to pass on an undivided domain – but he had no sons; so he passed his kingdom to his daughter, another Urraca (1109–26). Her reign was full of difficulties, but it showed that a lady could succeed to a throne.

The parallels to the career of Henry I are very striking: three brothers, one of them removed by sudden death, the other by imprisonment for life; a great inheritance united in a single hand; and a reign which ends with the inheritance being passed to a daughter. We have special reason to think that the early part of this story was known to his father. In or about 1072 two of the Spanish brothers competed for the hand of one of the Conqueror's daughters; a marriage was prevented by the lady's death.[148] In 1087, at the end of the Conqueror's life, when Henry was probably in attendance on him, William was offered Galicia by messengers from rebel nobles of that province. Nothing came of the proposal, but William and Henry doubtless meditated on the story which lay behind the offer.

If Henry were privy to a conspiracy to remove William Rufus, Alphonso's story would warn him of the need for caution. Alphonso was able to swear his innocence. But when Sancho was dead, Alphonso was undoubted heir of León. When William died, Henry's position, since he was still a younger brother, was much more doubtful; he could less afford to take risks. A breath of suspicion might have ruined his cause for ever. Spanish history contained sterner warnings of the danger of being suspected of fratricide. In 1076 Sancho of Navarre was murdered at the instigation of his brother Ramon; but Ramon did not succeed – he was rejected on account of his crime, and Navarre passed to the king of Aragon. In 1082 Ramon of Barcelona was murdered. His brother took over the government, although there was a son who could have succeeded. But he was proved guilty of complicity in Ramon's murder, was branded a fratricide, and eventually fled from Barcelona in 1096 under cover of the First Crusade.

These cases may have diverted Henry from fratricide; they would certainly make him most careful not to be found out. They show that fratricide (whether or not Henry was guilty of it) was by no means unknown among the kind of noblemen from whom William and Henry sprang.

On the whole, Henry I got a good press from the chroniclers of the day. In part this might be attributed to fear or hope of favour; in part to tact, since for example William of Malmesbury's *History* was dedicated (among other people) to Henry's most distinguished illegitimate son, Robert, earl of Gloucester. But these motives cannot be applied to writers like Abbot Suger, who wrote in Paris when Henry was safely dead, and who speaks warmly of a king who had never been a friend to his patron, King Louis. Nor do the chroniclers give the impression of fear or favour: several of them are frank about some of his weaknesses, all praise his virtues. God had endowed him, says Henry of Huntingdon, with the three gifts of wisdom, victory and riches; but these were offset by three vices, avarice, cruelty and lust.[149] His insatiable quest for money was

---

148 William of Poitiers, pp. 94–7 and nn.; Freeman 1867–79, IV, Appendix TT.
149 Henry of Huntingdon, pp. 698–701.

noted by several contemporaries, and has been revealed, quite starkly, from the official records of his exchequer (the Pipe Roll of 1130, the first exchequer account to survive). In this he followed the example of his father and his brother; nor was covetousness a rare vice among medieval kings and governments. What was striking was Henry's success in gathering and keeping treasure.

By his pious and popular first queen, Matilda, he had two children: the first, Matilda, outlived him; the second, William, died in the wreck of the White Ship in 1120. Besides these, he acknowledged upwards of twenty bastards, some, like Robert, earl of Gloucester, born before his marriage, many born while he was king, of a variety of mothers. Infidelity was far from rare in the circles in which Henry moved. He was unusual only in degree; and also, perhaps, in the generosity with which he acknowledged so many of his children. For some of them he seems to have cared deeply. But he never allowed any of them to imagine that he could succeed to England and Normandy. In 1118 Matilda died; in 1120 the sole male heir followed her; within three months Henry married again, but had no further legitimate children.

Thus far the accusations of avarice and lust; what of cruelty? As king, Henry was strong and ruthless, and not averse to savage punishment. The Conqueror is said to have abolished the death penalty, in preference for blinding and mutilation and other less fatal forms of punishment. Henry employed all these means. Thieves could be hanged; in 1124, forty-four of them were hanged in a day, and in the same year moneyers who issued false coin were mutilated – and in 1124–5 all the moneyers in England were mutilated without individual investigation of guilt or innocence. In later years, however, Henry became increasingly inclined, whether from avarice or humanity, to commute the more savage punishments for fines. The age was not squeamish, and Henry's agent in dealing with the moneyers was a bishop. His choice of penalties reveals, perhaps, no more than that he was particularly active, particularly unsqueamish, in meting out punishments which few seriously deplored. But the accusation of cruelty does not rest solely on these grounds. As a young man Henry had helped to suppress a revolt in Rouen, while assisting his brother Robert against his brother William. The final act came when Henry personally threw a wealthy citizen of Rouen, a leader in the revolt, from the battlements of the castle – or, as another chronicler has it, defenestrated him.[150] On another occasion two of his granddaughters (by his illegitimate daughter Juliana) were blinded by his permission

150   William of Malmesbury, *Gesta Regum*, I, 712–15; Orderic, IV, 226–7.

or on his orders. This was a case, quite literally, of an eye for an eye – they were hostages, being treated as their own father had treated the hostages for whom they had been exchanged – and Henry's grand-children must have been about as numerous as the English baronage. But it is clear that Henry was capable of real cruelty.

To the modern student, Henry is perhaps the most unattractive of his family. To his father's ruthlessness he added a strain of savagery – sufficient to make him feared, though not execrated by his contem-poraries. Rufus was open and generous; Henry had learned to keep his counsel, made much more show of conventional piety. Henry was sometimes generous: he bought many supporters by endowing them with baronies, and in some cases, most notably those of his son, Earl Robert, and his nephew, Count Stephen, an element of real affection seems to have entered into his generosity.[151] He does not seem to have refused responsibility for his children. He could somehow win men's trust, for he suffered very little from rebellion; but he also won their fear, and never lost the capacity for sudden, ruthless, effective action, or the strength of mind for extreme actions. 'His bodily frame was that of his family; thick-set and strongly made, of moderate height and inclining to fatness; but his black hair falling over his brow like that of Trajan, and the soft expression of his eyes, a contrast to the fierce look of Rufus, were points peculiar to himself': so Freeman, after William of Malmesbury and Orderic.[152] But his 'soft expression' does not deceive us; we still tremble before the lion of justice more than 800 years after his death.

Henry's cruelty helps us to answer the question, was he capable of planning his brother's death? We must not underestimate the serious-ness of the charge: a brother's murder, and the murder, furthermore, of his overlord. One can easily believe him capable of being privy to fratricide; less easily, perhaps, to treachery on the scale here involved. Perhaps one should allow something for the possibility that he ser-iously believed in his own claim to the throne. It is very hard for us to credit, but there are quite strong indications that Henry thought he and not William should be king.[153] This claim worked against Robert too. Like many kings whose own title was suspect, Henry was much concerned for his succession; and when all hope of a male heir failed, he tried to bind his barons by the strongest possible ties to his daughter Matilda. It is strange to us that a king who was not the obvious heir to his predecessor, whose elder brother was, indeed, still alive (Robert died in 1134), should have been so insistent on hereditary succession. His later years would have been far easier and more successful if he had settled for one of his nephews or even an illegitimate son; his heart seems to have been with them. This he refused to do; and his refusal is easier to understand if we take seriously the story that he himself claimed the throne as the eldest son 'born in the purple'.

Henry did not marry till after he became king. It is true that at that time his hand was not of high value in the marriage market, but his rapid marriage to a scion of the old English line after his accession seems premeditated. The effect, at least, was that all his legitimate children were 'born in the purple', and this may have strengthened the urgency of his wish for Matilda to succeed him. One could carry this speculation further, and say: if he had a brother's murder on his conscience, how much stronger would be the urge to establish the rule of porphyrogeniture, which made the murder of Rufus not an act of treachery but the removal of a blaspheming usurper.

Once again we are in the land of 'ifs'. The circumstantial evidence against Henry can be piled up; but of positive evidence there is none. (See p. 2.) Yet the notion of porphyrogeniture gives us one final, ironical twist. In 978 an elder brother had been murdered, and a younger brother succeeded, whose reign was clouded by the suspicion of his complicity in the murder. It was not a precedent likely to give Henry much joy. But there had been those who argued that the younger brother ought in any case to have been king; and in Henry's own lifetime, in Eadmer's *Life of St Dunstan*, it was alleged that the supporters of Ethelred, the younger son, had argued that his case was superior because his father was king when he was born, that he was *porphyrogenitus*.[154] Eadmer treated the argument with scant respect, but we may be sure that Henry, if he knew of it, did not. Like the Spanish precedent, the case of Ethelred may have warned him of the danger of fratricide, the need for concealment if one engaged in it. Ethelred may also have suggested to him a ground for believing that Henry not William was the true king. Along these lines one can reconstruct a frame of mind which might lead Henry to be accessory to murder, but there is no proof that he was. It is most probable that Rufus's death in August 1100 was an accident; and if so, Henry I was an exceptionally lucky man.

154 See above, p. 152 n. 146.

14

Stephen

Henry I died on 1 December 1135; by Christmas Stephen was installed in his place. The 'lover of peace', who had inherited the Conqueror's force and guile, but few of his redeeming features, was replaced by a dashing, gallant, baronial leader, the most attractive of the Norman kings. He was in many respects Henry's antithesis; and it may be that it was this very fact which had endeared Stephen to his uncle. There is little doubt that Stephen was one of Henry's favourite nephews; and it is likely enought that he felt for him a warmth of affection stronger than for any of his numerous children. It was Stephen's fate to pass his life surrounded by men and women of greater force and brilliance than himself – his uncle, Henry I, his brother, Henry of Blois, bishop of Winchester, his wife, Matilda of Boulogne, and his rival, the empress. In this gallery Stephen was wrongly cast in the role of king.

To his charm and good nature even his enemies bore witness. 'When he was a count', wrote William of Malmesbury, Stephen 'by his good nature and the way he would jest, sit and eat in the company even of the humblest, had earned great affection, so great that it can hardly be imagined.'[155] But he also implies that behind this façade Stephen was tricky and unreliable. He tells the story of how he laid an ambush for the earl of Gloucester, and when it failed, tried to laugh it off 'by a genial countenance and an unsolicited confession'. When he suspected treachery or was faced by rebellion, Stephen could act with great dash and bravery; but on several occasions he had his enemies suddenly arrested when they were in his court and ought to have been under his protection. Thus he arrested the bishop of Salisbury in 1139 and the earl of Chester in 1146. In both cases his own supporter, the author of the *Gesta Stephani*, ascribes the circumstances to the urgings of Stephen's supporters and implies that the situation was

155 William of Malmesbury, *Historia Novella*, pp. 32–3.

beyond the king's control. These are traditional excuses, but there seems in this case some justification for them. Stephen could be rash and precipitate; but his real weakness as king was that he could neither control his friends nor subdue his enemies. Events often got beyond his control. 'Yet he was not broken in spirit by any man's rebellion', says William of Malmesbury, 'but appeared suddenly now here, now there, and always settled the business with more loss to himself than to his opponents. For after expending many great efforts in vain, he would win a pretence of peace from them for a time, by the gift of honours or castles.'[156] Stephen was a brave and skilful warrior; he was usually loyal and generous, if not always trustworthy; he had the knightly qualities with a touch of warmth which was lacking in the Conqueror and his sons.

He was conventionally pious, and something more. At the end of the Furness peninsula, in Lancashire north of the sands, lies the town of Barrow, a monument to the seventh duke of Devonshire and his great effort to pay his father's debts. Nestling in a little valley still just hidden from the town are the splendid ruins of the great abbey of Furness, a monument to the young Stephen, and to the feeling he shared with so many of his colleagues that the prayers of the most fervent monks available were needed to save him from the consequences of his sins. Stephen was not so sensational a benefactor to the religious as King David of Scotland (1124–53), who founded or refounded over a dozen houses of various orders.[157] Stephen was the founder of three. His third foundation, Faversham Abbey in Kent, was planned by himself and his wife towards the end of their lives, in imitation of Reading Abbey, which had been founded as a Benedictine abbey following Cluniac customs by Henry I, and also as a royal mausoleum; both these functions Faversham was to follow, and it reveals the conventional side of Stephen's religion to the full. Furness is more remarkable: it was first established (on a different site) in 1124, and moved to its present home in 1127. Furness and Buckfast (Devon) were daughters of the Norman Savigny, which was already spreading the new ideas of monastic seclusion and asceticism which we more commonly associate with Cîteaux and the Cistercians. The houses of the order of Savigny were taken over by the Cistercians in the late 1140s; and so Furness, not without protest, became one of the leading English Cistercian houses. It remains one of the most considerable ruins in the north-west; in early days it was the chief centre of religious life in that part of England, and had many

156 William of Malmesbury, *Historia Novella*, pp. 40–1.
157 Brooke 1999, ch. 9.

links with Ireland and Man; and its granges and its sheep dominated the economic life of the Furness peninsula and the neighbouring fells. Stephen was an early and princely supporter of this novel fashion in the religious life.

He could afford to be generous in the 1120s. Originally indeed, he had had no English endowment. His father was count of Blois, his mother the Conqueror's daughter. But he was a younger son, and like many younger sons in the feudal world, like Henry I himself in early days, he was landless. But he was early received into the household of his royal uncle, and provided with substantial properties. The honour (or feudal complex) of Eye gave him scattered properties with a nucleus in the south-east; the honour of Lancaster gave him vast estates in the north-west, including the Furness Peninsula. The county of Mortain and much land once held by the family of Bellême-Montgomery made him the richest landlord in Normandy. In 1125 Henry married him to Matilda, daughter and heiress of Eustace, count of Boulogne. Matilda was a granddaughter of St Margaret of Scotland, and so descended from the Old English kings. She brought with her the substantial county of Boulogne, and the honour of 'Boulogne' in England, a very substantial group of properties which had been held by her father. Thus Stephen was by blood of the Conqueror's line, by marriage of the line of Cerdic and Alfred, and far and away the richest baron of England and Normandy. In 1127 he and Earl Robert of Gloucester, Henry's illegitimate son, were said to have disputed which of them should be the first of the lay barons (after David of Scotland) to swear allegiance to the Empress Matilda. It is clear that the two were rivals for Henry's affections; and by a crude material test one would judge Stephen the winner, since he was the better endowed; he had certainly won his place at court earlier than Robert.

It was perhaps partly out of affection for Stephen that Henry I brought Stephen's younger brother from the famous Burgundian abbey of Cluny and its modest English daughter, Montacute, in 1126 and placed him as abbot at Glastonbury.[158] In 1129 he promoted him to the bishopric of Winchester, and from then until his death in 1171 Henry of Blois held both the richest of English sees and one of the richest of English abbeys. He was at once a monk and a mandarin. He was a great financier; money poured into his hands, and was as rapidly spent in restoring the finances of Glastonbury and Winchester, and of Cluny itself, and in providing himself and his churches with lavish buildings and lavish ornaments. Glastonbury remembered his

158 For Henry as prior of Montacute, see Knowles, Brooke and London 2001, pp. 121, 269.

keen eye for good arable land, his fondness for the waving corn. Winchester recorded his fabulous gifts: which included gospel books and crosses encrusted with jewels, vestments, frontals, curtains, carpets, 'woollen cloth on which are embroidered the miracles of St Mary', and above all the great cross, adorned with over 200 precious stones, including a large sapphire of particular value, and containing within two relics of the True Cross, and relics of the Lord's Sepulchre, of the place of his Nativity, of his Ascension, of his manger, of Mount Calvary, of his cradle, of the Blessed Virgin's hair, of her Sepulchre, of Abraham, of Isaac, of Jacob, of St Bartholomew the Apostle, of St Matthew the Apostle, of St Stephen, of SS Sergius and Bacchus, of St George, of St Pantaleon, of the holy winding-sheet, of the stone which served Jacob for a pillow.[159] Henry of Blois was a man of large ideas, ambitious, grandiose, ostentatious, and yet devoted. He may have inspired his brother to become king; he certainly hoped to rule the English Church by his side. Stephen was largely dependent on him for the Church's aid in his early years, but he refused to be dominated by him. He would not have him as archbishop of Canterbury; as a compensation Henry was made papal legate, and ruled the English Church as the pope's representative from 1139 to 1143. When this lapsed, he tried to have Winchester made an archiepiscopal see, but with no success. Frustrated ambition combined with a genuine distrust of his brother's treatment of the Church made Henry's loyalty cool for a time. But as the years passed he mellowed; and in later life the brilliant prince-bishop became a revered elder statesman: no less wealthy, but more inclined to subdue his panache under the monastic habit which he never ceased to use.

Of those close to Stephen, his brother is the most exciting. Firmer in loyalty, more constant in good advice, but altogether remoter from our vision was Stephen's queen, Matilda of Boulogne. At the nadir of Stephen's fortunes, when he was imprisoned in 1141, she took over the reins of government. The two Matildas faced one another; and the irony is that the empress who had been groomed to rule England proved inferior in skill and personality to the queen whom no one had ever intended to be more than a consort. The queen's emergence was brief; but her determined loyalty to Stephen was one of the decisive factors in winning back his crown and so preparing the way for the quieter times of his later years.

The empress herself was the victim of the dynastic system into which she had been born. No career reveals the working of the system more clearly. She was born in 1102, betrothed at eight and married

---

159 Bishop 1918, pp. 392–401.

just before she was twelve to the Emperor Henry V. In 1110 she was shipped off to Germany, and was empress until her husband's death in 1125. By then she had grown accustomed to her new land, and had acquired much property there; England and her family were largely forgotten, and she had no wish to return. But she had the misfortune to be an eligible widow; and although she tried to resist her father's authority, it was a man's world, and Henry needed her for his schemes. Accustomed from her earliest years to the loftiest throne in Europe, she now found herself involved in the politics of a mere kingdom; and worse still, unequally yoked to a count considerably her junior. Matilda seems to have been endowed with some charm and considerable intelligence; at the end of her life she was able to give much good advice to her son, King Henry II, which he would have been well advised to follow. But she had been compelled too young to make what she could of a system which gave her grandeur without consulting her happiness or comfort. She had learned to enjoy being an empress, and she emerged haughty and self-centred, disinclined to control the swift temper of her family, unaccustomed to the need to conciliate her associates and subjects. Her second marriage was a miserable affair. She was married in 1128 to Geoffrey of Anjou, but soon left him. In 1131, however, they were reconciled, long enough to have three children; but they were never really happy together. In 1139 they agreed to dismember Stephen's domains: the empress was to invade England, Geoffrey to annex Normandy. This division of forces may or may not have been strategically sound; it certainly suited their domestic infelicity. Characteristically, Geoffrey succeeded, Matilda failed. She came very near to success, thanks to the skilful leadership of her half-brother, Robert of Gloucester; but in her hour of triumph her temperament, spoiled by grandeur and misery, proved Stephen's strongest weapon.

Early in 1136 the English leaders had rallied to Stephen, and it seemed as if he would become master of the kingdom. The barons who had hesitated, even Robert of Gloucester, eventually came to his court. In 1137 he was secure enough to cross to Normandy and enforce his rule on the rest of Henry I's domains. But unrest was already growing. The Church discovered that Stephen was unable to live up to his promises of good government; some barons found it difficult to forget that they had sworn an oath to the empress; others found it convenient to remember their oath when they observed that Stephen lacked the effectiveness of his uncle and grandfather. Stephen was a dashing, capable soldier; but he did not have the dogged persistence necessary to subdue a ring of baronial castles, and the ultimate ruthlessness needed to make himself feared. In September

1139 the empress came to England, and a group of barons led by Robert of Gloucester made her welcome. From 1139 to 1148 she stayed in England; throughout this time she had a secure base in the west country, especially in Bristol, her half-brother's headquarters.

Matilda's arrival was well-timed. Stephen had already shown that he had none of Henry I's flair for dissipating rebellion. He tried to hold his own by rapid manoeuvres; but never carried a plan through to the finish. In 1139 he imprisoned the bishop of Salisbury, the leading figure of Henry I's administration, and his relations, and dismantled their castles. He suspected them of treachery; he doubtless thought their disgrace would be popular with the barons they had oppressed. But the only visible result was that he became embroiled with the Church, and was forced to do penance by a council presided over by his own brother. While he was thus alienating the Church's leaders, who also included the most scrupulous of his followers, his weakness was also suggesting ideas to the most unscrupulous. The arrival of the empress gave them their opportunity. A baron of moderate wealth and no inhibitions called Geoffrey de Mandeville, by playing off one side against the other, built up an immense endowment of offices and land and won an earldom. Even grander was the position of the earl of Chester, who achieved a position of semi-regal independence by playing off one side against the other.

In 1141 Matilda found herself supported by the earl of Gloucester and the genuine Angevins,[160] by the earl of Chester and the leading turncoats, and by the bishop of Winchester. On 2 February Stephen was defeated and captured at the battle of Lincoln. For a few months it seemed as if Matilda's cause would triumph. Henry of Winchester proclaimed to a council at Winchester that 'God has executed his judgement on my brother in allowing him to fall into the power of the strong'; that it was the clergy's prerogative to choose (by which he clearly meant to have the first voice in electing) and consecrate a king; and that they had decided, calling God to their aid, to choose Matilda as lady of England and Normandy.[161] Next day the Londoners arrived to take their part in the election; but they merely requested King Stephen's release. It was already clear that a great number of people were not happy to see divine judgement in Stephen's capture at Lincoln. It was essential for the empress to proceed tactfully. Her notion of tact in this moment of opportunity was to proceed to

160   The supporters of the empress, and later of Henry II, were called Angevins, since she was countess of Anjou.
161   William of Malmesbury, *Historia Novella*, pp. 92–3. For a slightly more sympathetic account of Matilda's adventures in 1141, see Chibnall 1991, pp. 96–117.

London, show her most arrogant face to the Londoners and the baronial leaders, and levy a tax on the city. Very soon Henry of Winchester revised his notions of divine judgement. The empress was expelled from London; the bishop returned to Winchester; Stephen's queen gathered an army. The empress was determined to win back the bishop by force, and she hurried to Winchester and besieged the bishop in his palace, Wolvesey Castle. Presently the queen arrived, with a much larger army, and proceeded to besiege the empress and cut her communications. In this remarkable double siege it was the city which suffered most. The bishop's troops threw firebrands from their castle, which set light to the city; the convent of nuns near by, and Hyde Abbey outside the town, were burnt. Threatened by fire and famine Robert of Gloucester determined to break out and get his sister safe to the west country. This was accomplished by a series of sorties, most of them successful – though another convent, Wherwell Abbey in north Hampshire, was burnt in the fighting. The empress herself escaped; but Robert of Gloucester was captured. His loss was decisive; the Angevin party could not exist without him. He was exchanged for King Stephen, and with the king at liberty, Matilda's chance of victory was gone.

Matilda's power, however, was still formidable enough to prevent Stephen winning a complete victory. There were sporadic outbreaks of war in many parts of the country throughout the 1140s, though they grew weaker as time passed. The events of 1141 left Matilda in possession of the west country and of rather more than she had had before. She held Oxford as an outpost of power, a fortress covering the approaches to Bristol and Gloucester, which remained her headquarters. As autumn turned to winter in 1142 the king devised a plan for capturing Oxford with Matilda in it; and it very nearly succeeded. But just before Christmas, Matilda slipped out of the castle by night, accompanied by only three knights, and went six miles on foot, then took horse to Wallingford, through snow and ice, clad in white clothes to provide protective colouring. She soon reached the safety of the west. There she stayed, her power slowly diminishing, for five years; the king never had another chance of capturing his rival. In 1147 the earl of Gloucester died, and early in 1148 the empress retired to Normandy, which had been conquered, in the meantime, by her husband. With her departure the anarchy, which had oppressed England since her coming in 1139, finally subsided. But Stephen's hold on the English throne was still not undisputed.

In 1135 Matilda's eldest son, Henry, had been a child of two; when she left England he was a dashing young warrior of fourteen or fifteen. He had been partly brought up in England, and given a more through education than most laymen received at this time. But he also visited his father in Anjou and Normandy. In 1147, at fourteen, he made his first attempt on the English throne; in 1149 he made another. These were rapid and exciting adventures, with little prospect of success. But when he returned to the Continent in 1149, his father handed over to him the duchy of Normandy. The process had begun which was to convert Henry from the heir of a lost cause to one of the greatest dynasts in Europe. In 1152 the French king's marriage to the duchess of Aquitaine was annulled on the ground of consanguinity, and she immediately married Henry. In 1153 he invaded England again, in much greater strength than in 1149. Stephen fought stubbornly against him. But the Church had already prepared the way for a solution. Stephen's heir was his elder son Eustace, and he had tried to ensure Eustace's succession by having him crowned in his own lifetime. Archbishop Theobald, now in a position of effective leadership in the English Church, was always formally loyal to Stephen after 1141. But he was more concerned for the unity and peace of the kingdom than for the personal success of Stephen. It was no doubt largely his doing that the Church set its face against the coronation of Eustace, and in 1152 the pope formally forbade it. Stephen was accepted as *de facto* king; but the future was not to be mortgaged on this account. Not unnaturally, the relations between Stephen and Theobald deteriorated; but there was as yet no question of the archbishop turning traitor. In 1153, some months after Duke Henry's landing, Eustace suddenly died. This was the signal for a final offensive by the Church. Theobald of Canterbury and Henry of Winchester led a movement to bring Stephen and Henry together. They won over those leaders who wished for peace; and Henry, as duke of Normandy, had a blackmail hold over those, like the earl of Chester, who had large properties in Normandy. In November an arrangement was made that Stephen should be king until his death, that his younger son should inherit his baronies, and Henry his kingdom. On 25 October 1154 King Stephen died; on 19 December Henry II was crowned, and began to issue charters under the title 'king of the English, duke of the Normans and Aquitanians and Count of the Angevins'. By conquest, luck and marriage the inheritance of four great dynasties had fallen to one man's lot. Stephen was replaced by one of the strongest, most ruthless, most imaginative of medieval kings.

Stephen's reign was an interlude between the two Henrys; under both England was a comparatively peaceful, obedient land. Why did it relapse so rapidly into anarchy after 1135? The chronicler who described the nightmare of the nineteen winters of Stephen's reign exaggerated; anarchy only lasted from 1139 to 1145. In 1139 and the years which followed there was real anarchy: towns and fields were burned, castles were built without any control, and churches converted to fortresses; local feuds were freely pursued under cover of the civil war. But the anarchy never spread over the whole country, and after 1141 it gradually subsided, so that by 1145 war was an occasional rather than a normal thing.[162] Disorder, however, was sporadic till the end; Stephen was never firmly in control. The interlude of anarchy reveals many things about medieval kingship. It shows how powerful were the forces of disorder which the other Norman kings had held in check. It shows how much kingship owed to personal loyalty. It was the tight bond between king and barons – and between the king and the people at large – which kept England normally peaceful. This bond depended on the oath of homage, on the respect which his followers had for the king, above all on their admiration of his strength and fear of his anger. To all this was added the supernatural aura of monarchy – the 'divinity which doth hedge a king, rough-hew him how you will' as Mark Twain put it. But without the personal loyalty and the fear the bond was easily broken, the divinity quickly forgotten. Loyalty to Stephen was never complete. Archbishop Theobald was one of the very few great leaders who had never sworn allegiance to the empress while her father was alive. It is not entirely chance that he was almost the only one whose loyalty never wavered, except for a brief moment in 1141, and then with Stephen's permission. A disputed succession might on occasion have a chaotic effect on a kingdom. This may be obvious enough, but it helps to explain why such enormous precautions were taken to prevent it: precautions so elaborate that such an event was much rarer in English history than we should expect from the confusion of law and custom which surrounded the succession. Yet even so Stephen's failure is not entirely explained. He won the crown in 1135 as William Rufus had won it in 1087 or Henry I in 1100, while the obvious heir was alive and active. The situation was little if at all worse in 1135 than before. In what lay the difference?

The short answer is that Stephen had the qualities of Duke Robert, the unsuccessful eldest brother, not those of William and Henry. Robert's finest hour was on the First Crusade. He was not a distinguished general, but he was a brave knight and a reliable officer, trusted by his men. He had reached up to too high an office. Stephen

---

162   For a nuanced defence of the word 'anarchy', see Hollister 1994. Crouch 2000 argues against it, giving learned support to the attempts which have been made to diminish the disorder of the reign.

was admirably suited to be count of Mortain, count of Boulogne, lord of the honour of Lancaster, founder of Furness, a leader among the English barons. Brought up under the wing of Henry I, he had observed how men instinctively obeyed his uncle; he had also learned how oppressive his rule could be. But instinctive obedience was not automatically given to a king: he had to prove himself first. And Henry had proved himself by ruling with a heavy hand. Stephen lacked the final ruthlessness and persistence. William of Malmesbury was a supporter of the empress. None the less, he spoke for many when he said that Stephen 'was a man of energy but lacking in judgement, active in war, of extraordinary spirit in undertaking difficult tasks, lenient to his enemies and easily appeased, courteous to all: though you admired his kindness in promising, still you felt his words lacked truth and his promises fulfilment'.[163]

163   William of Malmesbury, *Historia Novella*, pp. 28–9.

15

Epilogue

While the visible power of the English monarchy was threatened with eclipse under King Stephen, the ideal image of English kingship was being boosted by the growth of two powerful legends. In 1138 Geoffrey of Monmouth issued his *History of the Kings of Britain*, whose central character is King Arthur, and Osbert de Clare, prior of Westminster, finished his *Life* of Edward the Confessor. Osbert's Edward naturally bore some relation to the Edward of history, even though the king's saintly qualities have notably increased and the tale of his miracles has grown much longer since the first *Life* was completed in or about 1067. The monks of Westminster had his relics, but they had not yet succeeded in having him canonized. Osbert's efforts were abortive; the pope refused the monks' petition. It was only in 1161, with the aid of Henry II, that the monks of Westminster eventually succeeded in promoting Edward to the calendar and converting the royal bones to holy relics. This campaign was the religious counterpart to the growing opinion that King Edward represented the tradition of Old England; that good law must be related to the 'law of King Edward' and good kings to his family. Henry I married his great-great-niece, Stephen his great-great-great-niece, Henry II was his great-great-great-great-nephew. After 1161 his relics presided in Westminster Abbey at the coronations of his successors; and in the thirteenth century King Henry III dedicated his best energies to rebuilding Edward's shrine and Edward's church, and gave the name Edward to his eldest son.

Edward I was not likely to forget that he had been named after the Confessor. But he seems personally to have been more interested in his other famous predecessor, Arthur; and there is no doubt that Edward III was more Arthurian than Edwardian. If Arthur existed, he was a leader in the reconquest of some large part of England about the year 500; but his existence is doubtful. Yet for centuries his legend grew slowly; and it was only in the twelfth century that he came to join

Charlemagne and Alexander the Great as the supreme legendary monarchs of European literature. His fame grew up, like so many of the legends which flourished in the twelfth century, in the Celtic lands. Its early history is quite obscure. But Arthur was made respectable very largely by the daring inventions of Geoffrey of Monmouth. Geoffrey was a Breton brought up in Wales, well acquainted with Celtic lore. He also had patronage from Anglo-Norman barons and bishops, and rose at the end of his life to be bishop of St Asaph, a diocese which proved, however, as imaginary as his *History of the Kings of Britain*. The *History* is mainly fiction; its central purpose seems to be to float legends and stories which Geoffrey delighted in as if they were sober history.[164] But in the process he succeeded in flattering the Celts by enormously magnifying their past, and flattering the Normans by revealing Arthur as in all essentials an Anglo-Norman king. In the midst of the book are some very strange prophecies, put into the mouth of the magician Merlin. It is not clear whether these forecast a wonderful Celtic revival, or the building up of a great British empire by Norman kings to come. The ambiguity is clearly deliberate; Geoffrey rejoiced in the mystification of his readers, and in leading serious historians by the nose. There is no doubt that the English kings, in the long run, were the gainers. The chief centre of the heroic epics of the early twelfth century was the court of Charlemagne. The kings of France and Germany could both claim to be Charlemagne's heirs, and bask in his reflected glory. In the second half of the twelfth century, in the courtly romances, Charlemagne was outstripped by Arthur, and the English kings basked in their stead.

The Arthur of Geoffrey's *History* and the legends of the Round Table was a princely overlord, who took counsel with his barons, and was condemned if he ignored their advice. In spite of this, his word was very nearly law; and it has often been observed that the tendency of the English monarchy in the twelfth century was towards despotism. This tendency was checked, and the direction reversed, in the thirteenth century. This is not to say that the barons who resisted John and Henry III created the limited, constitutional monarchy we know today. They had ideas of how to limit kingly power; more sophisticated notions were developed in the fourteenth century. But it was far from clear, between the fourteenth and the seventeenth centuries, that royal absolutism would not be reasserted. We have had no despots since James II, and our special brand of constitutional monarchy is something profoundly different from anything known in

164   Geoffrey of Monmouth; cf. Brooke 1986, ch. 4; and for recent discussions, esp. Gillingham 1990.

the Middle Ages. None the less, if it owes most of all to the traditions established between 1688 and 1901, it owes much to the divergent opinions, the controversies, the events of the four centuries which divided *Magna Carta* from the Civil War.

We cannot close a study of the English kings who reigned before the birth of John without asking what links there are between their monarchy and that of today. Most of the answer is implicit in the story that has been told. In the notion that a monarch is the symbol of many aspects of a people's life, in many of the trappings of monarchy, most notably in the service of anointing and coronation, the elements of continuity are striking. The most obvious difference is that it was essential that a king in the early Middle Ages should rule as well as reign; today it is essential that he or she should not. In the Middle Ages institutions and customs set some limit on royal absolutism; in the twenty-first century the royal office sets a limit to the republican tendency of our institutions, and performs a wholly new kind of function in relation to the Commonwealth. In these respects the institution in the early Middle Ages and today performs almost opposite tasks. But our kind of constitutional monarchy, or crowned republic, presupposes a long development both of representative and of monarchical institutions. Unlike Sir Robert Cotton we can no longer see the Witan as a kind of proto-Parliament. If we ask the question, from what roots did representative institutions spring in the thirteenth and fourteenth centuries, when they were born in England, as in almost every country in western Europe, the answer must be from the world of ideas and statecraft of the late twelfth and thirteenth centuries. But if we go on to ask why parliaments flourished in England more lastingly than elsewhere, a part of the answer must be that in England they grew out of institutions of local government already deeply planted. In Saxon times already royal representatives met the local communities in the shire courts and elsewhere. There was already present in germ the idea of 'self-government at the king's command' which is the special character of English government in the thirteenth and fourteenth centuries. In medieval conditions, it was only possible to govern effectively if remote local communities accepted and joined willingly in the work; and so an element of self-government was necessary to strong government. Self-government at the king's command helped the English kings to rule more effectively than those of most other European countries of the day. But it also meant that it was more difficult for English kings entirely to ignore the opinions of their influential subjects.

The effects of this lay far in the future in 1154; and the deepest interest of our story must be in the way changing ideas and circumstances moulded a powerful institution – ideas both primitive and sophisticated, working in the minds of men of the most varied outlook and accomplishment; and in how the institution grew and altered in the hands of kings often of most strongly marked individuality. As time passed, the individuality was better recorded, and so we can observe with some precision the impact of Alfred, Athelstan, Cnut, and the first three Norman kings on English kingship, and of English kingship on them. But even so we are constantly tantalized by problems we cannot solve; our early kings appear before us like a row of unfinished portraits. Sometimes they seem to come to life and step out of their frames. But the moment passes, the ghosts fade back into the wall, and we are left peering at the old, worn, unfinished canvases, searching for new evidence of how the artist meant the portrait to be completed.

Bibliography

For all topics relating to the period to 1066, see the invaluable *Blackwell Encyclopaedia of Anglo-Saxon England*, ed. M. Lapidge, J. Blair, S. Keynes and D. Scragg, Oxford, 1999. Accounts of many individual kings and queens will be found in A. Williams, A.P. Smyth and D.P. Kirby, *A Biographical Dictionary of Dark Age Britain*, London, 1991. Where no reference is given in the text, a relevant article in the *Blackwell Encyclopaedia* will commonly supply it. Much valuable detail can be found in the journals *Anglo-Saxon England* and *Anglo-Norman Studies*. Simon Keynes's *Anglo-Saxon History: A Select Bibliography*, 3rd edn, Kalamazoo, 1998, is a mine of useful information.

For lists of kings and queens, see *Handbook of British Chronology*, ed. E.B. Fryde, D.E. Greenway et al., 3rd edn, London, 1986, pp. 1–36 (David Dumville) and *Blackwell Encyclopaedia*, pp. 500–16 (Simon Keynes).

Abbreviations

ASC: *Anglo-Saxon Chronicle*.
Blackwell Encyclopaedia: see above.
EHD: *English Historical Documents*: see below.
NMT: Nelson's Medieval Texts.
OMT: Oxford Medieval Texts.

Sources

This book is mainly based on sources: those cited in the text are listed below. Useful collections in translation are *EHD* I and II: *English Historical Documents*, I, *c.500–1042*, ed. D. Whitelock, 2nd edn, London, 1979, and II, *1042–1189*, ed. D.C. Douglas and G.W. Greenaway, 2nd edn, London, 1981.

Ælfric, *Sermones Catholici*, ed. B. Thorpe, London, 1844–6.
Æthelweard, *The Chronicle of*, ed. and trans. B. Campbell, NMT, 1962.

Ailred of Rievaulx, *Genealogia Regum Anglorum*, in J.P. Migne, ed., *Patrologia Latina* 195, cols. 711–38.

Alfred's translations are quoted from the extracts in *EHD* I, 917–20, with references to full editions.

Annals of St Neot's: see under *ASC.*

ASC: Anglo-Saxon Chronicle, The: I have used the translation by G.N. Garmonsway, revised edn, London, 1960; also in *EHD* I to 1042, and other versions. Also ed. in the many volumes of *The Anglo-Saxon Chronicle: A Collaborative Edition*, esp. 3, *MS A*, ed. J. Bately, Cambridge, 1986; 17, *Annals of St Neot's*, ed. D. Dumville and M. Lapidge, Cambridge, 1985 – also in *Asser*, ed. Stevenson.

Ashdown, D., ed., 1930, *English and Norse Documents relating to the Reign of Ethelred the Unready*, Cambridge, 1930.

Asser: Asser's Life of King Alfred, ed. W.H. Stevenson, revised D. Whitelock, Oxford, 1959; also trans. in *Alfred the Great: Asser's 'Life of King Alfred' and Other Contemporary Sources*, by S. Keynes and M. Lapidge, Harmondsworth, 1983; 2nd edn, forthcoming.

Bayeux Tapestry, The, ed. F.M. Stenton, 2nd edn, London, 1965; ed. D.M. Wilson, London, 1985. See esp. articles by H.E. Walker and N.P. Brooks, C.R. Dodwell, R. Gameson and others, in *The Study of the Bayeux Tapestry*, ed. R. Gameson, Woodbridge, 1997.

Bede: Bede's Ecclesiastical History of the English People, ed. and trans. B. Colgrave and R.A.B. Mynors, rev. edn, OMT, 1992.

Bede's Ecclesiastical History of the English People: A Historical Commentary, by J.M. Wallace-Hadrill, OMT, 1988.

Beowulf and the Fight at Finnsburg, trans. D. Wright, Harmondsworth, 1957, etc.; standard edn ed. F. Klaeber, 3rd edn, Boston, 1950.

Byhrtferth, *Vita S. Oswaldi*, ed. J. Raine, *The Historians of the Church of York and its Archbishops*, I (Rolls Series, 1879), pp. 399–475 [a new edition by M. Lapidge is forthcoming in OMT].

Councils and Synods: Councils and Synods with other Documents relating to the English Church, I, 1, 871–1066, ed. D. Whitelock, Oxford, 1981.

Dunstan: Memorials of St Dunstan, ed. W. Stubbs, Rolls Series, 1874.

Eadmer, *Historia Novorum*, ed. M. Rule, Rolls Series, London, 1884; trans. G. Bosanquet, *Eadmer's History of Recent Events in England*, London, 1964.

Eadmer, *The Life of St Anselm, Archbishop of Canterbury*, ed. and trans. R.W. Southern, NMT, 1962; repr. OMT, 1972.

Edward the Confessor: The Life of King Edward who lies at Westminster, ed. and trans. F. Barlow, 2nd edn, OMT, 1992.

Encomium Emmae Reginae, ed. and trans. A. Campbell, rev. edn by S. Keynes, Cambridge, 1998.

Engels, L.J., 1973, 'De obitu Willelmi ducis Normannorum regisque Anglorum: texte, modèles, valeur et origine', *Mélanges Christine Mohrmann* (Utrecht, 1973), pp. 209–55.

Geoffrey of Monmouth, *Historia regum Brittaniae*, I–, ed. N. Wright, J. Crick et al., Woodbridge, 1985–; English trans. L. Thorpe, Harmondsworth, 1966.

Gesta Stephani, revised edn and trans. K.R. Potter and R.H.C. Davis, OMT, 1976.

Gilbert Foliot, *Letter and Charters*, ed. A. Morey and C.N.L. Brooke, Cambridge, 1967.

Gordon, R.K., 1954, *Anglo-Saxon Poetry*, revised edn, London, 1954.

Guy of Amiens, *Carmen de Hastingae Proelio*, ed. and trans. F. Barlow, 2nd edn, OMT, 1999.

Henry of Huntingdon, *Historia Anglorum: The History of the English People*, ed. and trans. D.E. Greenway, OMT, 1996.

John of Salisbury, *Historia Pontificalis* (*Memoirs of the Papal Court*), ed. and trans. M. Chibnall, NMT, 1956; repr. OMT, 1986.

——, *Vita S. Anselmi*, in J.P. Migne, ed., *Patrologia Latina* 199, cols. 1009–40.

John of Worcester, *Chronicle*, II–III, ed. and trans. R.R. Darlington, P. McGurk and J. Bray, OMT, 1995–8.

Orderic Vitalis, *Ecclesiastical History*, ed. and trans. M. Chibnall, OMT, 6 vols., 1968–80.

Regularis Concordia: The Monastic Agreement, ed. and trans. T. Symons, NMT, 1953.

Richard FitzNigel, *Dialogus de Scaccario*, ed. and trans. C. Johnson, 2nd edn, corr. by F.E.L. Carter and D.E. Greenway, OMT, 1983.

Sawyer, P.E., 1968, *Anglo-Saxon Charters: An Annotated List and Bibliography*, London, 1968.

Schramm, P.E., 1968, *Kaiser, Könige und Päpste*, II, Stuttgart, 1968.

Suger, *Vie de Louis VI le Gros*, ed. and French trans. H. Waquet, Paris, 1929.

Sutton Hoo: A.C. Evans, *The Sutton Hoo Ship Burial*, London, 1986; M.O.H. Carver, *Sutton Hoo: Burial Ground of Kings?*, London, 1998; M.O.H. Carver and M.R. Hummler, *Sutton Hoo: The Early Medieval Cemetery and its Context*, London, forthcoming.

Turgot, *Vita Sanctae Margaritae Reginae Scotiae*, here quoted from *Acta Sanctorum Bollandiana*, June, II (1698), 328–35; for other edns see Baker 1978, p. 129.

Vigfusson, G., and York Powell, F., eds., 1883, *Corpus Poeticum Boreale*, II, Oxford, 1883.

Walter Map, *De nugis curialium*, ed. and trans. M.R. James, C.N.L. Brooke and R.A.B. Mynors, OMT, 1983; repr. 1994.

Widukind, *Rerum gestarum Saxonicarum libri tres*, ed. H.E. Lohmann and P. Hirsch, *Monumenta Germaniae Historica, Scriptores Rerum Germanicarum*, Hanover, 1935.

William of Jumièges et al., *Gesta Normannorum Ducum*, ed. and trans. E.M.C. Van Houts, 2 vols., OMT, 1992–5.

William of Malmesbury, *Gesta Regum Anglorum: The History of the English Kings*, ed. and trans. R.A.B. Mynors, R.M. Thomson and M. Winterbottom, 2 vols., OMT, 1998–9.

William of Malmesbury, *Historia Novella: The Contemporary History*, ed. and trans. E. King and K.R. Potter, rev. edn, OMT, 1998.

William of Poitiers, *Gesta Guillelmi*, ed. R.H.C. Davis and M. Chibnall, OMT, 1998.

Yeavering: B. Hope-Taylor, *Yeavering: An Anglo-British Centre of Early Northumbria*, London, 1977.

Secondary Literature

Abels, R.P., 1998, *Alfred the Great*, Harlow, 1998.

Baker, D., 1978, 'A "nursery of saints": St Margaret of Scotland reconsidered', in *Medieval Women*, ed. D. Baker (Oxford, 1978), pp. 119–41.

Barlow, F., 1970, *Edward the Confessor*, London, 1970.

——, 1980, 'The king's evil', *English Historical Review*, 95 (1980), 3–27; repr. in Barlow, *The Norman Conquest and Beyond* (London, 1983), pp. 23–47.

——, 1983, *William Rufus*, London, 1983.

Bassett, S., ed., 1989, *The Origins of Anglo-Saxon Kingdoms*, London, 1989.

Bernstein, D.J., 1986, *The Mystery of the Bayeux Tapestry*, London, 1986.

Biddle, M., and Keene, D.J., 1976, 'Winchester in the eleventh and twelfth centuries', in F. Barlow et al., *Winchester in the Early Middle Ages, Winchester Studies*, ed. M. Biddle, I (Oxford, 1976), pp. 241–448.

Bishop, E., 1918, *Liturgica Historica*, Oxford, 1918.

Blunt, C.E., 1974, 'The coinage of Athelstan, 924–939: a survey', *British Numismatic Journal*, 42 (1974), 35–160.

Brooke, C.N.L., 1986, *The Church and the Welsh Border in the Central Middle Ages*, Woodbridge, 1986.

——, 1989, *The Medieval Idea of Marriage*, Oxford, 1989.

——, 1992, 'Aspects of John of Salisbury's *Historia Pontificalis*', in *Intellectual Life in the Middle Ages: Essays Presented to Margaret Gibson*, ed. L. Smith and B. Ward (London, 1992), pp. 185–95.

——, 1999, *Churches and Churchmen in Medieval Europe*, London, 1999, chs. 8–9 on the Norman kings and David I of Scotland as patrons of monasteries.

——, 2000, *Europe in the Central Middle Ages*, 3rd edn, Harlow, 2000, ch. 6, pp. 124–9 (queens and empresses), and ch. 10 (kingship and government).

Bruce-Mitford, R.L.S., 1975–83, *The Sutton Hoo Ship Burial*, 3 vols., London, 1975–83.

Carver, M.O.H., 1998, *Sutton Hoo: Burial Ground of Kings?*, London, 1998.

Cary, G., and Ross, D.J.A., 1956, *The Medieval Alexader*, Cambridge, 1956.

Chadwick, H.M., 1912, *The Heroic Age*, Cambridge, 1912.

Chibnall, M., 1991, *The Empress Matilda*, Oxford, 1991.

Crouch, D., 2000, *The Reign of King Stephen*, Harlow, 2000.

Davies, R.R., 1994–7, 'The peoples of Britain', I–IV, *Transactions of the Royal Historical Society*, 6th Series, 4 (1994), 1–20; 5 (1995), 1–20; 6 (1996), 1–23; 7 (1997), 1–24.

Davis, R.H.C., 1967, *King Stephen*, London, 1967.

——, 1976, *The Normans and their Myth*, London, 1976.

Dodd, C.H., 1944, *The Apostolic Preaching and its Developments*, 2nd edn, London, 1944.

Douglas, D.C., 1964, *William the Conqueror*, London, 1964.

Duggan, A.J., ed., 1997, *Queens and Queenship in Medieval Europe*, Woodbridge, 1997.

Dumville, D.N., 1976, 'The Anglian collection of royal genealogies and regnal lists', *Anglo-Saxon England*, 5 (1976), 23–50.

——, *Wessex and England from Alfred to Edgar*, Woodbridge, 1992.

Fox, C., 1955, *Offa's Dyke*, London, 1955.

Freeman, E.A., 1867–79, *The History of the Norman Conquest*, 6 vols., Oxford, 1867–79.

Gameson, R., ed., 1997, *The Study of the Bayeux Tapestry*, Woodbridge, 1997.

Garnett, G., 1986, 'Coronation and propaganda: some implications of the Norman claim to the throne of England in 1066', *Transactions of the Royal Historical Society*, 5th Series, 36 (1986), 91–116.

Gillingham, J., 1990, 'The context and purposes of Geoffrey of Monmouth's *History of the Kings of Britain*', *Anglo-Norman Studies*, 13 (1990), 99–118.

Grape, W., 1994, *The Bayeux Tapestry: Monument to a Norman Triumph*, Munich, 1994.

Green, J.A., 1986, *The Government of England under Henry I*, Cambridge, 1986.

Hill, D., 2000, 'Offa's dyke: pattern and purpose', *Antiquaries Journal*, 80 (2000), 195–206.

Hollister, C.W., 1986, 'The strange death of William Rufus', *Speculum*, 48 (1973), 637–53; repr. in Hollister, *Magnates and Institutions of the Anglo-Norman World* (London, 1986), pp. 59–76.

——, 1994, 'The aristocracy', in King 1994, pp. 37–66.

Huneycutt, L.L., 1990, 'The idea of the perfect princess: the Life of St Margaret in the reign of Matilda II (1100–18)', *Anglo-Norman Studies*, 12 (1990), 81–97.

Keynes, S., 1978, 'The declining reputation of King Æthelred the Unready', in *Ethelred the Unready*, ed. D. Hill (Oxford, 1978), pp. 227–53.

——, 1980, *The Diplomas of King Æthelred the Unready*, Cambridge, 1980.

——, 1996, ed., *The Liber Vitae of the New Minster and Hyde Abbey, Winchester*, Early English Manuscripts in Facsimile, Copenhagen, 1996.

For Keynes and Lapidge on Alfred, see under sources, *Asser*.

Kiernan, K.S., 1984, *Beowulf and the Beowulf Manuscript*, New Brunswick, 1984.

King, E., ed., 1994, *The Anarchy of King Stephen's Reign*, Oxford, 1994.

Kirby, D.P., 1991, *The Earliest English Kings*, London, 1991.

Knowles, D., Brooke, C.N.L., and London, V.C.M., 2001, *The Heads of Religious Houses, England and Wales, 940–1216*, 2nd edn, Cambridge, 2001.

Lapidge, M., 2000, 'The archetype of Beowulf', *Anglo-Saxon England*, 29 (2000), 5–41. See also Asser, *Blackwell Encyclopaedia* (pp. 174–5).

Loyn, H.R., 1962, *Anglo-Saxon England and Norman Conquest*, London, 1962.

——, 1984, *The Governance of Anglo-Saxon England*, London, 1984.

Morey, A., and Brooke, C.N.L., 1965, *Gilbert Foliot and his Letters*, Cambridge, 1965, ch. 7, for Matilda's case against Stephen.

Murray, M., 1931, *The God of the Witches*, London, 1931.

Nelson, J.L., 1986, '"A king across the sea": Alfred in continental perspective', *Transactions of the Royal Historical Society*, 5th Series, 36 (1986), 45–68.

——, 1986, *Politics and Ritual in Early Medieval Europe*, London, 1986.

——, and see Parsons 1994.

Owen-Crocker, G.R., and Graham, T., eds., 1998, *Medieval Art: Recent Perspectives: A Memorial Tribute to C.R. Dodwell*, Manchester, 1998.

Parsons, J.C., ed., 1994, *Medieval Queenship*, London, 1994, esp. chs. by P. Stafford and J.L. Nelson.

Poole, A.L., 1951, *From Domesday Book to Magna Carta*, Oxford, 1951.

Robinson, J.A., 1923, *The Times of St Dunstan*, Oxford, 1923.

Roffe, D., 2000, *Domesday, the Inquest and the Book*, Oxford, 2000.

Round, J.H., 1895, *Feudal England*, London, 1895.

Sharpe, R., 1997, *A Handlist of the Latin Writers of Great Britain and Ireland before 1540*, Turnhout, 1997.

Sims-Williams, P., 1998, 'Genetics, linguistics and prehistory: thinking big and thinking straight', *Antiquity*, 72 (1998), 505–27.

Sisam, K., 1953, 'Anglo-Saxon royal genealogies', *Proceedings of the British Academy*, 39 (1953), 287–348.

Southern, R.W., 1963, *St Anselm and his Biographer*, Cambridge, 1963.

——, 1970, 'The place of Henry I in English history', in Southern, *Medieval Humanism and Other Studies* (Oxford, 1970), ch. 11.

Stafford, P., 1983, *Queens, Concubines and Dowagers: The King's Wife in the Early Middle Ages*, London, 1983.

——, 1997, *Queen Emma and Queen Edith*, Oxford, 1997.

——, and see Parsons 1994.

Stenton, F.M., 1927, 'Lindsey and its kings', in *Essays in History Presented to Reginald Lane Poole*, ed. H.W.C. Davis (Oxford, 1927), pp. 136–50; repr. in Stenton, *Preparatory to Anglo-Saxon England*, ed. D.M. Stenton (Oxford, 1970), pp. 127–35.

——, 1971, *Anglo-Saxon England*, 3rd edn, Oxford, 1971.

Stubbs, W., 1874, *Constitutional History of England*, I, Oxford, 1874.

Van Houts, E., 1992, 'Women and the writing of history in the early Middle Ages', *Early Medieval Europe*, 1 (1992), 53–68.

Vince, A., ed., 1993, *Pre-Viking Lindsey*, Lincoln, 1993.

Walker, H.E., 1956, 'Bede and the Gewissae', *Cambridge Historical Journal*, 12, 2 (1956), 174–86.

Walker, I.W., 1997, *Harold: The Last Anglo-Saxon King*, Stroud, 1997.

Wall, V., 1997, 'Queen Margaret of Scotland (1070–1093): burying the past, enshrining the future', in Duggan 1997, pp. 27–38.

Wallace-Hadrill, J.M., 1971, *Early Germanic Kingship in England and on the Continent*, Oxford, 1971.

Wood, M., 1983, 'The making of Aethelstan's empire: an English Charlemagne?', in *Ideal and Reality in Frankish and Anglo-Saxon Society*, ed. P. Wormald (Oxford, 1983), pp. 250–72.

Wormald, P., 1983, 'Bede, the *Bretwaldas* and the origins of the Gens Anglorum', in *Ideal and Reality* (as above), pp. 99–129.

Yorke, B., 1990, *Kings and Kingdoms of Early Anglo-Saxon England*, London, 1990.

——, 1995, *Wessex in the Early Middle Ages*, London, 1995.

Genealogical Tables

The following are simplified versions of the genealogies of the kings of Northumbria, Mercia, Wessex and England – simplified, because there are many problems and discrepancies in the early sources, which I have had to ignore. A glance at the entries in the *Anglo-Saxon Chronicle* Ā for 597, 674, 676, 685 and 688 (trans. Garmonsway, pp. 20, 34, 38, 40) relating to the West Saxon line will illustrate a number of the discrepancies. I have reproduced the genealogies as they were in 1963, based on careful study of Sisam 1953 and the sources indicated there; but I have corrected the dates of the kings. For references to full lists of kings and queens, see p. 174; there is a useful set of family trees in Kirby 1991, Appendix. The early names are of doubtful historicity, and the earliest ones almost certainly fictitious: for the significance of these genealogies, see pp. 74–5.

For the rich modern literature on the genealogies, see esp. Dumville 1976 and other references given in the article by D.E. Thornton in *Blackwell Encyclopaedia*, pp. 199–200.

Often in early times a family group reigned simultaneously; this tends to be hidden in these tables: it is not possible to give all the known colleagues without making the tables wholly unintelligible. Many younger brothers and cadet branches are not shown.

Names in capital letters are mentioned in the text of the book. Those with dates were certainly kings (etc.); of those without dates some probably held kingly rank, many may have done, some certainly did not.

1 *Northumbria* (down to 729)

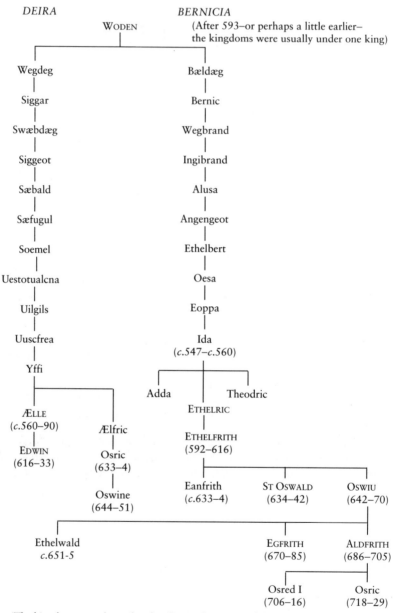

DEIRA

BERNICIA
(After 593–or perhaps a little earlier–
the kingdoms were usually under one king)

WODEN

Wegdeg

Siggar

Swæbdæg

Siggeot

Sæbald

Sæfugul

Soemel

Uestotualcna

Uilgils

Uuscfrea

Yffi

ÆLLE
(c.560–90)

EDWIN
(616–33)

Bældæg

Bernic

Wegbrand

Ingibrand

Alusa

Angengeot

Ethelbert

Oesa

Eoppa

Ida
(c.547–c.560)

Adda   Theodric

ETHELRIC

ETHELFRITH
(592–616)

Ælfric

Osric
(633–4)

Oswine
(644–51)

Eanfrith
(c.633–4)

ST OSWALD
(634–42)

OSWIU
(642–70)

Ethelwald
c.651-5

EGFRITH
(670–85)

ALDFRITH
(686–705)

Osred I
(706–16)

Osric
(718–29)

(The kingdom passed to other families in the course of the early eighth century;
but survived until about 875, when it was conquered by the Vikings, who set up
a kingdom based on York which lasted until the mid-tenth century.)

2 *Mercia*

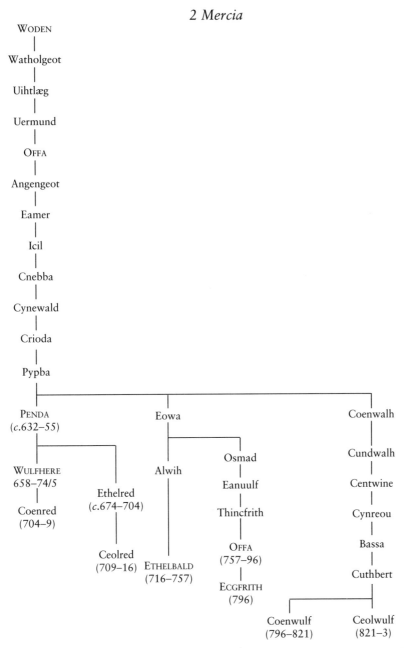

WODEN
|
Watholgeot
|
Uihtlæg
|
Uermund
|
OFFA
|
Angengeot
|
Eamer
|
Icil
|
Cnebba
|
Cynewald
|
Crioda
|
Pypba

PENDA
(*c.*632–55)

WULFHERE
658–74/5

Coenred
(704–9)

Ethelred
(*c.*674–704)

Ceolred
(709–16)

Eowa

Alwih

Osmad

Eanuulf

Thincfrith

ETHELBALD
(716–757)

OFFA
(757–96)

ECGFRITH
(796)

Coenwalh

Cundwalh

Centwine

Cynreou

Bassa

Cuthbert

Coenwulf
(796–821)

Ceolwulf
(821–3)

(Followed by a succession of kings of
unknown origin)

3 Wessex

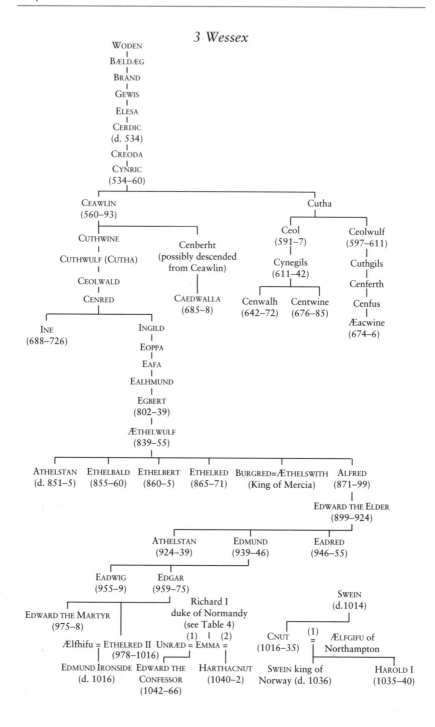

4 The Norman Kings

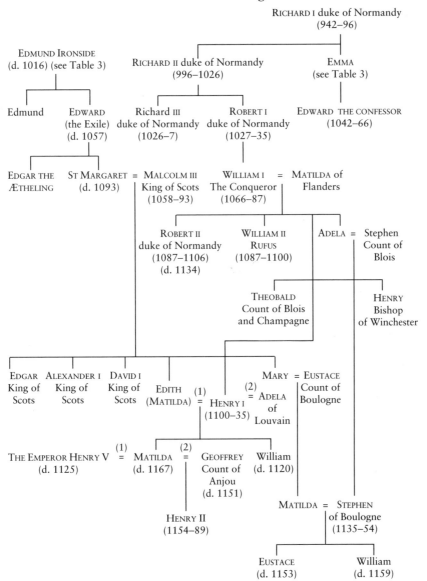

Index

People who lived before 1200 are normally entered under their Christian names.